The Fiddle Handbook

CHRIS**HAIGH**

The Fiddle Handbook

CHRIS**HAIGH**

A BACKBEAT BOOK
First edition 2009
Published by Backbeat Books
An Imprint of Hal Leonard Corporation
7777 West Bluemound Road,
Milwaukee, WI 53213
www.backbeatbooks.com

Devised and produced for Backbeat Books by
Outline Press Ltd
2A Union Court, 20-22 Union Road,
London SW4 6JP, England
www.jawbonepress.com

ISBN: 978-0-87930-978-7

A catalogue record for this book is available from the British Library.

DESIGN: Paul Cooper Design
EDITOR: John Morrish

Origination and print by Colorprint Offset China

09 10 11 12 13 5 4 3 2 1

c

introduction

This book answers once and for all that hoary old question, "What's the difference between a fiddle and a violin?" The answer, of course, is that fiddle players have more fun. They're the rascals, rogues, chancers, and jokers of the violin world. They answer to no composer or conductor, and they make up their own rules. They play from the heart, from memory, from the noisiest corner of the pub.

Violinists have to behave, sit up straight, watch their backs, and never make a single mistake. Fiddlers on the other hand ... I well remember one of my many trips to the Shetland Folk Festival in Scotland. The 'session' started in the pub in Aberdeen, continued on the boat all the way to Lerwick, and never stopped during the four days on the islands, continuing in pubs, car parks, changing rooms, on traffic roundabouts and coaches, not to mention at all the gigs. When you put a critical mass of fiddlers together you get an explosion of excitement and enthusiasm, a cross-fertilisation of ideas, and a swapping of tunes, techniques, and tall tales. And not a beta-blocker in sight – though there may be the odd dram or can of the good stuff going around.

That's what this book is all about. The world is full of fiddles and fiddlers, sawing away at Celtic, American, blues, jazz, Gypsy tunes, and everything in between. No instrument is more adaptable, more challenging, and more exciting than the fiddle.

This book is a treasure trove of information spanning the whole range of fiddle playing, from the spike fiddles of Africa and Asia to the Chinese erhu, the fabulous Indian sarangi and the mysterious Norwegian hardingfele, favourite of spirits and trolls.

We look in detail at the most commonly played styles among today's fiddlers. From America there's old time, bluegrass, Cajun, western swing, country, blues, rock, klezmer, and jazz. From the British Isles there's Irish, Scottish, and English. And we also take a quick romp through Eastern Europe.

Time was when the kind of fiddle music you played depended on where you were brought up. Being from the mill town of

Huddersfield in Yorkshire, England, would have qualified me to play 'On Ilkley Moor Bah T'at' (don't ask!) and 'Scarborough Fair', but not a lot else. In this postmodern world things are a bit different. Nowadays there are great bluegrass players in Japan. Tango is huge in Finland. The choice is there for everyone to make. And what choice did I make? Like a greedy child gaping open-mouthed at a table full of delicious desserts, faced with the choice of deciding where to start, I took a sly look around, and then grabbed the lot. I'm still eating.

Along with solid facts on the origins of different fiddle styles, and the different instruments, techniques, and repertoires involved, comes the piquant sauce of fiddlers' gossip, scandal, and blatant speculation. You'll meet the first fiddle player to set foot in America, discover how Mary Queen of Scots escaped from 500 fiddle players, and who really wrote 'Orange Blossom Special'. In the company of the ghost of Cecil Sharp, we'll find out how it all went wrong for English fiddle playing at the Battle of Waterloo, and we'll uncover the crimes against music perpetrated by the Soviet dictator Joseph Stalin. We'll rub shoulders with the Bishop of Galway, and find out why you're not likely to meet him at a ceilidh. We'll share a merry tune with Henry Ford.

We'll find out how to play on four strings at once, how to cheat at fiddle contests, and how to put yourself into a trance. We'll meet fiddlers on horseback, on the gallows, and on acid. We'll throw caution to the wind and name the best fiddle player in the world, and the worst, as well as the finest and most dismal rock violin solos of all time. We'll even find out what happened when the Devil came back to Georgia.

As if this wasn't enough, there is a wealth of musical examples of ornaments, bowing patterns, scales, modes, exercises, and complete tunes to give you a taste of each style, most of them faithfully reproduced on the accompanying CDs.

This is one fiddle book that won't gather dust on your shelf.

introducing the fiddle

The history ■
Fiddles of the world ■
Fiddle-playing basics ■
Learning the fiddle ■

introducing the fiddle

The history

Rather like the family tree of some medieval monarch, the genealogy of the fiddle is long, rambling, and often bitterly disputed, an ancestry littered with foreign potentates, pretenders, wicked uncles, and princes in the tower.

Early precursors

The earliest contender for the fiddle's ancestor must be the 'ravanastron', a rather mysterious stringed instrument for which the bow is said to have been invented by King Ravan of Ceylon before 3000BC. The significance of the claim comes from the fact that this was the first recorded use of the bow on a stringed instrument. It is a long, thin instrument with two gazelle-gut strings stretched over a wooden body. It is still used today by Buddhist monks. It seems likely that while the name of the instrument may indeed date back thousands of years, its use with a bow probably does not; if the bow had been invented so early, it would almost certainly have spread throughout Asia and Europe soon afterwards, which it failed to do. The ravanastron's claim is further weakened by the fact that all illustrations of it show a completely different instrument, the Chinese 'erhu'. This is a publisher's mistake, probably made decades ago, and faithfully and unquestioningly copied ever since.

A more widely accepted view of the bow's origin is that it was invented by the horse-riding warrior nomads of central Asia in the 8th century or shortly before. They would certainly have had ready access to horsehair, the military bow was in constant use, and rosin was essential for maintaining the strings of these bows. The Chinese certainly credit the 'barbarians' on their western border for the origin of their 'huqin' group of bowed instruments. The bow rapidly spread in the 10th century along the Silk Road and through the Islamic countries of North Africa and the Near East.

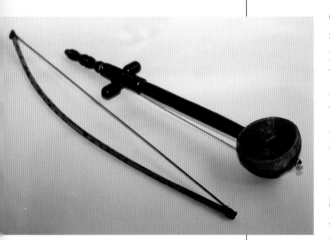

ABOVE: **a rebab and bow from Egypt.**

RIGHT: **a 19th-century Welsh crwth.**

Another early precursor of the fiddle is the 'rebab'. This term is used to include a large and diverse group of bowed stringed instruments. A particular pear-shaped variant, found in Persia, Arabia, and North Africa, was first used with a bow in Arab countries in the late 8th century; by the 10th or 11th century it had been brought into Moorish Spain. The first crusade, around 1100AD, saw its first widespread introduction to Northern Europe. By the Middle Ages it was in widespread use throughout Europe. Until this time no bowed instruments were known here, and it is likely that when the bow arrived with the rebab, musicians would have experimented with using it on pre-existing indigenous instruments (such as the Welsh 'crwth' or 'crowd') that would previously have been plucked.

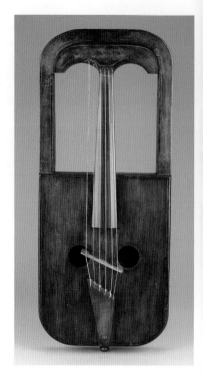

Both the ravanastron and the rebab, together with many other Mediterranean and Balkan fiddles, are played vertically on the lap or knee. It seems that in Europe there was a tradition of playing standing rather than sitting, for which a horizontal position, with the fiddle resting on the chest or shoulder, is more convenient.

Medieval ancestors

By medieval times, Europe had two principal fiddles. The first grew directly out of the rebab and the second developed as a result of the arrival of the bow.

The 'rebec' is an instrument with a pear-shaped body or resonance box, a flat top or belly, and a narrow neck that curves seamlessly into the body. It developed out of the rebab when that arrived in Europe. It had three or six strings (as opposed to the two or four on the rebab), and the body was made of wood (in the rebab it was usually made from a gourd, with a skin face). The strings were attached on the body to a bridge or endpin, and at the neck end were tuned by pegs. It had two soundholes, usually semicircular.

On its introduction to Europe in the 11th century, the rebec was

LEFT: **two modern reproduction rebecs.** BELOW: **a modern vielle based on an instrument shown in a 15th century Flemish painting.**

seen as a high-class instrument much in favour in royal courts, played either solo or in consorts (groups). During the 13th century it was adopted as an accompaniment to church services. It eventually declined in the 15th century, facing competition from the vielle, and, in the 16th century, the violin, which eventually replaced it entirely.

The 'vielle' (medieval fiddle) had a distinct neck, and a slightly arched belly connected to a flat back by ribs. It superseded the Welsh lyre-like instrument, the 'crwth' (also known as the 'crowd', 'rote', or 'rota'), in the 12th century. The number of strings on the vielle grew from one or two to five. The strings were of gut, and were tuned GCCGE or CGCGC. It was said to be the most common stringed instrument of the time, being loud and with a good dynamic range. Two examples of this medieval fiddle were found on the wreck of the *Mary Rose*.

The vielle would have probably played melody with one or more drones. It had a mellow tone compared to that of the more shrill rebec.

Evolution

The vielle continued to develop with the addition of a tailpiece and bridge. The bridge gradually got higher, and a curve was added so that the strings could be played individually. Eventually it gave way to the Renaissance 'viol'; this started with a round opening or sound-hole, which was later replaced by two separate, crescent-shaped holes that foreshadowed the current f-holes. The arched top was more marked than previously. The viol had a soft and sonorous tone, and was ideal for accompaniment of the singing voice.

By 1500 the 'viola da braccio' had developed. It was held against the

shoulder, and it was from this that the violin evolved. It had three or four strings, tuned in fifths, rather than five (on the vielle), and like the rebec had tuning pegs set in a pegbox. It had increasingly marked 'cutouts' – the 'waist' of the instrument – allowing the upper and lower strings to be bowed at a steeper angle to the belly. The soundholes started to take on an f-shape.

By the 16th century, the terms 'vyollon' and 'violon' were being used in France, and 'violino' in Italy. The word 'violin' is first recorded in England in the 1570s.

The violin in its more or less modern form emerged in Milan in northern Italy between 1520 and 1550. With a sound brighter and louder than that of the viol, the violin was ideal for dance music, and was quickly adopted for high-class balls, played in a consort by professional musicians. Some considered it, however, something of an upstart, without the class and pedigree of the now venerable viol. The fact that it was also quickly adopted by illiterate, possibly itinerant, and certainly disreputable folk musicians or fiddlers did little to help its cause in polite society.

An interesting variation on the modern fiddle, dating from the 17th and 18th centuries is the 'dancing master's fiddle' also known as the 'kit' or, from the French, the 'pochette'. This was a fiddle with a cut-down body small enough to fit in the (admittedly voluminous) pocket of a coat. It would have been used by a professional dance instructor who would use it for personal instruction to people in their own homes. Its small body size made it too quiet for use in a proper dance. The earliest models were boat-shaped, a late descendant of the rebec, but this eventually gave way to a cut-down model of the standard violin.

ABOVE RIGHT: **a vielle player, from a painting by Giotto (1267-1337).**
BELOW: **troubadours playing lute and vielle during a knighting ceremony, from an illuminated manuscript of the 15th century.**

THE FIDDLE HANDBOOK

Where did the names 'violin' and 'fiddle' come from?

I learned at school that, since the Norman Conquest, many words for types of meat have two names in English, one deriving from the French, and one from the Anglo-Saxon. Thus the Anglo-Saxon peasants got to tend and feed, though perhaps not to eat, 'the pig', whilst the snooty Norman overlord got to eat 'le porc'. So it is with the fiddle and the violin. The source of both words is the Latin 'vitula', a stringed instrument like a lyre, but also the name of a Roman Goddess. When this was taken by the Romans to Germany, it was called first a 'fidula', then 'fiedel', and finally, on arriving in Britain (in the hands, no doubt, of some itinerant ne'er-do-well), the fiddle.

ABOVE: **Dancing master's fiddles from the 17th and (right) 18th centuries.**

In Spain, however, the vitula passed its name on to a lute-like instrument, the 'vihuela'. On arrival in Italy this became the bowed instrument, the viol, and hence the violino (little viol). Finally arriving on these shores in the possession of some haughty merchant or noble, it became the violin.

Initially the violin would have been a rare and expensive instrument, but as it became cheaper and more easily available, the less sophisticated medieval fiddle gave ground and virtually disappeared. Within a short time the fiddle and violin had become the same instrument, identifiable not by what was in the case, but by what manner of person was carrying it.

The fiddler as rogue or devil

Today the violin, has became, perhaps along with the piano, the key instrument of orchestral art music; the head of the first violin section is regarded as the leader of an orchestra, and top violinists such as Heifetz, Zukerman, or Menuhin are cultural icons. On the other hand, in the possession of a minstrel, itinerant, busker, or vagabond, the fiddle – as essential for a party as a disco or sound system is today – was a symbol of low living and licentiousness. At least, that's what I was promised when I took it up!

Poetry, literature, and art in the 16th, 17th, and 18th centuries are full of images of fiddlers: impoverished, blind, drunk (and blind drunk), and generally a nuisance. This was a favourite theme of the 18th century artist and illustrator William Hogarth; no fairground, ale-house or riotous mob was complete without a fiddler. In 'Hudibras', a 17th-century satirical poem by Samuel Butler, the principal figure, a pompous aristocrat called Sir Hudibras, confronts a "rustic, bear-baiting mob" led by Crowdero, a bearded, one-legged fiddler, described thus:

A squeaking engine he apply'd
Unto his neck, on north east side …

His grisly beard was long and thick,
With which he strung his fiddle-stick …

He, and that engine of vile noise
On which illegally he plays …

Stephen Gosson, a poet and dramatist, complained in 1579 that "London is so full of unprofitable pipers and fiddlers, that a man can no sooner enter a tavern, than two or three cast of them hang at his heels, to give him a dance before he departs."

Such was considered to be the nuisance caused by fiddlers that in 1656 a law was passed prohibiting "all persons commonly called fiddlers or minstrels" from "playing, fiddling, and making music in any inn, alehouse, or tavern".

This image of fiddler as rascal and troublemaker was brought into stark relief in the Puritan era in Europe and America. Drinking, dancing, and any kind of music outside the church were seen as the road to hell, with the fiddler most definitely leading the way. It became seen by many as the Devil's instrument (often referred to as "the Devil's box") and as late as the 19th century fiddles were publicly burned in Scotland and Norway; there are many stories of fiddles being buried or hidden inside walls to prevent their destruction. The Norwegian Hardanger fiddle, in particular, was banned from churches; it had always been linked with legends of trolls and devils, with specific 'devils' tunes' and 'devils' tunings' openly used. There are legends throughout Northern Europe, America, and Asia of fiddles or fiddlers being possessed by the Devil; just as today gangsters may use drugs to entice young people into a life of crime, so the Devil clearly saw the fiddle as the key to ensnaring human souls. In Poland, priests often refused to bury fiddlers in their churchyards. In Shetland, by way of retribution, fiddlers play a tune called 'De'il Stick Da Minister', and many other tunes refer to the Devil in some way: 'The Devil's Dream', 'The De'il Among The Tailors', 'Devil In The Strawsack', and so on. Robert Burns mocked the notion that fiddle music was the Devil's work in his song 'The De'il's Awa' Wi' The Exciseman", in which the Devil "cam' fiddlin' thro' the toun, an' danced awa' wi' the Exciseman".

Probably the most famous modern rendering of the demonic fiddler tale is Charlie Daniels' song 'The Devil Went Down To Georgia', in which the Devil, on the lookout for a "soul to steal", meets Johnny, "Sawin' on a fiddle and playin' it hot". The devil thinks it will be a safe bet to challenge Johnny to a fiddle contest; "I bet a fiddle of gold against your soul, 'cos I think I'm better than you!" Satan leads off with a demonic solo that sounds like Arnold Schoenberg on acid, whilst Johnny counters, and wins, with some hot-to-trot bluegrass licks and a tune stolen from Vassar Clements. You will no doubt have heard this song, and if you're a fiddle player yourself will be more than familiar with people asking if you can play it, but if you haven't yet heard it, you must also check out 'The Devil Came Back To Georgia', sung by Johnny Cash. In this version the Devil comes back for another go, but this time squares up against session supremo Mark O'Connor. After practising his scales and limbering up, O'Connor comes up with a technically mind-blowing finale, which sends Old Nick once more back to hell with his tail between his legs.

ABOVE: the legendary Norwegian fiddler Myllarguten (1801-1872) playing the Hardanger fiddle.

Fiddles of the world

In this book we will look in detail at fiddle styles from around North America and Europe. All these styles can be readily played on the standard violin, and can be written to some degree in standard notation. Your average modern urban western fiddler has a sporting chance of being able to learn them. However, the fiddling world is far wider, stranger, and more mysterious than the safe confines of the front-porch picker. Across the world are a baffling array of fiddles, some bearing little resemblance to the violin, and often steeped in history, myth, and mysticism.

So your first question has to be, if it doesn't look like a violin, how do you define a fiddle?

Stringed instruments as a whole can be divided into five groups.

- The musical bow. At its simplest, this is a single piece of wood, bent into an arch, with the two ends joined by a single string that can be plucked.
- The lyre. This has a four-sided frame. One side comprises a soundbox; two arms come out from this, joined on the fourth side by a crossbar. Strings stretch from the crossbar to the soundbox.
- The harp. This has a soundbox and a single diagonal arm, with strings of different lengths between the two.
- The lute. This has a body or belly, a neck, and some kind of head. The strings run along the full length of the neck.
- The zither. This has a rectangular body, with strings stretched across most of its length and width.

All of these families of instrument existed in some form before the fiddle, and all were designed to be plucked. The crucial invention was that of the bow. When drawn across the strings, it could create a sustained sound quite different from the plucked sound. Whilst a plucked string can create music, a bowed string can do far more: it can imitate the timbre of the human voice. The idea of at least trying the newfangled bow would have been irresistible to anyone who played a stringed instrument.

The harp and zither, by nature of their construction, and mostly because there were too many strings all lying parallel, could not be effectively bowed. The musical bow could itself be played with a smaller bow, but lacking a resonating chamber could never produce a powerful note. This leaves the lyre and the lute, both of which, with a little modification, could be bowed. Which brings us to an all-encompassing definition of the fiddle, as any lute- or lyre-like instrument which is bowed.

You may never get to play any of the wild and wonderful instruments described here, but they are all important. Whenever the standard fiddle co-exists with or replaces an ancient folk fiddle, it will take on or inherit many of the characteristics of the older fiddle, in bowing technique, tunings, scale, intonation, or repertoire. To understand fully a folk fiddling style it is often necessary to know something about these sometimes cranky, often difficult, but always fascinating older relatives.

We have identified central Asia as the possible source of the bow, so here might be a good place to start a whirlwind tour of world fiddles. Mongolia has as its national instrument the 'morin khuur', also known as the horse-head fiddle. It is full of magic and symbolism, representing the nomad's love of his horse and his lifestyle amid the wide-open spaces of Asia. A square box-like body is held upright between the knees, a little like a cello. The long neck has two strings; the thicker or male string is made from 130 hairs from a stallion's tail, whilst the thinner, female string has 105 mare's tail hairs. I suspect the offer of a set of Thomastik Spirocore would be politely declined. Instead of a scroll, the neck is topped with a carved horse's head, not unlike those found on the staffs of shamen, who were said to have the power to journey into the spirit world.

The sound of the morin khuur is deep, rich, and highly expressive, and the music produced deliberately imitates horses neighing, hooves galloping, and the wind sighing through the grasses. Legend tells that the first morin khuur was made by Kuku Namjil, a Mongolian shepherd, who received from the gods a gift of a magical winged horse to allow him to fly at night to visit his distant beloved. A jealous rival cut the wings off the horse, causing it to fall to the earth and die. From the body, the distraught Kuku built the morin khuur and used it to create tragic songs of loss and longing. From the design of his instrument, one assumes that he missed the horse more than the girl.

China has an instrument closely related to the morin khuur, the 'erhu'; it is one of a family of instruments called the 'huqin', meaning "two-stringed barbarian instrument". Earliest records of the erhu come from the 5th-century Song dynasty, but this version was bowed with a strip of bamboo; the horsehair bow, which probably came in along the Silk Road, again from central Asia, arrived around the 11th century. It is a rather more delicate instrument than the morin khuur, with a small, usually six-sided bowl-like body of wood, and a belly of python skin. The strings were originally of silk but are now usually of steel. Both strings are fingered simultaneously with the back of the nail, with the angle and pressure of the bow determining which string is sounded. Unusually for such an instrument, the playing style is not based on drones and is capable of great delicacy and sensitivity. Also very unusual is the fact that the hairs of the bow, instead of being laid in top of the strings, are permanently fitted between the strings. For centuries the erhu was seen, perhaps because of its barbarian origins, as a low-class instrument suitable for beggars and musicians in folk-

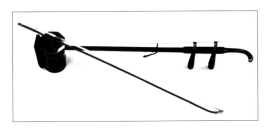

operas. In the 20th century it was elevated to the highest status, and playing techniques took great leaps forward, to the extent that it can now be heard playing everything from

ABOVE: **a Mongolian musician playing the morin khuur.**

BELOW LEFT: **a Chinese erhu.**

Thelonious Monk's *Round Midnight* to the *Paganini Variations*, all with the hauntingly beautiful tone immediately evocative of China.

India has one of the strangest looking fiddles in the 'sarangi', with its squat rectangular box-like body, three melody strings, and up to 40 sympathetic strings which ring on their own, giving a resonant, whining sound to the instrument. The name means "a hundred colours", giving some idea of the expressiveness of the instrument; Yehudi Menuhin described it as "the very soul of Indian feeling and thought". It is widely found in the Hindustani area of north India and it is said that the first one was built by a wandering doctor, who woke from sleeping under a tree to be startled by an eerie noise from above; it turned out to be the wind blowing over the dried skin of a dead monkey.

The western violin was probably introduced to India around 1790 by British bandsmen stationed at Fort St George in Madras. The Indian musician Baluswami Dikshitar learned the violin, and quickly recognized its potential value in Carnatic (south Indian) classical music. This is the 'raga' tradition of improvisation around a set of around 72 scales ('melakartas') and 35 rhythms ('talas'). A key aim of instrumentalists is the imitation of the human voice, for which the violin is uniquely suited. The violin was soon adopted on a large scale, and playing techniques were modified to suit the new demands of Indian music. Players sit cross-legged on the floor, the violin pointing downwards with the scroll resting firmly on the right ankle. Open tunings are used, such as DADA or FCFC, and there is a great deal of precise sliding between notes, with the middle finger sliding up and the index finger sliding down. The whole hand moves with the slide.

In the late 20th century, Indian violin took great strides when musical contact was made with such western rock or jazz musicians as George Harrison and John McLaughlin. Indian musicians began fusing their own tradition with western styles, to devastating effect. When I first heard L. Shankar playing with McLaughlin's group, Shakti, I was startled by the speed, accuracy, and invention of his playing. I was convinced that this was surely the best fiddle player in the world, bar none, and have yet to be convinced otherwise.

Not satisfied with mastering four strings, L. Shankar designed, with the help of American guitar-maker Ken Parker, a truly audacious instrument: a ten-stringed, double-necked electric violin. This enabled him to play the full range of the violin family, right down to the double bass. If he ever sits in on your old-time picking session, I suggest you beat a hasty retreat to the bar.

The bow travelled in both directions along the Silk Road from central Asia, and one of the first beneficiaries was the Islamic world of Persia and Arabia. The first fiddle to be developed here was the 'rebab';

ABOVE: **Dilshad Khan playing the sarangi.**
OPPOSITE PAGE TOP: **a North African rebab.**
OPPOSITE PAGE BOTTOM: **the Persian kemance.**

a simple instrument with a small rounded body (often a gourd or coconut shell) and some kind of skin belly, a long stick neck, and a pegbox to which up to three strings could be attached. Such instruments circulated widely throughout the Middle East, Far East and North Africa. The body would often have a spike coming out of its bottom end, hence the common generic name of spike fiddle.

A slightly more sophisticated fiddle is the 'kemance', developed in Persia. The name comes from 'keman', meaning bow or violin (the two words, interestingly, seem to be interchangeable), and 'ce', small. (There are at least six different spellings of kemance in common use.) The advantage of this instrument over the rebab is that it has a proper fingerboard, so that the strings can be fingered with greater ease, accuracy, and range. In Greece and Turkey the kemance has a confusing, promiscuous, and incestuous relationship with the 'lyra'; in some cases the same instrument may share both names, the Turkish 'klassikkemenche' being referred to by Greeks as the 'politiki lyra'. There are two common body types. The first is a so-called boat shape, as represented by the 'Black Sea fiddle' or 'Pontic lyra'. This is found mainly around the town of Trabzon, formerly settled by Greeks but now in north-east Turkey. The three strings are tuned in fourths and are usually double stopped, giving it a distinctive and strangely archaic sound. Having a proper fingerboard, this is one of the easiest such instruments for a fumbling western fiddle player to make sense of. If you've ever taken a holiday on the beautiful Greek island of Crete, you may have come across the 'Cretan lyra', which has the second of the main body types, the pear shape. This is used for the accompaniment of dancing and singing. Like all the rest of the family it is played vertically, and can be used either standing or sitting. It is a robust instrument with a powerful, nasal tone. Most of the melody is played on the top string of three (usually tuned GDA). When playing for celebrations such as weddings, the lyra player may be expected to play for many hours at time without a break. To ease the workload of the bowing arm, when a change of string is required the whole lyra is rotated rather than the right arm having to change position.

A long drive north takes us to Scandinavia, a land of ice and snow, mountains, forests, trolls, legends – and fiddles. The standard violin is in use throughout the region, but south-west Norway is home to one of the most fascinating of fiddle variants, the Hardanger fiddle or 'hardingfele'. Whilst this looks superficially like a violin, and is played in the same position, there are many subtle differences. Most important is the presence of four or five sympathetic strings, which lie underneath the fingerboard. The neck is slightly shorter, the body deeper, the bridge flatter and the f-holes wider than normal; the body

ABOVE: **A Hardanger fiddle made in Norway in the 19th century.**

is elaborately decorated with black ink, the fingerboard inlaid with mother of pearl, and the scroll carved into a lion or dragon. One of the most fascinating aspects of the hardingfele is the many cross-tunings that are used, and the names which they are given. Most common is the 'high bass', ADAE, followed by standard tuning, GDAE. There are around 24 more tunings, many of which are named for colours of the sky; light blue, twilight grey, semi-grey and so on. As with the ragas of India, where different scales are used at different times of the day, so in Norway the tuning may change as the evening progresses and the sky darkens. On winter nights, when the stars are out, the fire has burned down, the listeners have fallen asleep, and the beer has run out, the fiddler may switch to 'half-troll tuning' or the infamous AEAC♯ – the Devil's tuning. The Devil and his minions play leading roles in the many legends associated with Norwegian fiddling. With the instrument in the devil's tuning, you can play 'rammeslatter', hypnotic tunes with the power to send people into a trance. It is said that once playing such a tune the fiddler may be unable to stop, and the instrument has to be pulled off him. Sometimes the Devil himself may appear at a dance, grab the fiddler's instrument and play with such power that the dancers will dance themselves to death; their skeletons will continue dancing until their skulls fall off and roll down the hill.

Among the Devil's earthly representatives are the sprites and trolls who live under bridges in mountain streams. If you want to gain supernatural fiddling abilities, there's one very easy way to do it. Go to a bridge at midnight, and hang your fiddle underneath, then go home and try to get a good night's sleep. In the morning, go back to your fiddle. The troll will have retuned it, played one of his unearthly tunes, and put all his magic into your fiddle. He will also have hung his own instrument, identical in every way, next to yours. Pick your own fiddle and you have all the troll's magical command of the fiddle. Pick the wrong one and the Devil gets your soul.

The basics of fiddle playing

In this section we will look at some of the basics of fiddle playing. They include buying and maintaining a fiddle; the parts of a fiddle; the accessories that go with it; amplifying it; and learning and developing as a fiddle player.

Buying an instrument

There is a huge choice of fiddles available, and a lot of decisions to make. Should you buy a new, factory-made instrument, or one newly hand-made? If you want something older, will it make a difference if it's 100 years old or 300? Should you go for French, German, or Italian?

If you're a beginner, and this is your first fiddle, my advice is not to worry about getting a quality violin. Let's face it, for the first few months this is going to seem like an instrument of torture to those around you, if not to yourself, and not even a Stradivarius is going to ameliorate the pain and suffering you're going to cause. (OK, maybe I exaggerate slightly.)

Go for a new, cheap, factory-made instrument. That way, you'll get your violin, strings, case, and bow all in good working order, and probably for less than £100/$150. If you have a friend who's an experienced fiddler who can come with you to the music shop, ask him or her to try out half a dozen different instruments for you; you'll probably find that some are quite a lot better than others, even within a batch of apparently identical instruments from the same factory.

After a year or so you'll either have realised that playing an iPod is a lot easier than a fiddle and taken it down to the charity shop, or you'll have made sufficient progress that you're starting to see the limitations of your instrument, and you can start thinking about buying something with a bit more quality. Something attractive to look at, with a bit of history to it and with a tone – bright, mellow, sweet, powerful – that suits your musical temperament.

The bow

Just as violins may be highly valued both for their quality as musical instruments and as objets d'art by famous makers, so the bow can be a highly prized object. It is easily possible for a bow to be worth a great deal more than the violin it is playing on, and in the hands of a skilled player it can make a great deal of difference to the sound produced.

So what do you need to know about your bow? Firstly, as with a young lady checking out a suitor, make sure it has a reasonably full head of hair. The white horsehair strands stretched down the length of the bow are what cause the vibration on the violin strings, creating your sweet, sweet music. Over time these will break, one by one. If your playing ranges from timid to genteel, this may take years, but if your playing is more in the aggressive to manic range, it may be more like weeks. When a hair breaks, you generally pull out what's left to keep the bow looking tidy (though I did know a devil-may-care Cajun fiddler who deliberately left the loose hairs on so that they would flap around dramatically as he was playing). When you've lost about a quarter of the hairs, it's time, not to get a new bow, but to get the bow rehaired. This is a job for which you need to take it to a violin shop, repairer, or bow specialist. The job will take a couple of days and will cost maybe £20-30/$30-45. If you're playing every day this can be a bit of an inconvenience, which is why fiddlers often carry two bows with them in the case, so there's always a spare.

At the heel, or hand-end of the bow, you'll notice at the very end a section that rotates. You use this to tighten or loosen the hairs of the bow. When you put the instrument away, loosen the hairs, otherwise your bow will suffer from prolonged tension. When you are about to use it, tighten the hairs up enough so that, with your right hand in playing position on the bow, you can just about push the wood of the bow down onto the violin strings; if this is too easy, the hair isn't tight enough; if it's too hard, the hairs are too tight. And don't forget your rosin. Without it the hairs of the bow will slide over the strings without any grip, and you'll not get much sound out of the fiddle. Rub the bow hairs over the rosin, end to end, maybe 20 times. This coats the hairs with the sticky particles (made from pine tree resin), enabling the bow to get a firm grip on the strings.

Strings

The four strings of a fiddle are tuned G, D, A, and E, E being the thinnest and highest in pitch. To put a string on, first loosen the peg (at the head of the fiddle), and thread the tip of the string through an inch or so. Then, holding the string tight with one hand, wind the peg round a few times. Still holding it tight, position the string over the appropriate groove in the bridge, and attach the other end (usually the ring or hook) to the fine tuner or the hole in the tailpiece. Tighten it to approximately the right pitch using the peg, and then do the final tuning with the tuner. You'll find the string will keep going flat for an hour or so after putting it on, until it's finished stretching.

Classical players tend to use three gut strings (which do not use fine tuners), with only the E being metal with a tuner, whilst fiddlers usually use all four metal strings and use four tuners. Metal strings are more durable, and can last for months. You know that a string needs changing either when it starts to sound very dull, when you find it difficult to play it in tune (more difficult than usual, that is), or when the winding starts to give way (you'll feel an unevenness under your finger as you play). When this happens, the string is going to break in the near future.

Always to carry at least one set of spare strings; at the very least carry a set of old strings as an emergency back-up. It's a good idea to change all four at once, since a new string sounds a lot brighter than an old one, and the fiddle will have an uneven tone with one new string and three old ones. When you change your strings, don't take all the old ones off together. If you do, the bridge will collapse; the

THE FROG

THE HEAD

THE BOW
1 Button
2 Ebony body
3 Ferrule
4 Throat
5 Leather band
6 Lapping
7 Head mortise
8 Face/head plate
9 Ridge
10 Throat
11 Hair

THE FIDDLE
1 Scroll
2 Pegbox
3 Pegs
4 Nut
5 Fingerboard
6 Table
7 Nicks
8 F-hole
9 Finial
10 Bridge
11 Tailpiece

12 Saddle
13 Tailgut
14 Purfling
15 Neck
16 Button
17 Top bout
18 C-bout
19 Corner
20 Lower bout
21 Back
22 End button
23 Edge

strings are all that's holding it in place. Instead, replace each string as you take it off.

Some fiddlers like to experiment with alternative tunings, raising or lowering the pitch of strings to allow different tonalities and make possible different types of drone. This can be a risky business, as neither the strings nor the bridge are designed to take more tension than they are already under. Anything more than a tone higher than normal, and a string is liable to snap in protest at your heathen practices.

Tuning

If you have perfect pitch you'll know instinctively what pitch a string is, and what it should be, without any external point of reference. But perfect pitch is very rare, so you will probably need something to tune to. This could be a tuning fork, tapped against your knee (ouch) and then held on the bridge of the fiddle; it will then ring loudly enough to tune to. Alternatively you can get a note from a piano or, increasingly nowadays, use an electronic tuner.

The general practice is to get the A string right first, then tune the others to this. Some people (most classical players) do this by bowing two adjacent strings simultaneously, and listening to the interval (which should be a perfect fifth). An alternative method of tuning is to play harmonics on both strings; in this way it is possible to play the same pitch on the two strings and compare them directly.

The bridge

It looks a simple enough thing – an arched piece of wood with four notches – but the bridge is a complex piece of engineering and not to be taken lightly. If you buy a new bridge, let's say to put on an old fiddle that came without any strings, it will come uncut. It needs to be shaped to fit the individual fiddle and positioned in exactly the right place. In short, like the extraction of nuclear fuel rods, or open-heart surgery, it's best left to an expert. Once on, a bridge should last several years without any attention. However it has a lot of work to do supporting the tension of the strings, and eventually it may start to sag. Look at it sideways on. It should be dead straight and vertical. If, on the other hand, it's slightly bent, and leaning forwards at the top, then it's not happy and needs some attention. Loosen all the strings slightly. Then, using two fingers and two thumbs, you should be able to straighten it out. Keep an eye on it; if it keeps sagging, get it replaced.

Shoulder rest

In the old days, fiddlers used to hold the fiddle low down on the chest. This made it easy to walk or even dance when playing, and also sing

(I'm not sure about juggling live eels). However, it meant that the weight of the fiddle was supported by the left hand, which also of course has the job of fingering. As long as the hand is clamped in the same place, that's not a problem, but if you want to change position (about which, more later), it's a big problem. For this reason the chinrest was created, allowing the fiddle to be clamped comfortably under the chin, with the weight supported by the collar bone or shoulder. However, this still isn't very comfortable. What you need is a shoulder rest. This clamps on to the bottom of the fiddle and raises it above the shoulder. It's now possible comfortably to hold the instrument horizontal without taking any weight on the left hand at all. This frees the hand to move up and down the neck from first to ninth position without any trouble (easier said than done of course, but let's think positive).

Mute

Small, cheap, but potentially very important; it could mean the difference between marriage and divorce, between a regular practice routine and an old-fashioned lynching. A mute is a little device that clamps on to the bridge, damping the vibrations and making the fiddle quieter; a great idea if you share a flat with non-musicians, or have thin walls and unsympathetic neighbours. It also gives a much softer tone; Stéphane Grappelli often used one when playing delicate ballads.

Amplification

Throughout most of its history the fiddle has been played unamplified; even at large, lively dances the fiddler would have to rely on his own sweat and elbow-grease to make sure he was heard above the hubbub of voices, clinking glasses, and stomping feet. Nowadays there are many options for amplification, and since audiences are so used to hearing amplified music virtually wherever they go, it is rare to play at any but the smallest of dances without amplification.

So what are the options?

Playing through a microphone on a stand

This is a good option where the rest of the band is relatively quiet. With a decent mic and PA system this can give a very good representation of the true sound of the fiddle; all that is required of the fiddler is to place his instrument the right distance from the mic. Traditional bluegrass bands make an art-form of playing round a single mic, stepping backwards and forwards to balance the sound. The chief drawback of a microphone is that if there is too much volume on the stage (if there's a drummer, for example) you are liable to get feedback, an unpleasant and persistent howling that continues even after the bagpipe player has left the stage. Feedback occurs because the mic will pick up the drummer as well as the fiddle, not to mention the guitarist (whose amp volume control is stuck on 11). That volume will come back into the mic, increasing your own volume and setting up an uncontrollable howl. If you're in a werewolf/industrial/grunge metal band this may be just the effect you're after. If not, you're going to want either a pickup or an electric violin.

Using a dedicated, close-up fiddle microphone

These are tiny microphones mounted on the body of the fiddle. A good system can be unobtrusive and can give a clean, warm sound, but there will always be the danger of some feedback on a noisy stage. They are often used in professional theatre and orchestral situations; they are ideal for this because they can be very quickly and easily attached to the instrument without otherwise affecting it in any way. One of the leading models is the DPA, which clips just behind the bridge. I've tried one of these, and it gave the best representation of the acoustic sound that I have heard. Of course, nothing is perfect; I found it somewhat prone to feedback on a noisy stage. I was also worried that the thin cable would have a short working life, but have been assured that it is practically indestructible.

Using a pickup, sometimes called a bug

These come in various shapes and sizes; most pickups are 'piezo-electric transducers', sensitive crystals that convert vibrations into an electrical signal. Some pickups attach to the body of the violin, for example the Ashworth AJ11, but the majority of pickups are attached to the bridge, which is the part of the instrument where the vibrations are most focused. The pickup might stick on to the bridge and be removable, as for example with the Barcus Berry; the old models used to stick on with a kind of Blu-Tack or adhesive putty, whilst the newer models are screwed on. The Fishman is designed to slip into the slot in the bridge. The makers recommend using the slot on the treble side, but with many years of using this system I found the bass side gave a much better tone.

The chief advantage of a pickup system is that feedback is a lot less likely, and you are free to move about the stage. The two potential problems with pickups are that, firstly, the pickup may cause some acoustic damping of the fiddle, so that when played acoustically (but with the pickup still attached) the fiddle may not be quite as loud. I have never found this a problem. Secondly, it can be difficult to get a true representation of the tone of the fiddle.

Most pickups are removable. There are two disadvantages to removing your pickup often. Firstly, the wires are often very fragile and may become damaged after a few years of use. Secondly, even a tiny difference in the positioning of a bridge pickup may make a big difference to the tone.

Some pickups are built into the bridge itself; one such is the L.R. Baggs, which I use myself; it gives a very balanced sound, a powerful signal, and works well without a preamp. The downside of this is that once it's on, you're committed to this system; taking the bridge on and off is a job for a violin shop, not for your average player. Some makers produce bridges with multiple transducers. The Barbera bridge, for example, comes with a pickup on each string; these bridges are incorporated in electric violins by Wood and Jordan, among others.

Most pickups benefit from a pre-amp. The signal produced by a pickup is very small, so it needs to be increased before going to the amp or mixing desk. You may well find, particularly with an older or cheaper pickup, that if you plug directly into an amp you have firstly to turn the gain right up and secondly turn most or all of the treble off. This means that you need a pre-amp. This will boost the output volume and also help to regulate the tone, giving you more of the warmer mid and bass frequencies and less of the harsh upper end. Most companies that produce pickups also make their own preamps, which should be well matched to the needs of that particular pickup. A preamp is also a good idea because it gives you a degree of local, independent control over your tone and volume. Otherwise you either have to go backwards and forwards to your amp or, worse still, rely on the soundman being awake, sober, and receptive to your frantic signals.

An important consideration for any type of pickup is the connection socket (jack) that you use to plug into the amp. The socket/jack may be for a mini-jack cable, usually mounted on the tailpiece. Years of experience with this system leads me to plead with you not to use one. Cables with a mini-jack are lightweight and for a gigging musician last no time at all. I used to have a whole suitcase full of old, broken mini-jack cables, all of which had failed during a gig. Far better to get a 'carpenter jack' system fitted. This is a quarter-inch jack socket that mounts on the side of the fiddle with the same fittings as a standard chinrest; it allows you to use a full size guitar cable, which will last much longer and is much easier to find.

Using an electric violin
The next possibility is some kind of electric violin. At its crudest this

can be nothing more than a normal violin stuffed with filling to stop any natural vibrations and eliminate feedback and then mounted with a pickup. With a dedicated instrument you can fit a preamp inside and put a volume and tone control on the body. Barcus Berry were one of the first companies to produce electric violins. As soon as you lose the natural vibrations of a violin body, the tone produced is bound to change. Some electric violin makers go out of their way to try and produce as natural a sound as possible. An example would be Skyinbow, based in the Shetland Isles, Scotland, which provides fiddles for many folk players. In the rock and jazz fields, the edgy and more cutting tone produced by many electric violins is seen as an advantage; much of the subtlety of the true violin sound is wasted amid the rough and tumble of drums and electric guitars.

A possibility that opens up with electric violins is the use of extra strings. Barcus Berry introduced a lower C string to some of their early electric violins, whilst Violectra have produced a seven-string model. The lower strings would be virtually inaudible acoustically, but when amplified they can sound very dramatic.

Once you're relying for the sound purely on the bridge, and the acoustic properties of the violin body are no longer being used, the field is open in terms of design. Solid bodies, clear Perspex, and dynamic colour schemes become possible. The greater weight of a solid body is a problem easily surmounted by removing all of the extraneous structure; all you really need is the points of contact with left hand, chin and shoulder. Elegant and often striking stick or skeletal body shapes are a strong selling feature for many electrics; for many rock players the appearance of the instrument is as important as the sound. If you're into glam rock or heavy metal, and really fancy yourself as a four-string guitar hero, the Viper, Stingray, or Sabre shape of Mark Wood's violins might be just the thing for you.

A bonus feature of possessing an electric violin is that you can practise silently, using headphones; the relatively cheap Yamaha SV-120K is produced with this in mind. A silent fiddle is a must if you're stuck in a bedsit with thin walls, a tour bus, a hotel room, or a jail cell.

MIDI violins

Perhaps the final frontier in electric violin design is the use of MIDI; this enables the violinist to control a separate sound module, producing a virtually limitless palette of sounds. MIDI is also a useful tool in writing and recording, since the MIDI signal can be translated directly into musical notation. Market leader in the MIDI violin is Zeta. The Zeta bridge has two piezo-electric pickups for each string, allowing the individual string volumes to be balanced for analogue use, and allowing clean separation so that each string can give its own MIDI signal. Zeta produces its own rack-mountable MIDI controller, the Synthony II. Other MIDI converters are available, for example by Roland or Yamaha, but the Zeta violin will only produce MIDI through the Synthony II.

Learning the fiddle

The violin is a notoriously difficult instrument for a beginner. Whereas any fool can get a sweet, clean note out of a piano, the odds are stacked against getting a decent note on the fiddle. Playing the note in tune depends on getting your fingertip in exactly the right place on the fingerboard, whilst playing it clearly depends on just the right movement and pressure with the bow. Too little pressure and it will whistle; too much and it will screech or growl in a most unbecoming fashion. In short, don't expect too much from yourself too soon.

It's a good idea to have some plan and sense of direction to your learning. Of the styles described in this book, not all would be recommended for beginners. There's no point, for example, in trying to play jazz, western swing, or bluegrass until you've mastered a lot of the basics. Old time, Cajun, or Irish make far fewer technical demands on the player. That is not to say there's anything inferior about these styles, but you could say they have their feet more firmly on the ground.

How to go about learning? Traditionally fiddlers would learn by listening to and imitating their parents, siblings, friends or neighbours, possibly augmented at some point by some lessons. Nowadays there is also the option of listening to and playing along with CDs, as well as learning from tutor books or DVDs, or attending fiddle camps or courses. Even a generation ago it was difficult to learn any style of fiddle playing that wasn't available in your own neighbourhood. Nowadays there's nothing to stop someone in the Appalachian mountains from learning klezmer fiddle, or someone from the glens of Scotland learning jazz.

It's important to start off with a good posture when learning the fiddle. A bent back, hunched shoulders, and a stiff neck not only look and feel bad, they mean that ten years down the line you could end up with serious health problems. Keep your feet apart and your shoulders in the same axis; don't twist, don't rest unevenly on one foot. Keep your head upright, the violin horizontal (not pointing downwards), and angled slightly to the left. It's important to be relaxed, with your head upright and your back straight.

Don't rely on your left hand to support the weight of the violin; the instrument should be held firmly between your chin and shoulder.

Keep your left wrist straight, and your hand well up so that your fingers are coming down onto the fingerboard nearly vertically, rather than horizontally from the side.

The fingers of your right hand should all be bent; your three middle fingers wrap around the wood of the bow; the little finger remains on the top, and the thumb hooks underneath, in the notch of the frog. Many traditional players hold the bow some way up from the frog, effectively shortening the bow. They may feel that this gives them more control, but it also limits them to a fairly narrow range of possible bowing techniques.

All in all, fiddle players are notorious for getting at least some of these things wrong; when you teach yourself from scratch, and spend most of your playing time sitting in a pub or at a festival campsite, it's easy to let such things go. My recommendation would be that when you're starting off, even if you intend to teach yourself, you should have at least one lesson to show you everything you need to know about standing and holding the instrument correctly.

Should you learn to read music? As a violinist there is no question that you have to become musically literate at the same time as learning to play. For a fiddle player there's more of a choice; many traditional players manage perfectly well playing by ear and relying on a good memory. Uncle Jimmy Thompson, the first fiddler to play on WSM Barn Dance, the radio show that was the precursor to the Grand Old Opry, said "I'd just as soon look a mule in the ass as look at a sheet of music!" However, there's no doubt that there are many advantages to learning to read music, particularly if you intend to play gigs. It makes it a great deal easier to access a large and perhaps diverse repertoire, and makes it easier to pass tunes from person to person without a lot of tedious repetition. Being a good reader is a great asset in all kinds of professional settings, and in styles such as jazz an understanding of the music itself is tied in with musical theory – and you can't really understand theory without reading music.

Many people switch to the fiddle after having learned the classical violin. In this case you're faced with quite a different set of challenges. You will find you have to 'unlearn' a lot of the techniques that came with classical discipline. Classical players, for example, generally use far too much vibrato for any fiddle style, and play bows which are much too long. Concepts such as 'playing dirty' and improvising are also quite foreign.

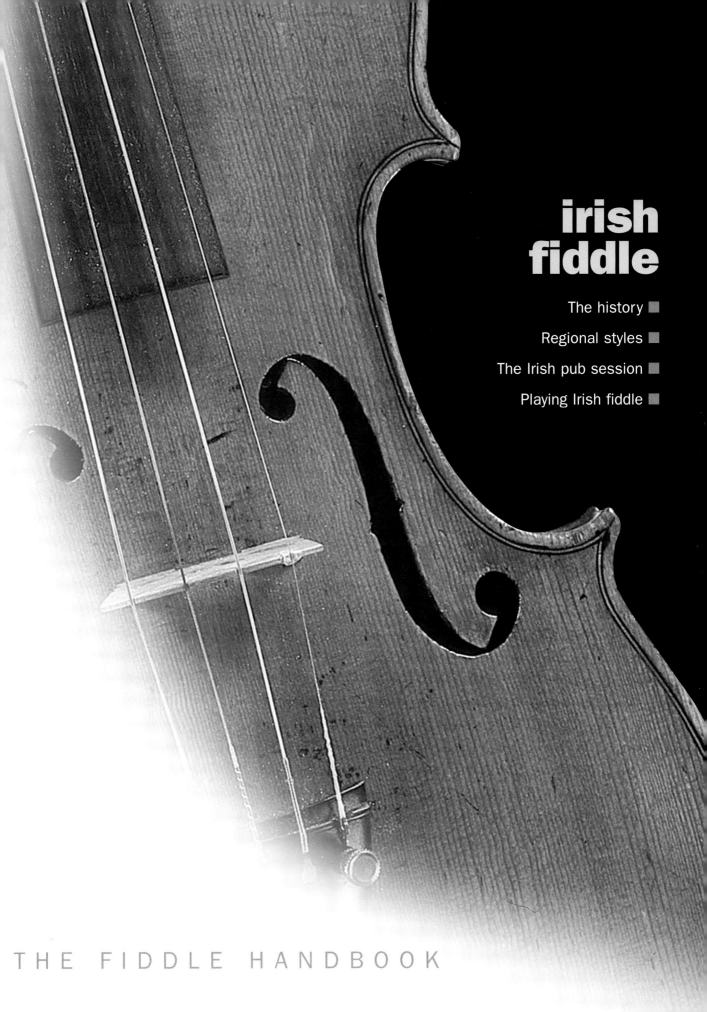

irish fiddle

The history ■

Regional styles ■

The Irish pub session ■

Playing Irish fiddle ■

THE FIDDLE HANDBOOK

irish fiddle

When it comes to fiddle playing, the Irish wrote the book. Or more to the point, Chicago Police Chief Francis O'Neill wrote the book, at the start of the 20th century. Born near Bantry in west Cork in 1848, O'Neill was an energetic and ambitious man. He went to sea as cabin boy on a British merchant ship at the age of 16, eventually settling, along with many thousands of his fellow countrymen, in the city of Chicago.

Here he joined the ranks of the police force, rising to become its chief in 1901. Although he was no slouch as a policeman (a newspaper carried the story that three notorious thieves left Chicago because "this town is too tough for graft while O'Neill is chief of police"), his ruling passion was Irish dance music. Like émigrés everywhere, he saw the music of his homeland as an emotional and symbolic lifeline to everything he had left behind.

Worried that this music was in decline, he enlisted the aid of fellow policeman and namesake James O'Neill, from County Down, to transcribe what he could remember of the tunes he had heard as a boy. Though a talented flautist, the chief could not write music. James, on the other hand, was a trained violinist and had both the patience and enthusiasm to write down the tunes his friend played. Soon this endeavour became known to other musicians in Chicago, and in no time fiddlers, pipers and flautist were lining up to have their tunes copied in this way. The chief would book them in, and the three would sit together, with James annotating the tune then playing it back to the performer, who could comment on and correct the transcription. O'Neill was always on the lookout for new blood, and as soon as he heard of a new musician arriving in the country, he would invite him to Chicago, often with the offer of a job on the force. Of the approximately 3,000 officers on the force at the time, around two thirds were said to be Irish.

His collection grew rapidly, and more than 2000 tunes were published in two collections; *The Music of Ireland* in 1903, and *Dance Music Of Ireland* in 1907. The significance of these collections cannot be over-emphasised. Whilst others had tried similar endeavours before

(Edward Bunting published a set of Harp tunes in 1792, and George Petrie followed in the early 19th century with several collections of Irish airs), these earlier collectors had little real understanding of the music they were listening to. Intended for the drawing rooms of the nobility, these collections ended up with tunes written in the wrong key, with inappropriate accidentals and piano accompaniments. For actual practitioners of folk music they were next to useless.

O'Neill, on the other hand, was surrounded by such practitioners, and went to great pains to get as accurate as possible a record of the tunes as actually played.

In doing so he had to get to grips with a series of problems that are central to all types of folk music in terms of copying, learning, and reproducing the style of traditional performance. A classical composer can write and publish his music, using the elaborate and precise methodology of classical notation. Once it's 'out there', any trained, competent musician can perform the tune pretty well exactly as the composer intended, even centuries later. Traditional music, the province of the fiddle player, is another kettle of fish. For a start, with a few notable exceptions, the original composer of the tunes is usually unknown, and they have been handed down by ear, over generations. At every turn, when a jig or reel passes from one person to the next, there is the possibility, even the likelihood, that something is going to change in the telling. Thus a note, a phrase, a whole section can change, as well as the title and form. In an essay on 'The Development Of Traditional Irish Music', O'Neill, perhaps stung by a criticism that some of his transcriptions were inaccurate or inauthentic, presented previously published versions of the same tunes, demonstrating how over the years a single tune could be given two different titles, or could change from a jig to a reel, or a reel to a hornpipe.

After many amusing or perhaps frustrating transcriptions, in which the written version never seemed to quite match what was played, O'Neill eventually realised that some players, notably the fiddler John McFadden, could never play a tune without some element of improvisation and variation. Once the structure of a tune is firmly in a fiddler's head, he can vary the ornamentation, substitute one phrase for another, or even create elaborate variations, all with the greatest of ease and possibly without even realising. Unlike with classical music, where there is a one right way and a million wrong ways to play a tune, a traditional melody in the hands of a skilled fiddler is a living, breathing thing that belongs as much to the performer as it does to the composer, if such a single person ever existed.

Again in the words of O'Neill, "Traditional music, unlike any form of modern composition, is not the work of one man but many. Indeed it can hardly be said to have been composed at all. It is simply a growth to a certain extent subject to … heredity, environment, natural selection, and survival of the fittest."

The history of Irish fiddling

Irish fiddling, indeed Irish folk music in general, centres around the traditional Irish pub session, where musicians relax around a table heaving with foaming pints, laughing, chatting, and swapping tunes as they have for centuries, right? Wrong! Many aspects of what we see and hear today in the performance of Irish music are not traditional at all.

Before the 20th century most folk music (or what might be better defined as working-class music) in Ireland was performed solo, not by enthusiastic amateurs but by professional musicians scraping a living (pun not intended) at cattle fairs, horse races, markets, and so on. It was a tough living, and the money earned was scarcely enough for one musician, never mind a group. When you look at a tune book today it will often have chords written above the melody. In terms of Irish music these are a very modern invention; we may today see those chords implied by the sequence of notes, but most traditional players wouldn't have recognised a chord if it slapped them in the face. The nearest thing to a pub session would have been the 'céilí', (in Scotland the spelling 'ceilidh' is used), a small dance in someone's kitchen. A very relaxed and enjoyable affair, no doubt, but again probably with just the one musician, a fiddler or a piper. Individual tunes were played repeatedly for a dance, and variation and extemporisation would have been common; in such a situation two fiddles playing together would have been an awkward situation and unison would probably have been impossible. Professional jealousy may also have been a factor in keeping performers apart. Although music would have been highly valued, learning and performing was not something done as a leisure activity. The profession of musician would often have been hereditary, with children learning both technique and repertoire from elders of their own family, or at least someone in the local area.

In such a situation, and in an era where there was little opportunity or need for the average person to travel, regional and even local variations in style and repertoire would have been very marked. Like Darwin's island finches, separated by stretches of ocean, fiddling would have evolved in a hundred different ways across Ireland.

One of the first great upheavals to disturb this status quo was the great famine of 1845-49, when the staple food crop of Ireland was destroyed by the potato mould. Faced with starvation and eviction by unsympathetic landlords, those with enough remaining strength and money emigrated, many of them to the United States. Here, in Eastern cities such as New York, Boston, and Chicago, although life remained a struggle, there was a great deal more opportunity to earn a decent living. Fiddlers found a ready audience in minstrel companies (of which there were more than 100 in the 1860s), variety theatres, and vaudeville shows, feeding an insatiable nostalgia for the 'old country'. In common with most other émigrés, people in the Great Melting Pot found their identity not always diluted, but often reinforced by separation from the homeland. With more money and perhaps a little more leisure time, the idea of playing fiddle purely for enjoyment took hold. Now it was possible for Irish Americans to hear and learn from fiddlers not just from their own village, but potentially from all over Ireland.

By the 1920s the recording industry was taking off in America, and the new recording companies knew that there was a ready market for music representing all the different ethnic groups still flooding into the country. First off the block was fiddler Patrick Clancy, who in 1919 recorded four medleys for the Victor Talking Machine Company. Also among the first Irish fiddlers to join this trend, and certainly the most influential, was Michael Coleman. He was a highly gifted fiddler, his Sligo style highly ornamented and expressive. Along with others such as James Morrison and Paddy Killoran, he put down 78 rpm recordings of fiddle with (often ham-fisted) piano accompaniment, and sometimes with other instruments such as pipes, banjo, accordion, or flute. This new combination of instruments, along with the time limitations of the 78 rpm disc, meant that the old idea of extended repetition with variations was a thing of the past. Snappy arrangements were created with maybe two tunes each played twice through.

These recordings were hugely popular both in America and back in Ireland. Their significance in terms of the development of Irish fiddling was huge. Here suddenly was a standardised format of style, arrangement, and repertoire that was available not just to the audience at a céilí or fair, but to thousands, musicians and non-musicians alike. The downside was that the 'New York style' – an amalgamation of all Irish styles (but, due to the towering presence of Michael Coleman, with a strong bias towards Sligo) – began to erode and eventually largely destroy the huge and diverse patchwork quilt of styles that had developed across Ireland. Almost everyone who heard these recordings saw the future of Irish music staring them in the face, and that was how they wanted to play from now on. The upside was that a new generation of fiddlers could learn not just at their father's knee, but from the exciting and invigorating music of master musicians. Fiddlers found a new pride and respect for what was rapidly becoming seen as a performance art, worthy not just of the kitchen but perhaps of the concert hall as well.

At around the same time the first actual céilí bands were being created to perform at public dances. The term 'céilí band' was probably coined by Frank Lee, whose Tara Céilí Band came together to celebrate St Patrick's Day in London's Notting Hill in 1918.

In 1926 the recently formed Irish Free State, anxious to bolster the spirit of Irish nationalism, created its own radio station. By the following year there were regular broadcasts of traditional music, featuring Dick Smith's Céilí Trio of fiddle, piano, and flute. Soon céilí bands were appearing all across Ireland as well as in America and England. Alarmed at the prospect of the good people of Ireland having too much fun, the Catholic church and the Irish government colluded to ban unlicensed house dances under the Dance Halls Act of 1935. In 1924 the Bishop of Galway, not mincing his words, had stated that "The dances indulged in are not the clean, healthy national dances but importations from the vilest dens of London, Paris, and New York, direct and unmistakable incitements to evil thoughts and evil desires." Nice one, Bishop. Though music as such was not specifically proscribed by this ban, it obviously had a severe effect on musicians, particularly in terms of morale, and many left for America.

In common with many other kinds of traditional music, Irish music

The Chieftains, including fiddlers Séan Keane and Martin Fay.

took a big downturn in the 40s and 50s as swing, rock'n'roll, and general postwar optimism encouraged a new generation to turn their backs on what was seen as a tired and outdated genre. Concerned by the decline and potential demise of traditional playing, a group of musicians got together in Dublin in 1951 and formed Comhaltas Ceoltóirí Éireann ('gathering of musicians of Ireland'), commonly referred to as just Comhaltas (key-ol-tas). Their aim was to promote Irish traditional music, dancing, language, and culture, and to establish an annual national festival and competition, the Fleadh. From small beginnings this festival grew rapidly and branches of Comholtas were established throughout Ireland and overseas. Classes teaching instruments and dance to young children became widespread, and the competitions have consistently driven up the overall standard of playing.

A key figure in the modern development of Irish music was Seán Ó Riáda. Born in 1931 in Cork, he was one of the first musicians to learn traditional music before moving on to a thorough classical training. Writing for film, radio, and theatre, he gave Irish music a higher status among connoisseurs of the arts than it had ever achieved. The ensemble he put together for live performance, Ceoltóirí Chualann, included fiddlers Séan Keane, Martin Fay, and John Kelly. It broke new ground in its presentation of Irish traditional music almost as chamber music, with rich new textures, harmonies, and arrangements. Although a leading champion of Irish music, he was no fan of céilí bands, likening them to the buzz of a bluebottle in an upturned jam-jar. While his group was short-lived, it produced an offshoot in the form of The Chieftains, which became arguably the most successful traditional Irish band ever. The band, led by the jovial piper Paddy Moloney, included fiddler Martin Fay, who was joined and eventually replaced by Séan Keane. Since their first album release in 1964, The Chieftains have travelled the world, including making a notable trip to China in 1983, and have frequently collaborated with musicians and singers from widely different genres and cultures.

In the late 60s, along with peace, love, and The Beatles, came a new enthusiasm for all things down-home, wholesome, and folky. With armies of young people now playing instruments, the pub session finally became established in Ireland; it had been around since the 40s among expatriates in London and the US. And a new market opened up for bands playing not just the old traditional Irish music, but experimenting with new instruments, sounds, and textures. The accordion, guitar, and later the bouzouki were added to the musicians' armoury, and bands like Planxty and The Bothy Band found new ways of mixing and incorporating songs and instrumentals. Fiddlers such as Tommy Peoples, Paddy Glackin, and Kevin Burke all served time in Planxty, while Mairéad Ní Mhaonaigh

ABOVE: **The Bothy Band.**
BELOW: **Mairéad Ní Mhaonaigh of Altan.**

REGIONAL FIDDLE STYLES

Much as spoken dialect varies across the length of a country, so does the style of traditional music playing. In the case of Irish fiddling, the regional variations have been well studied and documented. Distinct geographical boundaries, such as rivers or mountain ranges can be mirrored by boundaries between fiddle styles. At one time hundreds of such styles would have existed. These musical barriers could only last as long as the communities remained largely isolated. By the start of the 20th century the distinctiveness inevitably started to decline. Today only a few distinct styles remain. It should be noted that there has always been variation between individual fiddlers, so that it would be wrong to expect, even within an isolated community, all the fiddlers to use the same bowing and ornamentation. However, certain characteristics of a general nature can be discerned.

The style of Donegal, in the wild north-west corner of Ireland is fast and aggressive, with an emphasis on short, powerful bow strokes and frequent bowed triplets. Fingered ornamentations such as rolls are sparse. Reels are played unswung. Droning and double-stopping reflect the influence of piping, while schottisches and strathspeys betray the strong Scottish influence. Mazurkas and highlands (similar to strathspeys) are often played here, but rarely elsewhere in Ireland. Among the leading exponents of this style today are Tommy Peoples, Paddy Glackin and Mairead Ni Mhaonaigh.

hit the world with her group Altan, and Frankie Gavin with De Dannan. Such supergroups were and still are able to sell bucket-loads of records, and play to packed venues all over the world, with a standard of playing, whether in terms of precision, performance, imagination, or expression, that would have been unthinkable in previous generations.

Finally, there's no escaping *Riverdance*. Composer Bill Whelan produced a masterful score which saw Irish music breaking out of the straitjacket of 4/4 and 6/8 and rubbing shoulders seductively with the hot rhythms of flamenco, the Balkans, and Russia. Irish/American fiddle player Eileen Ivers was more than equal to the challenges of the fiddle part, and *Riverdance* exploded in a wave of Celtic optimism and new-found confidence throughout the 90s.

There are now unprecedented resources available to anyone learning Irish fiddle, whether it's CDs, tutor books, DVDs, regular classes, workshops, or summer schools. As more and more people have

Sligo has a fast, light, bouncy style, rich in ornaments and combining the bowed triplets of Donegal with much of the rolling and slurring found further south. Influential players included Michael Coleman, Paddy Killoran, and James Morrison. Among the leading players today is Kevin Burke, an alumnus of The Bothy Band, and more recently acclaimed for his work with Patrick Street and the Celtic Fiddle Festival.

In Galway the tunes are played much slower than in Sligo, and with a more reflective character. Galway has many fiddle tunes, unusually, in the keys of E and B-flat. This style is exemplified by Frankie Gavin of DeDannan and Paddy Fahey.

The Clare style is different again, and is particularly characterised by the relaxed tempos, the subtlety of ornamentation, the preponderance of the reel, and the use of long, fluid bow-strokes covering many notes at a time. Sliding up to notes is common and there is a degree of improvisation. Master of the style is Martin Hayes.

Limerick, Cork, and Kerry; a region sometimes known as the Sliabh Luachra, in the south-west. Here there is a strong tradition of slide and polka playing, with a simple but very rhythmic style ideal for dancing. Dennis Murphy has given his name to numerous polkas, while Matt Cranitch from Cork is noted for his playing of slow airs.

started taking seriously the study, teaching, and performance of Irish fiddling there is every sign that the decline of regional diversity has been halted. Teachers are deliberately disseminating their local styles, and people are focusing on them consciously, choosing which suits them best, while many professional performers take pride in being exponents of the tradition of their particular region. The future for Irish fiddling has never been brighter, and nowadays there's no excuse not to learn. You don't even have to be Irish.

The Irish pub session

More perhaps than in any other style of folk music, the 'session' is the heart and soul of Irish traditional music. Everyone from beginners to the top professionals spends time at these informal gatherings, learning and swapping tunes. They take place almost exclusively in pubs or bars. The musicians will take over a corner which will be theirs for the evening. Those taking part do so largely for their own enjoyment. The other drinkers in the pub will not have paid to get in, and will not generally be expected to keep quiet, despite the fact that there will be no amplification. Some will hardly notice the music, but the landlord obviously believes that the overall ambience benefits from them being there; a steady supply of Guinness may well be supplied 'on the house' to keep things going.

Sessions are a curious mixture of informality and etiquette. In any given town or village, the regular players will know that certain pubs will have sessions on a certain night of the week, but this will almost certainly change over time; some will fall by the wayside only to reappear somewhere else. There is often a core group, maybe just of a couple of people who have arranged things with the landlord, and can be expected to be there most weeks. Sometimes they'll be virtually on their own; some weeks the place will be heaving. Strangers are welcomed, but it's always a good idea to ask if it's OK before you get out your fiddle and join in. It's also wise to take note of the standard of playing before you consider playing; if the other players are all experts, rattling away at the most demanding tunes with obvious ease, then a near beginner is obviously going to cramp their style. Conversely, if the other players are plodding carefully through 'The Boys Of Bluehill' at half the normal speed, they may not be impressed if you launch into a high-powered 'Mason's Apron' with all the trimmings, which is obviously going to leave them standing. The general aim is to find a level at which most of the players can join in together. Everyone respects good players, but egos, along with firearms, are generally left at the door.

There is a repertoire common to players all over the world; regular session-goers will know hundreds of tunes, some of which will be considered 'overplayed' and will therefore be rarely heard in a 'happening' session, whilst new material, either newly written or recently recorded by a popular artist, will suddenly be all the rage.

Someone will usually start a 'set' just by launching into a tune, probably without comment or introduction; everyone who knows the tune will immediately join in, and run it round two or three times, at which point someone – usually the person who started the set – will change tunes without break or pause. Often there will be an established order for the tunes of a set, so that people have a good idea of what might be coming next. This order will take into account continuity of style, feel, and tempo, and a natural progression of keys. It's normal for some people to drop out when the tune changes, or for others to join in. It's not a concert, and a bit of hesitation or deviation is fine, but if you don't know a tune, it's not a good idea to blaze away regardless; either play very quietly, or not at all. Variation, improvisation or plain noodling will get you some black looks. Unison is the order of the day, and even well thought-out harmonies may be frowned upon. The end of a set will generally come when the person who started, perhaps with a nod to the others, ends a tune without starting another. After a pause for a drink and a chat, it will then be someone else's turn to kick off. And so it goes, for maybe hours on end.

If you're new to the session, don't kick off a tune yourself unless invited to; think of the session as if you were sitting down at someone else's picnic. Sometimes, maybe on request, a player may do a solo party-piece that the others will all listen to, and there may be the odd song. Fiddles, flutes, whistles, uilleann pipes, accordions, and bodhrans are all common at sessions, and, since the 'folk revival' of the 60s, guitars, four-string banjos, and even bouzoukis. Irish traditional tunes will predominate, but increasingly you may hear something more exotic, whether American, French Canadian, or Balkan. The highly unconventional 'Music For A Found Harmonium' by the Penguin Cafe Orchestra has entered the regular repertoire since it was recorded by the band Patrick Street.

Irish-American fiddling

Well before Chief O'Neill began his tune collection, back at the start of the 20th century, Irish fiddling was thriving in America. The recordings of Michael Coleman, James Morrison, and others showed that America was not merely a lost backwater of traditional music, but that here were world-class players in a stimulating environment and with a huge and eager audience on their own doorstep. Today many of the top players in the music are second or third generation Irish. Not least among these is Liz Carroll. She was born in Chicago to parents who were both from Ireland. She grew up in the 60s amid a resurgent traditional music scene with many fine local players as role models, including Johnny McGreevy, a Sligo-influenced fiddler. The Irish music organization Comholtas also arranged tours of musicians from Ireland, so Liz was able to see such fiddlers as Paddy Glackin, Seamus Connolly, and Sean McGuire. She was always able to pick up on the best qualities of the fiddlers she saw, and incorporate them into her own playing; from McGuire, for example, she picked up the forcefulness of his bowing. From her earliest time playing music she has written tunes, many of which are widely played in sessions. One of the best known is her three-part jig 'The Diplodocus'.

The most convincing way for an American fiddler to prove his or her worth is to go to Ireland and compete in the national championships. That is exactly what Liz Carroll did in 1974, winning the under-18 title; the following year she won the All-Ireland Senior

Championship. In 1979 she recorded her first solo album, and by the 90s she was being showered with awards, including the proclamation by Mayor Daley of Chicago of an official Liz Carroll day on September 18 1999.

If you need any persuading that environment can affect your playing style, look no further than Eileen Ivers. Though her parents were Irish through and through, she grew up in the cultural melting pot of New York, and on the way through the Bronx to her Irish fiddle classes the eight-year-old Ivers would be hearing the sounds of Latin, rock, reggae, and African music from every street corner. Little wonder that these influences were eventually to find their way into her own playing. She learned initially from Limerick-born Martin Mulvilhill, a renowned teacher who inspired a generation of young fiddlers in New York, Philadelphia, and Washington. Soon she was spending her summers in Ireland, stacking up a heap of contest titles, including no less than nine All-Ireland Fiddle Championships. There was a time when Americans entering competitions in Ireland were viewed with suspicion as a possible threat to the cultural purity of the tradition, but there is today more of an acceptance that the diaspora is an equal and valued part of the body of Irish music.

She began to build a solid reputation touring with Mick Moloney's group Green Fields Of America, and then with Cherish The Ladies, as well as with an increasingly diverse range of other musical projects. Her first taste of life in the fast lane outside of Irish music came with a year-long world tour with rock superstars Hall & Oates. She wasn't back home long before the phone was ringing again; this time it was composer Bill Whelan asking if she would come over to London to perform in his new show, *Riverdance*, stepping into the shoes of the original fiddler Máire Breathnach. This was to be her biggest break, putting her at the forefront of the biggest international showcase Irish music had ever had. Aware that Ivers was no ordinary fiddler, Whelan gave her an on-stage solo where her virtuosity, exuberant performance style and all-encompassing musical influences could be best displayed. Her custom-made blue electric Zeta fiddle became something of a trademark, (now available at a store near you as the Zeta Eileen Ivers Signature Series). This fiddle appears on the cover of her groundbreaking 1996 album *Wild Blue*; emboldened by her success with Riverdance, she was able to indulge herself to the full extent of her stylistic creativity. This masterful romp through rock, jazz, and world music no doubt offended many traditionalists, whose worst fears about the invasion of Ireland by American musical imperialism had now surely been vindicated. Whatever your opinion on such questions, there's no denying the purity of style at the core of her playing, the clarity and beauty of her tone, or the surefootedness with which she gives vent to her imagination in any direction she chooses.

Some Irish fiddlers are respected, admired, even marveled at. Martin Hayes is revered. He was born in County Clare into a family as musical as they come; his uncle Paddy Canny was a famous fiddler and his father P J Hayes, also a fiddler, ran the Tulla Céilí Band, which in the 50s and 60s virtually defined céilí music. Martin was soon playing in his father's band and winning contests, including two All-Ireland Senior Fiddle Championships. After attending college he moved to America, first to Chicago and eventually to Seattle where he now lives. It was in Chicago that he met the guitarist Dennis Cahill, with whom he was to have a long and intense musical relationship. At first they had little sense of musical direction; they formed Midnight Court, a jazz/rock/fusion band, taking any gig and exploring any musical direction that came their way. Eventually they turned back to their traditional roots, where they have remained ever since, working mostly as a duo and developing an almost telepathic understanding of each other's playing. Albums such as *The Lonesome Touch* and *Live In Seattle* have made them a household name among Irish music fans. The initial experimentation has left its mark on Hayes's playing style, with a lot of jazzy sliding and syncopation in his playing. However, he has made a deliberate decision to centre his playing on the lyrical East Clare fiddle style. Though he has mastered high positions and vibrato and is very aware of many non-traditional styles, he avoids using them, concentrating instead on the simple goal of finding self-expression within a traditional framework. He rejects the use of flashy technique to impress, but never fails to capture an audience with the beauty and

ABOVE: **Eileen Ivers.**

BELOW: **Martin Hayes and Dennis Cahill.**

honesty of his playing. Not for him the Perspex violin, Latin rhythm section, and full-on rock histrionics. He has become an articulate and passionate spokesman for maintaining the purity and soul at the heart of Irish traditional music.

PLAYING IRISH FIDDLE
The anatomy of a tune

A great deal of fiddle music occurs in simple and well-ordered formats. The more of a particular type of tune in a particular genre that you play, the more familiar you'll become with the format, and the easier the tunes will be to read, learn, and play.

EXAMPLE 1.1

CD 1 TRACK 1

Here's a typical Irish polka.

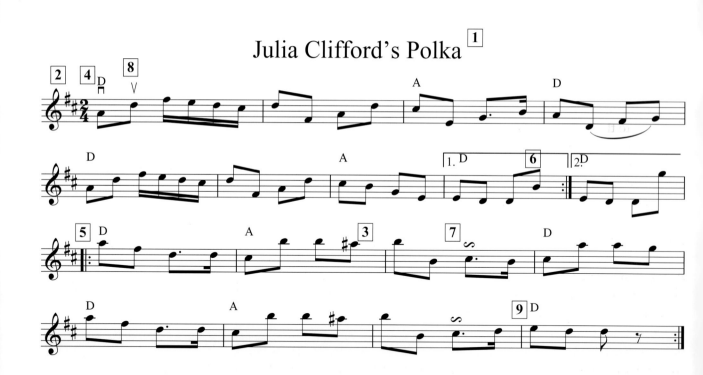

Julia Clifford's Polka

Here are some things to notice.

1.The title. With a traditional tune you can always take this with a pinch of salt. To quote Chief Francis O'Neill: "The bewildering variety of settings or versions of traditional Irish tunes is fully equalled by the confusing diversity of names by which many of them are known." The optimist's outlook on this is that it means that you can never be accused and found guilty of having the wrong title or the wrong version of a tune.

2. The key signature. This is a handy device that saves you having to write in lots of sharps and/or flats all over the music. The number of sharps or flats will tell you what key a tune is in:

- No sharps or flats = C major or A minor
- One sharp (F-sharp) = G major or E minor
- Two sharps (F-sharp, C-sharp) = D major or B minor
- And so on … See the Appendix for the whole list.

If there are two sharps in the key signature, these will be F-sharp and C-sharp; this means that every time an F or C note occurs in the tune, it will be sharpened, unless you're told otherwise. Because of the way scales work, this also means that the tune is in the key of D major or B minor. Every major key has a relative minor three semitones (half-steps) below, so the relative minor of E would be C-sharp.

3. Accidentals. If you see a sharp or flat sign on the actual music (as opposed to the key signature), it means that that note, and every other note of the same pitch in the same bar, is altered either up a half-step (for a sharp) or down a half-step (for a flat). If the altered note was already sharpened or flattened by the key signature, the accidental may appear as a natural sign. When you get to the next bar, unless the accidental is marked again, you can assume the note goes back to what it would have been without the accidental.

4. The time signature. This tells you how many beats there are in a bar, and gives you some idea about the rhythm of the tune. It consists of two numbers; eg, 2/4. The first number refers to the number of beats in a bar; the second refers to the length of one beat. In this case the 4 is a quarter-note or crotchet, and there are two in each bar; in Irish music 2/4 often means a polka. An 8 is an eighth-note or quaver, half the length of a quarter-note. So 6/8 would mean six eighth-notes to the bar, which in Irish music means a jig. A piece in 9/8 is a special kind of jig called a slip jig, with nine eighth-notes to the bar.

5. Repeats. Most Irish tunes, and indeed most of the tunes you'll come across in this book, have a format of eight bars repeated (the A section) followed by another eight bars, repeated (the B section). Older Irish musicians refer to these parts as "the first part" and "the turn". Repeat marks show you where to repeat from and to. If there is a repeat at the end of the A section, don't panic if you don't see one at the beginning; it looks messy to start a tune with a repeat sign, so it is left out.

6. First and second time bars. Sometimes the last bar of an A section leads naturally back to the repeat of the section, but doesn't follow smoothly into the B section. If that's the case you'll have two alternatives; a first time bar (which you play the first time you do this section) and the second time bar ('nuff said).

7. Grace notes or ornaments. These are 'little' notes. In a sense they are not essential to the melody, and they are the one element of a traditional tune which may be readily varied and swapped around. They are however vital to making a tune sound authentic. If none are written in, it's up to you to put them in yourself.

8. Bowing marks. The 'goalpost' symbol means a down bow, the V an up bow. You usually aim to start a tune or phrase with a down bow. If bowings are written in, after the first couple of notes it's assumed that every bow will be an alternate up and down, unless you're told otherwise by slur marks (as in bar four), or further bowing marks. Unlike in orchestral music, bowing directions are optional; if two fiddlers are playing in unison, eyebrows will not be raised if the bows are not moving perfectly together.

9. Chords. Until the mid 20th century, chords had little relevance to Irish music. When guitarists began playing the music, publishers started adding simple chord accompaniments to tune collections. Unless the tune is a recent composition by someone with firm ideas about chords, take them with a pinch of salt. With any three accompanists you'll usually get at least four different variations.

Tune types in Irish music

The Irish repertoire consists of several different types of tune; here are some of the main ones.

- Reels are fast tunes in 4/4 time. They were imported from Scotland in the late 18th century, but have now developed their own style in Ireland, and make up a large part of the repertoire. They are made up mostly of quavers (eighth-notes) which may be played straight, or given a swing a bit like hornpipes. Patterns in which the bow rocks across two strings are common in reels.

- Hornpipes were introduced from England. They are similar to reels, but with a bouncy rhythm created by lengthening the first of each pair of quavers (eighth-notes), and shortening the second. They tend to be played slower than reels, particularly for dancing. A hornpipe can be reliably identified if the eight-bar line ends with three even crotchets (quarter-notes), as for example in 'The Sailor's Hornpipe'). Hornpipes tend to be more melodic than reels, with more harmonic interest, and frequent triplets are a common feature.

- Polkas have a more steady tempo, in 2/4 time. They are often very simple melodies, and are particularly prevalent in the South of Ireland.

- Jigs, among the oldest form of Irish dance tune, have a bouncy 6/8 rhythm, with a stress at the beginning of each three notes. The rhythm sounds like this: "rashers and sausages". You may sometimes hear the term double jig; this is in fact the normal form. A single jig has a simpler rhythm: "boil the eggs and cook the bacon".

- Slip jigs are far less common than ordinary jigs. They have a similar feel but are in 9/8: "cooking my rashers and sausages". The slip jig is used for a graceful soft-shoe stepdance, usually danced by women only, and also for the céilí dance 'Strip The Willow'. Among the best known slip jigs are 'The Butterfly', 'Drops Of Brandy', 'The Kid On The Mountain', and 'The Foxhunter's Jig'.

- Slides. Similar to jigs again, but in a brisk 12/8 time; found only in the south-west of Ireland. They can be distinguished from jigs by the long melodic phrases which would not fit into a bar of 6/8: "cooking my taters and rashers and sausages". Examples include 'Star Above The Garter' and 'Kelfenora Jig'.

We're now going to look at some of the techniques and common forms of ornament used in Irish music.

Once you've mastered these, you'll recognise their use when you hear or see fiddlers playing traditional tunes. If you're learning a new tune it's a good idea to learn the style and ornamentation that's commonly used in that tune, but always bear in mind that you should be able to separate them from the tune, applying them at will wherever you feel it appropriate.

Bowing

A good bowing technique is essential if you're going to get the right feel for Irish music. We're going to concentrate here on the bowing for a jig; a gently rolling rhythm in 6/8 time.

Try this:

EXAMPLE 1.2

CD 1 TRACK 2

Notice the bowing symbols; the goalpost is the sign for a down-bow (starting nearer the frog), and the flying V is an up-bow (starting nearer the tip). The sign underneath the stave indicates an accent. On the accented notes the bow should move faster and should dig in. Try and make sure nearly all the movement comes from the wrist; if the whole upper arm is moving from the elbow, with the wrist rigid, then you're working a great deal harder than you need to. Keep the bows short; those with an accent need be no more than two inches, the others a lot shorter still.

EXAMPLE 1.3

CD 1 TRACK 3

Now let's try a scale using the same pattern:

Notice that this is a G major scale, even though we're starting from D. Play it steadily at first. As you get familiar with the bowing action, increase the speed and try to make the movement fully automatic. Once you have a proper melody to deal with you won't want to be thinking too much about the bowing arm.

Many tunes use a rocking bow, with the bow alternating between two strings:

EXAMPLE 1.4

CD 1 TRACK 4

As a rule, most fiddlers prefer to start a phrase, pattern or line with a down-bow, and end each phrase with an up, leaving the bow in place to start again on a down.

However, there will often be places where an up-bow is easier or more appropriate, so it's good to practise the patterns in reverse. Try this one, a rocking bow with a bit more melodic movement, starting each bar with an up-bow.

EXAMPLE 1.5

CD 1 TRACK 5

Fingered ornamentation

Ornaments or grace notes are the little patterns which are superimposed on the melody. Whilst being superficial to the tune itself, they are crucial to making your playing sound authentic, and they provide the main vehicle for variation and personal expression within Irish fiddle playing.

The slide

Instead of hitting the note squarely, the Irish fiddler will sometimes approach the note from below, starting maybe half a semitone down and sliding swiftly and smoothly up to the correct pitch. The slide is most commonly used at the start of a phrase, and will be applied to just one or two key notes in a tune.

EXAMPLE 1.6

CD 1 TRACK 6

The single grace note or 'cut'

The cut is often used to separate two notes of the same pitch that lie together in a tune. The second of the pair is preceded by a slight flick of a higher note.

Here is an unornamented phrase:

EXAMPLE 1.7

CD 1 TRACK 7

Use your third finger to flick the A string. You touch the string as if you were playing a D note, but you don't apply enough pressure to make it sound clearly:

EXAMPLE 1.8

CD 1 TRACK 8

The idea is not to hear the extra note, but just to interrupt the notes on either side of it. The grace note is not bowed separately, but slurred into the note it precedes.

EXAMPLE 1.9

CD 1 TRACK 8

It doesn't really matter which finger you use for the extra note, so long as it doesn't actually sound. You can try the next finger up in each case (eg, second finger to grace a first finger note); I prefer to use the third finger to grace the first finger note.

Try this scale to practise the cut on each note:

EXAMPLE 1.10

CD 1 TRACK 9

The double cut

This involves two extra notes instead of one, and unlike the single cut, is not used to separate two notes of the same pitch.

Here's the unornamented phrase:

EXAMPLE 1.11

CD 1 TRACK 10

It could become this:

EXAMPLE 1.12

CD 1 TRACK 11

Here the B is the note to be cut; a very short B note is played, then a higher D note (only a flick, as in the single cut), then the target note B again.

Here's a scale to practise the double cut.

EXAMPLE 1.13

CD 1 TRACK 12

The long roll

This is one of the most important ornaments in Irish music, and a particular feature of the playing of Michael Coleman. A dotted crotchet or three quavers are split into five notes, as follows.

If we start with the phrase:

or it could be written

EXAMPLE 1.14

CD 1 TRACK 13

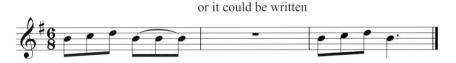

The note to be rolled is B. The B is sounded, followed by the note above, sometimes called the 'cut' (in this case C or D), another B, the note below, sometimes referred to as the 'tip' (A), and the B again to finish. It could be written as:

or

EXAMPLE 1.15

CD 1 TRACK 14

The five notes of the roll are not necessarily played equally; often the first note will be given most stress, perhaps more like this:

EXAMPLE 1.16

CD 1 TRACK 15

It is important to play the roll smoothly and always slurred into a single bow. Try this exercise:

EXAMPLE 1.17

CD 1 TRACK 16

Notice how the last roll (on the A) is different. Because it is an open string, you can't do a conventional roll without crossing to the lower string, which would break up the flow. Instead you roll with the first and third finger on the A string.

Long rolls are most common in jigs, but can also occur in reels or polkas:

EXAMPLE 1.18

CD 1 TRACK 17

An important feature of rolls is that with second and third finger rolls the lower note is a semitone (half-step) below the main note, regardless of key. Thus in the key of G, if you're rolling on a D, the lower note will be C-sharp despite the fact that the key signature dictates a C-natural.

EXAMPLE 1.19

CD 1 TRACK 18

If the roll is written, the sharp may not necessarily be written in as an accidental; it'll be assumed that you know it should be sharp.

The short roll
A short roll is exactly like the long roll, except that the five notes are squeezed into a crotchet instead of a dotted crotchet.
Try these examples:

EXAMPLE 1.20

CD 1 TRACK 19

Bowed ornamentation
The most common bowed ornament is the bowed triplet or treble. Here a note, usually a crotchet, is split into three very short, individually bowed notes. The effect is actually more of a flick or stutter than three clearly discernable bows. It's usually bowed down-up-down, but up-down-up is also used. This ornament, which is

interchangeable with the short roll, is most common in the Donegal style of fiddling.

Try this as a repeating pattern:

EXAMPLE 1.21

CD 1 TRACK 20

Here's a tune which uses a slide (eg, bar one), a long roll (eg, bar one) and a double cut (eg, bar four).

EXAMPLE 1.22

CD 1 TRACK 21

Paddy Fahey's Jig

scottish fiddle

The history ■

Scottish fiddle today ■

Regional styles ■

Playing Scottish fiddle ■

THE FIDDLE HANDBOOK

scottish fiddle

The year is 1700, and William McPherson is in trouble. Famous throughout Scotland as a Highland clan chief, swordsman, fiddler, bandit, and raider of Lowland cattle farms, he has had one adventure too many and is standing on the scaffold in Banff, found guilty of brigandage. Aware that a pardon is on its way on a fast horse from Aberdeen, the local sheriff, determined to be rid once and for all of this marauding menace, has put the clocks forward. McPherson had spent the previous night in the cells composing a tune on his fiddle (which he presumably had on him, even when fighting or cattle raiding). Realising that the game was up, he asked the executioner to allow him to play this final tune. Undaunted by the desperate circumstances, or the largely unsympathetic audience (mostly Lowlanders who had little reason to mourn his passing), he gave a bold and impassioned performance of his tune. Realising that his fiddle would soon be without an owner, he demanded of the crowd who would take the instrument. When there were no takers, he angrily broke it over his knee and threw the shattered pieces to the ground, before going steadfastly to meet his maker.

The tale is still often told, the remains of the fiddle lie today in the clan museum, and the tune, 'McPherson's Lament', is still widely played. This is just one example of the way in which the fiddle is woven deep into the fabric of Scottish history, myth, and folklore, as far back as medieval times.

The history of Scottish fiddling

The titles of Scottish fiddle tunes read like a mixture of a history lesson, a travel brochure, and a Who's Who of Scotland. Consider such titles as 'The Marquis of Huntley's Farewell', 'Mr Murray of Pittendreich', 'The Battle of Harlaw', 'Culloden', 'Rousing The Nation', 'Bridge Of Perth', 'King Robert The Bruce', 'Well May Charlie Wear the Crown' …

It is told that the good people of Edinburgh, on the occasion of a visit by Mary Queen of Scots to Holyrood Castle, chose to show their devotion by serenading her with their fiddles, en masse, beneath the castle walls. It is perhaps less often mentioned that, dismayed by the vile noise of 500 fiddles and rebecs (and we can assume they didn't spend a lot of time rehearsing or tuning up), she demanded to be given a room at the rear of the castle, as far away as possible.

The violin had probably been introduced to Scotland from England, and was much prized among the nobility (though perhaps not by Mary). It rubbed shoulders with its medieval ancestors, the rebec and vielle, before finally replacing them, owing to its superior tone and playability. When King Charles II, the so-called 'Merrie Monarch', came down from Edinburgh to take the English throne in 1661, one of his first acts was to bring his band of 24 fiddle players, led by a German violinist called Thomas Baltzar. By this time the nobility were more interested in European music than traditional Scots tunes, but throughout Scotland fiddling was about to enter its Golden Age.

Across the sea in Ireland, English invasion and repression had led to virtually the entire Irish aristocracy leaving the country, in what was called The Flight Of The Earls (1607) and The Flight Of The Wild Geese (1691). The working class was left impoverished, and there was little or no indigenous middle class. Centuries of Celtic culture and music were fractured from their roots, and fiddling was the domain of the poor, the illiterate, and often the blind.

In Scotland, by contrast, notwithstanding the Jacobite Rebellions and the Highland Clearances, there was a thriving economy, an articulate and well-educated middle class, and an aristocracy that was happy to sponsor and patronise the arts. Following a century of religious repression during the Reformation, the whole of Scottish society returned with enthusiasm to the arts, music, and dancing, and most specifically fiddling.

Whereas in Ireland the best fiddlers of the 18th and 19th Centuries, and those who composed the great body of today's repertoire, remained largely anonymous, in Scotland a host of fiddlers made their mark on history. Almost all of the great fiddlers were also composers, and their tunes, instead of being passed on aurally, were named, written down (often with detailed annotation on ornamentation and bowing), and published in collections.

Among the earliest of these was a collection of tunes entitled *The Caledonian Pocket Companion*. This was published in 12 volumes over a number of years by James Oswald. Born in Fife in 1710, Oswald was a gifted and industrious man, a cello player who discovered a talent for composition and publication. Following the Union of Parliaments in 1707, when the Scottish and English states were unified, Scotland saw a renewed interest in its national culture, and Oswald was among the first to translate this enthusiasm into something practical. His successful first effort was *A Curious Collection Of Scots Tunes*, which he published in 1740. Emboldened by the very respectable sales of this volume, he moved from Edinburgh down to London, where he attempted to set himself up teaching, composing and, once more, publishing. His timing was unfortunate; in 1745, not long after his arrival, the second Jacobite Rebellion took place; Bonnie Prince Charlie landed on the west coast of Scotland in an attempt to regain the thrones of Scotland and England, which had been taken from his family, the Stuarts, in the Glorious Revolution of 1688. As a Scot living in London, Oswald was obviously under suspicion, particularly as his chief Scottish patron, the Duke of Perth, had been a prominent supporter of the rebellion. Ever the pragmatist, Oswald, correctly predicting that the rebellion would fail, took the bold step of reprinting his *Curious Collection*, this time with a dedication to Frederick, Prince of Wales, thereby demonstrating his allegiance to the British crown.

His gamble was successful; the book sold well, and he followed it up with a series of volumes called *The Caledonian Pocket Companion*, starting in 1745. The first of these publications was aimed at flautists, but he soon realised that the fiddle was a much more popular vehicle for the playing of Scottish music, and future volumes were targeted much more in this direction. Along with traditional tunes, many of his own compositions were included, including some, such as 'The East Neuk Of Fife', that are still popular today.

The Jacobite rebellion was crushed at the Battle of Culloden in 1746, and was followed by parliamentary acts designed to stamp out symbols of Scottish independence, including the wearing of tartan and, more significantly, the playing of the Highland bagpipes. This led to a considerable transfer of both repertoire and playing techniques from the pipes to the fiddle (which fortunately was not banned). This move was reflected by Oswald, who began transcribing famous pipe tunes such as 'McIntosh's Lament' (a 200-year-old 'pibroch' – a type of extended improvisation – in memory of a dead clan chief). Since pipers had always learned and played by ear, such tunes had never been written down. Oswald reproduced the effect of the pipe's drones by using an open tuning (AEAC♯). The survival of these ancient tunes was therefore assured, along with many of the details of performance and ornamentation.

Oswald died in 1769 and his books were not reprinted, but there were enough in circulation to assure that the next generation of fiddlers were aware both of the repertoire he had collected and of the not inconsiderable profits that could be made by such endeavours.

Among the many people to own and treasure the *Pocket Companion* was Scotland's national poet, Robert Burns. Born in 1759, Burns was a fiddler himself, though not to any great standard. He quickly found a gift for putting words to fiddle tunes; it was no mean task to match the rhythm of such tunes with meaningful and poetic lyrics, especially with the complex phrasing of the newest form of tune, the strathspey. Among the songs he wrote to tunes from Oswald are 'The Deil's Awa' With The Exciseman' and 'Ae Fond Kiss'.

Another source of tunes for Burns was his friend and contemporary Niel Gow, among the greatest of all Scots fiddle players. Gow was born in the Perthshire village of Strathbraan in 1727 and initially trained in his father's trade of weaving. However, at an early age he showed great aptitude for the fiddle, and by 18 was able to demonstrate his prowess by winning an open competition in Perth. He was already well known for his powerful and highly distinctive bowing style, to the extent that the judge, a blind fiddler, specially chosen so that he would not show favouritism to the young lad, was able to state that he "would ken his bow hand among a hunder players" (recognise Gow's style among 100 players). The competition took place in 1745, the year of the Jacobite uprising. The Duke of Atholl, who was to become a lifelong friend and patron of Niel Gow, was one of many among the Scottish nobility who opted not to back the uprising, but hurried off to London to avoid any trouble.

The Duke's brother William opted to stay, and hired Gow for a grand ball in honour of Bonnie Prince Charlie when he stayed there on his march to Edinburgh. The fiddler may also have been among those Atholl tenants conscripted or persuaded to join the march; if so, he was also among the many to abandon it in short order, thereby avoiding the final massacre at Culloden. Over his lifetime Niel Gow enjoyed the patronage of three succeeding Dukes of Atholl, and was guaranteed a steady supply of work at balls and dances both near and far. He performed in a small band, often with a second fiddle player and with his brother Donald on cello. They would often walk miles to perform at some great house, drink rather too much, and then stagger home in the wee hours; referring to such a journey home he would complain that "it wasna the length of the road but the breadth o' it" that worried him (since he had a hard job keeping in a straight line).

He was highly respected by all classes not only for his fiery playing and his memorable and prolific compositions, but also for his sense of humour, and his honest and straightforward manner. Robert Burns, who visited him in 1787, described him as "A short, stout-built honest Highland figure, with his greyish hair shed on his honest social brow; an interesting face, marking strong sense, kind openheartedness mixed with unmistrusting simplicity". Niel Gow is often credited with inventing, or at least popularising the famous 'Scotch snap' which has become perhaps the trademark feature of Scottish fiddle playing, and was famous for his 'updriven bow', a style which emphasised the up-bow in reel and strathspey playing more than the down-bow.

Among his most famous compositions was the beautiful air 'Niel Gow's Lament For The Death Of His Second Wife', along with the reels 'Farewell To Whisky' (written in dismay at the failure in the barley crop in 1799), and 'Mrs McLeod's Reel'. He died in 1807 at the ripe old age of 80; his tombstone, with a humour befitting the man, read "Time and Gow are even now; Gow beat time, now time's beat Gow".

Niel Gow's legacy lay not just with his reputation and his published tune collections, but also with his sons, two of whom led fashionable bands in Edinburgh. Nathaniel Gow, the fourth son, inherited all his father's genius as a composer (he is credited with such classics as 'The Fairy Dance', 'Gallowglass', and so on), and went on to be a highly successful publisher in his own right.

The 18th and 19th centuries saw many gifted, skilful, and celebrated fiddlers, including such names as William Marshall (1748-1833), Simon Fraser (1773-1852), Isaac Cooper (1755-?), and Charles Grant (1806-1892). None, however, could compare either for fame or notoriety with James Scott Skinner, 'The Strathspey King'.

He was born in 1843, with a chip on his shoulder. He had an extremely hard upbringing, and was regularly bullied and beaten by his mother, stepfather, brother, and schoolteacher. Much of the success he eventually achieved seems to have been driven by a desperate need to prove himself to one and all. In contrast to the amiable and modest Niel Gow, Skinner was a self-important and somewhat pompous figure who never missed an opportunity to blow his own trumpet or talk down a rival.

He was taught by his older brother to play the violin and cello. A precocious student, at the age of eight he was accompanying the noted fiddler Peter Milne at local dances, earning himself the princely fee of five shillings a month. As was the custom at the time, they would have to walk home after the performances, and Skinner recalled that he was sometimes so exhausted on his return that he would fall asleep outside his own front door.

At the age of 11 he was taken on by a touring boys' group, Dr Mark's Little Men, with whom he performed on violin and cello around Britain for a number of years until he was dismissed after a fight with one of the other boys. At some point he was given classical lessons and taught to read and write music by the French violinist Charles Rougier; a valuable skill, as he had always played by ear up to this point. On returning home to Scotland in 1861 he was taken under the wing of William Scott, who taught him to dance and trained him to be a professional dancing-master. Skinner was so grateful for this help and kindness that he adopted Scott as his middle name (a more cynical view would be that this was merely an excuse to incorporate in his name an association with Sir Walter Scott, the great romantic poet, or indeed with Scotland itself).

In 1862 J. Scott Skinner, as he was now known, won a Highland dancing competition in Ireland (accompanying himself on the fiddle, which must have been quite a sight), and the following year he triumphed at a violin contest in Inverness. By this time he had become a fearsome and highly individual player, incorporating many classical techniques he had learned from Rougier: fancy bowing, use of vibrato, arpeggios, harmonics, and bold adventures into the higher positions. He began producing compositions which, whilst being within the traditional Scottish genre (airs, marches, reels, and strathspeys), were deliberately designed as vehicles to show off his superior technique to the other 'country bumpkin' fiddlers. Referring to his predecessor Niel Gow, he said he "did good work, but would have soared even higher if [he had] received a good sound training".

His work as a dancing master gradually gave way to proper performance work as his fame spread; he was perhaps the first Scottish fiddler to present Scottish traditional music not as something for the village hall dance-floor but for the listening appreciation of the discerning concert audience. His performances included Scottish tunes alongside his own compositions and others by Paganini and Mozart.

Following a tour of America and Canada in 1893, he took to wearing the kilt and full Highland regalia as his regular outfit for performance, and he began to take on the mantle of a self-appointed icon and ambassador of the Victorian ideal of Scottish romanticism. He became the first Scottish fiddler (I believe he would have thought of himself very much as a violinist rather than fiddler) to be recorded, and appeared at the Albert Hall and the London Palladium. He produced a huge output of compositions, and along with his many tune collections (the most famous being *Harp And Claymore* of 1904), he wrote *A Guide To Bowing* and his typically overblown memoirs, *My Life And Adventures*. A taste of the latter is given by his comment, "I have no intention of wearying my readers with the details of my life's output of original music, which, frankly speaking, has been colossal."

His death in 1927 left behind both a valuable legacy and a lasting controversy. His tunes still make up a sizeable part of the repertoire played today, from relatively straightforward reels ('The Spey In Spate', 'Mrs Forbes Leith', 'James Hardie'), stately airs ('The Music O' Spey'), and strathspeys ('Glenlivet') to technically challenging pieces such as 'The Mathematician' (peppered with triplet runs and ascending casually to sixth position), 'Madame Vanoni' (a showcase for artificial harmonics) and 'The President' (a full blown symphonic fantasy of a fiddle tune – the first bar is enough to scare me off!). His published tunes, both of his own work and that of others, are given detailed and specific annotation as to bowing and ornamentation; to work through a number of his tunes is akin to a degree course in advanced bowing and fingering. He undoubtedly (and, he would have added, single-handedly) raised the overall standard and expectations of Scottish fiddle playing, and demonstrated that it can sit proudly alongside Paganini and Mozart as a true art music. On the other side of the coin, he introduced a strong element of elitism and snobbery, encouraging showy technique over emotion. When Irish fiddling today is compared to Scottish fiddling, much of the difference and contrast in approach can be put down to the influence of Skinner.

Scottish fiddle in the 20th century

The fiddle continued to be popular through the 20th century, with strathspey and reel societies being established in most Scottish cities. Meetings of such groups see large numbers of fiddlers playing written arrangements of tunes in unison. The fact that the majority of players read music (as is perhaps not the case among traditional players in Ireland), and the relatively sparse use of fingered ornamentation in the Scottish genre, makes such unison playing a practical possibility. Fiddlers' rallies have become popular, occasional or one-off events where even larger numbers of fiddlers (often up to 100) get together to play, and one such rally was the starting point for the Scottish Fiddle Orchestra. This ambitious project, launched in 1980, sees up to 150 amateur players of all ages performing before a conductor in concert halls throughout Scotland and abroad. Many, however, weaned on the traditional Irish pub session, with its marked informality, find such rallies, societies, and orchestras anathema. Slightly less formal are the fiddle clubs which have sprung up throughout Scotland (where there are now more than 50) and also in the US and Canada.

Although fiddling is not as competitive in Scotland as in Ireland or the US, there is an equivalent to the Irish Comholtas festival/competitions. This is the Gaelic Mod, established in 1891 to preserve and promote Gaelic culture. There is a Royal National Mod, held annually, in a different location each year. Competitions include solo and choral singing, and Highland dancing, as well as playing of the bagpipes, 'clarsach' (harp), and fiddle. Despite having been originally started by a church choir, this hugely popular event has for some reason acquired the alternative title of the Whisky Olympics!

The link with dancing, always important with Scottish fiddling, was maintained through the 20th century with the rising popularity of Scottish country dancing, as exemplified by the Jimmy Shand group. With a typical line-up of fiddle, accordion, piano, and drums, such groups perform for social dancing. This probably reached its peak in the 50s and 60s when *The White Heather Club*, presented by Andy Stewart, was a regular feature of BBC broadcasting, attracting up to 10 million viewers across Britain. The suffocating effect of accordion and drums left little room for expression or virtuosity on the part of the fiddler, and together with the strait-laced, och-aye-the-noo presentation, it is an aspect of Scottish music that leaves many fiddlers today with a shudder. Personally, I have no shame; this year (and every year) on Burns Night I'll be scraping away to 'The Dashing White Sergeant,' eating my haggis and wearing my tartan with the best of them.

Scottish fiddle today

The past 30 years have seen great strides forward in Scottish music. The general folk revival seen throughout Europe and America has coincided with a reawakening of nationalist sentiment in Scotland, and the National Party political administration has seen folk music as a handy and distinctive symbol of Scottish pride. Funding has therefore been available for grandiose classical/folk productions such as the accordionist Phil Cunningham's *Highlands And Islands Suite*, incorporating the Scottish Chamber Orchestra, the Glasgow Phoenix choir, and a 30-piece Highland fiddle orchestra, as well as star fiddle soloists such as Aly Bain and Bruce McGregor.

There are now many professional Scottish fiddle players performing everywhere from local dances, folk clubs, and arts centres up to high profile festivals such as the Edinburgh Folk Festival (which has run on and off since the 50s) and Glasgow's Celtic Connections (started 1994) Every possible facet of Scottish fiddling has been explored in recent years, and maybe a few impossible ones. The Perthshire fiddler Pete Clark has made a special study of the playing of Niel Gow, recorded many of his tunes, and has performed on Gow's original fiddle, now held at Blair Castle. At the other end of the spectrum, a vibrant and exciting fusion of Scottish music with jazz was begun in 1984 with the creation of The Easy Club, playing "Scottish rhythm and swing" – a heady brew of swinging jazz guitar, cittern, bodhran, and the fiddle of John Martin. Though short lived, this band paved the way for such exotic creations as the Cauld Blast Orchestra, Salsa Celtica and Shooglenifty. Alisdair Fraser, born in Scotland but now living in California, looks both backwards and forwards; he has studied and recorded music reflecting the roots of Scottish fiddling, but also experiments with modern sounds and textures with his group Skydance. Martyn Bennett, before his untimely death in 1995, took Scottish music to a whole new place with his bizarre yet beautiful electronic soundscapes draped around his own superb bagpipe and fiddle playing.

Regional styles

As we saw with Irish fiddle playing, there existed in past centuries a whole patchwork of regional styles covering Scotland. The effect of widespread tune publication, the overriding influence of Scott Skinner, improvements in transport and communication, and more recently the universal availability of CDs, tutor books, fiddle schools, and YouTube have all had the effect of ironing out the local variations in style, creating a universal, 'syncretic' Scottish fiddle style. Nevertheless, it is still possible to identify and describe a number of regional styles distinguished by their repertoire and ornamentation, and preserved and disseminated by committed and outstanding players in each genre.

The Shetland Isles

The Shetland Isles, by virtue of their remoteness (out in the middle of the North Sea, as close to Scandinavia as they are to Scotland) have always had a distinctive sound to their music. The Isles belonged to Norway until 1469, and the cultural links have remained strong ever since. The Norwegian national instrument is the Hardanger fiddle, characterised by its four or five sympathetic strings which run underneath the fingerboard. Though this instrument, "da muckle fiddle wi mony strings", is not played in Shetland, the 'ringing strings' find distinct echoes in Shetland fiddling. This is achieved by use of use of open tunings, drones, and octaves. The most common open tunings are AEAE and ADAE. Shetland players such as Catriona MacDonald have done much to reaffirm the Norwegian links. She was given a Hardanger fiddle by her teacher, Tom Anderson, on the understanding that she would go to Norway to learn to play it properly. This was a promise she kept, and numerous trips north have led to a firm musical alliance with one of the leading young Hardanger players, Annbjorg Lien.

The type of tune most often played in Shetland is the reel. Whilst many of these are shared with the mainland, there is still a large body of "auld reels" or "muckle reels" inherited from the Norwegians, or older still, the "Trowie tunes" originally played by fairies or trolls (or so I'm told).

There is a strong element of accent and syncopation in Shetland fiddling, as exemplified by the tune 'Willafjord', said to have been brought back from Iceland on whaling ships. This syncopation naturally lends itself to a more modern swing feel, and the Django-influenced guitar playing of the late Peerie Willie Johnson provided the ideal accompaniment. His unique 'dumchuck' vamping style has been passed on to a generation of Shetland children; it is not unusual to see a bunch of ten-year-old kids at a traditional session in Lerwick hammering away on guitars, dashing off passing chords and moving basslines that would bring tears to the eyes of a hardened London jazzer.

Shetland fiddling in its present form owes a huge debt to Tom Anderson (1910-1991). He was a fine fiddler and a prolific composer of tunes, his best known being the heartbreaking slow march or air, 'Da Slockit Light'. From around 1945 he took it upon himself to protect and preserve the unique local fiddling tradition. He recorded many of the old fiddlers on the islands. In 1960 he formed The Shetland Fiddlers Society, informally known as Da Forty Fiddlers (and referred to by the broadcaster Magnus Magnusson, even more informally, as "Da Forty Fartin' Fiddlers").

He campaigned to get traditional fiddling onto the school curriculum, eventually succeeding in the 70s when he became the first of many to teach fiddle in Shetland schools; his students have included Catriona MacDonald and the great Aly Bain. In 1980 he formed a performing group from among his students, Shetland's Young Heritage, which has since gone on to record and tour internationally. There can be few local fiddle traditions more vigorous and fighting fit than that of Shetland.

The East And North-East

The east coast style of fiddling is perhaps the most representative of Scottish fiddle as a whole; many of the great names of 18th and 19th century fiddling came from this area, from Aberdeen down to Perth, including William Marshall, Niel and Nathaniel Gow, and J. Scott Skinner. The style includes many elements of classical influence. A strong vibrato is often used, as are chromatic passages and high position work; 'The Mathematician' by Scott Skinner is a good place to start, or possibly abandon fiddling altogether! Unlike on the west coast, where many tunes were inherited from the piping tradition, the majority of east coast tunes were written and published by and for fiddlers. These are often annotated with very precise bowing marks and ornaments. Scott Skinner was fond of adding graphic comments such as "these rants require physical force – plenty of go!" Slow airs, and especially strathspeys are widely played. Intonation and rhythm are very precise. Tunes may be written in difficult flat keys, and various classical staccato and bouncing bowing techniques are often employed. William Marshall, when questioned as to the difficulty of some of his tunes, retorted that he "did not write music for bunglers".

A good representative of the contemporary north-east style would be Bruce MacGregor from Inverness, founder of the Scottish fiddle supergroup Blazin' Fiddles.

The Highlands And West Coast

Whereas both Shetland and the north-east have a well preserved and largely unbroken tradition of fiddling, things have not gone so well in the wild upland areas of western Scotland. Here Gaelic was the chief language, and the region was isolated both physically and culturally. After the Reformation this was the area most affected by the strong disapproval of the Kirk (the church) of all things to do with sinful enjoyment: dancing, drinking, and fiddle music. Fiddles were actually burned, broken, or hidden away. The repression following the Jacobite rebellions, the break-up of the centuries-old clan system, and the notorious Highland Clearances, all led to the widespread fracturing of communities and the depopulation of large areas. Many moved to lowland or coastal areas, and still more emigrated to America. As a result of all this little is known about the role of the fiddle, or the way in which it was played in the 18th and 19th centuries. Undoubtedly the fiddle took on some of the repertoire and playing characteristics of the bagpipes, which were officially banned for a period after 1747. Many pipers actually switched to the fiddle at this point.

Drones and fast, florid grace-notes are a direct imitation of piping style, as is the use of the bagpipe mode (approximating to the Mixolydian, with a flattened seventh note compared to the major scale; the bagpipe in A cannot play a G-sharp note). When playing a tune in the key of A, some players will deliberately play the G note neither sharp nor flat (G-natural) but 'blunt'; that is to say, somewhere in between the two. This gives an effect very much like that of a bagpipe: either exquisite or agonising, depending on your point of view.

Triplets and 'birls' (a very fast bowed stutter or shiver) are often used, and jigs are played with a strong accent on the first of each three quavers. If strathspeys are the domain of the north-east, the 2/4 pipe march is the most characteristic of the Highlands. Though I've yet to hear exactly how, it's commonly said that the Gaelic language itself is an important factor in influencing the inflection and phrasing of this style of fiddling.

If you want a contemporary representative of west-coast fiddling, look no further than the Grant family. Angus Grant senior (Aonghas to his friends), "the left-handed fiddler of Lochaber", is a Gaelic speaker himself, and learned fiddle from his father and uncle. Typical of his tradition, he plays by ear and has never learned to read music. In his own words, he says of such players, "None of them knew anything of written music, but they were natural musicians who used complex bowing patterns, mordents, acciaccatura ornamentation and vibrato in some cases. They did so as a matter of course …" His son is also Angus Grant, the "hirsute and obliquely spoken" wild man of the Highland fiddle, fronting the magnificently adventurous Shooglenifty.

Iain McLachlan, from the bleak island of Benbecula, is another fine exponent of this distinctly old-world style of playing; he is best known for his composition, frequently assumed to be traditional, the mysterious 'Dark Island'. The American fiddler Bonnie Rideout, three times US National Scottish Fiddle Championship winner, has made a study of west coast fiddling, discovering a long-lost hoard of tunes, *The Patrick MacDonald Collection*. This manuscript, from 1781, contains Gaelic airs and melodies from the Scottish Highlands and west coast. She has also resurrected the art of playing pibrochs on the fiddle. These consist of a slow theme or 'urlar', followed by a complex set of variations. Many were written for the fiddle in the 18th century, or else transposed from bagpipe players, but by the end of the 19th century this practice had completely died out among fiddlers, no doubt due to the level of concentration required by both player and listener alike.

Cape Breton

This might be a good moment to rush to the atlas and confirm that, as you suspected, Cape Breton isn't exactly part of Scotland, and is in fact on the wrong side of the Atlantic Ocean, on the Canadian east coast. So how can I possibly include Cape Breton as a regional style of Scottish fiddling? For a start, you'll see signs around the place hailing it as "The Home of Celtic Music", and a quick browse through a telephone directory will show enough MacDonalds to fill Loch Lomond. Back in the early 19th century around 25,000 Gaelic-speaking Scots emigrated to Cape Breton from the Highlands and Islands, victims of the Clearances. Perched out on the edge of the country, there was little incentive to integrate with the rest of Canada, particularly as whole communities had often emigrated together. And, as the song goes, 'There's None So Scots As The Scots Abroad'. Fiddling is one of many aspects of the culture that the islanders have hung on to with messianic zeal, and the recent discovery that this could actually be a big economic selling point for a growing tourist industry has only further raised its profile. Fiddlers have always been in demand

NATALIE MACMASTER

Growing up in the village of Troy, on the southwest shore of Cape Breton Island, Natalie MacMaster was steeped from the earliest age in traditional Scottish music and dance. By the time great-uncle Charlie MacMaster sent a three-quarter size fiddle for Natalie and her siblings to try, she was already step-dancing, singing Gaelic, and playing piano. And with a famous uncle, Buddy, as role model it's little wonder that she took to the fiddle instantly, and was recording and performing by her early teens. The simultaneous fiddling and step dancing, along with her charm and sunny personality, made her an ideal figurehead for Cape Breton music in the wider world.

In 1995 she was signed by Warner Brothers, and has since produced a string of influential and highly acclaimed albums. Her 2002 album *Blueprint* was produced by fiddle maestro Darol Anger and, with an interesting twist to her Cape Breton/Scottish roots, used some of America's finest bluegrass players (they don't come any better than Jerry Douglas, Sam Bush, and Edgar Meyer). Her albums draw on a variety of 'outside' influences but remain very much rooted in the jigs, reels, strathspeys, airs, and hornpipes or her native tradition. Typical of the welcome and generosity of that tradition is that on her website you will find free sheet music to most of the tunes she has recorded. She is married to fellow fiddler Donnell Leahy, and though the two have separate musical careers they are often able to guest with each other's bands.

Natalie MacMaster

DONNELL LEAHY

Fiddler Donnell Leahy is part of the Canadian folk group Leahy. If you're looking for wholesome Celtic-flavoured family entertainment, this is it. The group consists of no fewer than eight siblings from a farm in Lakefield, Ontario. Their Irish father and Cape Breton Scottish mother taught them fiddle and step dancing from an early age. They performed from the early 80s as The Leahy Family, relaunching in 1997 as Leahy. They had a hit with the song 'A Call to Dance', and a year later they landed the job of support act for fellow Canadian Shania Twain.

Their set features the Cape Breton staples of fiddles (lots of them), piano, and step dancing, along with drums, guitar, mandolin, and vocals. Donnell Leahy's playing is by no means purely traditional; you can hear both Scottish and Irish influences in the bowing and ornamentation, but also country in the frequent double stops and drones. Traditional material is mixed with contemporary tunes and songs, plus crowd-pleasers such as 'Czardas' and 'The Orange Blossom Special'.

ALY BAIN

Arguably the most famous contemporary Scottish fiddler is Aly Bain. Born in Shetland in 1946, he started playing at the age of 11, learning the traditional Shetland style from the great master Tom Anderson, and also developing an outstanding and distinctive technique. This includes a beautiful clear tone, a rich vibrato, and a mastery of bouncing bowing. He has a particular talent for moving and emotional playing on slow airs and waltzes, but his show-stopping party piece is the all-action 'Hangman's Reel' or 'Le Reel Du Pendu', a mysterious tune in Norwegian troll tuning (AEAC♯) that features left-hand pizzicato. After moving to the mainland in his early twenties, he helped to form Boys Of The Lough, a groundbreaking and highly successful group with whom he toured and recorded for over 30 years. He also has a longstanding partnership with ex-Silly Wizard accordionist Phil Cunningham. Among their many achievements together was being chosen to play for the opening of the new Scottish Parliament.

He has always had an interest in fiddle music from outside Scotland, and has presented numerous TV series that have acquired virtually cult status, including *Down Home*, exploring the links between Shetland fiddling and the various branches of American fiddling. This 1985 series featured relaxed and highly entertaining sessions where he played along with such stars as Mark O'Connor, Johnny Gimble and Junior Daugherty. Other series in a similar vein were *Aly Meets The Cajuns*, *The Shetland Sessions* and *The Transatlantic Sessions*. He is described back in his home town of Lerwick as "the best fiddle player in the world, possibly even in Shetland".

Aly Bain with Phil Cunningham

for the local dances that remain an important part of community life, but in recent years the rest of the world has discovered the hidden gem that is Cape Breton fiddling. In fact the style found here is often described as being a living fossil, a segment of Scottish fiddling preserved in amber for two centuries, untarnished by the gentrification of Scott Skinner and his ilk.

Players like Buddy MacMaster grew up playing strathspeys and reels for square dances, and only towards the end of his career was there sufficient outside interest for him to start recording or doing proper concert work. A 1972 Canadian Broadcasting Corporation documentary,

The Vanishing Cape Breton Fiddler, put forward the idea, hotly contested by some on the island, that fiddling was dying out. In response a concerted effort was made to revitalise something that had perhaps been taken too much for granted. A fiddlers society was established, a fiddle festival, a 'ceilidh trail', and, since 1996, the Celtic Colours International Festival. Buddy's niece Natalie MacMaster is one of a growing number of young fiddlers, along with cousins Wendy MacIsaac and Ashley MacIsaac, who have had the benefit of a Cape Breton cultural revival, and found a ready market at home, throughout Canada, and abroad. Various artists, including Alisdair Fraser, have made successful efforts to re-introduce the Cape Breton style to Scotland, through concerts and workshops. Fraser states on his *Driven Bow* album of 1988, "Fortunately the fiddle and dance traditions of Cape Breton … provide us with a window which sheds light on the way 18th and 19th century dance fiddlers such as Niel Gow used to play in the Highlands of Scotland. … Let's hope that some of the great fiddle and dance tradition that has been absent from Scotland for so many years can be restored."

Apart from the repertoire of reels and strathspeys, there are many stylistic similarities with the Scottish Highland and west coast style. As in the Highlands, players see a rhythmic link with the Gaelic language; it is a great compliment to be told you "have a lot of Gaelic in your playing", though in the present generation there has been a great decline in use of the language. Open tunings such as ADAE are often used in long medleys of tunes in the key of A, and grace notes and drones can be traced back to the piping tradition. One distinctive feature of Cape Breton is that the piano has become an almost inseparable partner to the fiddle, with a busy chromatic and syncopated style.

PLAYING SCOTTISH FIDDLE
Modes
In the last chapter, under 'Anatomy Of A Tune', I told you that the number of sharps and flats in the key signature would tell you what key a tune is in, so that two sharps, for example, would always mean D major or B minor. I lied!

Many folk tunes, not least in Scottish traditional music, use 'modes', in which the key of a tune is not necessarily that indicated by the sharps or flats in the key signature. We're going to come across this again in many of the forthcoming chapters, so now is the time to get to grips with it.

So what is meant by a mode? This is easiest to demonstrate if you have a piano or keyboard to hand; if not the fiddle will do.

Play the 'white notes' from C to C:

EXAMPLE 2.1

CD 1 TRACK 22

This is the C major scale; it's a major scale because of the intervals: tone, tone, semitone, tone, tone, tone, semitone (whole-step, whole-step, half-step, whole-step, whole-step, whole-step, half-step). A tune constructed out of these notes will naturally have the 'home note' or tonal centre of C; any phrase will sound finished and settled if it ends on C. (Note: as with any scale, by transposing all the intervals together to another key, you keep the same kind of scale. If you started on F, for example, but kept the same set of intervals, you'd still have a major scale. This is important to understand because using the white notes of a piano is just an easy way to illustrate modes; ultimately, it's the intervals, not the notes that are important.)

Now, still using just the white notes, play a scale from D to D:

EXAMPLE 2.2

CD 1 TRACK 23

We're using all the same notes, just starting and ending in a different place. Does it sound major or minor? The intervals are tone, semitone, tone, tone, tone, semitone, tone (whole-step, half-step, whole-step, whole-step, whole-step, half-step, whole-step). The semitone interval between the second and third note defines this as a minor scale. If you noodle up and down the scale, you'll see that any melody or phrase will want to end on D. If you try to put a piano or guitar chord to it, it will be D minor:

EXAMPLE 2.3

CD 1 TRACK 24

Nothing sounds unusual about this phrase, except for the rather dreamy sounding B-natural (a raised sixth), but look at the key signature. According to standard western classical theory, no sharps or flats means C major or its relative minor, A minor. If you paid good money for violin lessons, go and ask for a refund! This special scale, from D to D, is a mode, called the Dorian mode. The names of modes come from the ancient Greeks, who thought they could identify different modes from different regions of their country. The modes were later taken up by medieval western church music, but subsequently largely abandoned, except, unwittingly, by folk musicians.

The Dorian mode is very common in Celtic music.

Let's try the next mode, E to E:

EXAMPLE 2.4

CD 1 TRACK 25

This is the Phrygian mode. A quick run up and down this will show that use of it constitutes a cruel and unnatural practice. If you can get a meaningful tune out of it you're a better man than me!

Swiftly on to the next one, F to F:

EXAMPLE 2.5

CD 1 TRACK 26

This is the Lydian mode. Pretty weird again. Three tones in a row at the start is unusual but not entirely unusable. You'll find it in music from Norway and from the Tatra mountains of Poland. The interval of three tones is called a a tritone. Because it sounds so wild and untamed, it was considered to be 'the devil's interval' – you'll hear it played on the ribcage of a skeleton at the start of Saint-Saëns's *Danse Macabre*. Oh, and listen out for it at the start of the theme tune of *The Simpsons*!

Now play G to G:

EXAMPLE 2.6

CD 1 TRACK 27

This is the Mixolydian mode. It sounds altogether more reassuring. It's exactly like a normal major scale, except for the seventh note, the F natural. Normally a major scale has a seventh a half-step (a semitone) below the top (root) note, but in a Mixolydian mode it's flattened. This mode has particular significance for Scottish music, because this is the mode played by bagpipes; not being chromatic, they can't play all twelve possible notes of a scale. This mode is also widespread in American old-time and bluegrass. You'll often hear people, particularly in reference to American old-time music, talking about a tune in "A modal". Give them a slap on the wrist from me, and tell them it should really be called A Mixolydian.

Let's interrupt our tour of the Greek provinces with a west Highland tune in the Mixolydian mode. It's in the key of A, but all the G notes are flattened to G natural. This tune, 'I Prefer The Kilt', is also known as the song 'The Keel Row'.

EXAMPLE 2.7

CD 1 TRACK 28

I Prefer The Kilt

Returning to the modes, A to A gives the Aeolian mode; this is the same as the standard natural minor, or descending melodic minor:

EXAMPLE 2.8

CD 1 TRACK 29

Because this is so common in classical music it is not really considered a mode. (Or to be more precise, a tune with this scale would not be considered to be modal.)

B to B provides another weird and unusable mode, the Locrian.

EXAMPLE 2.9

CD 1 TRACK 30

Finally back to C to C, which we started with. This is also called the Ionian mode; it is the 'standard' major scale, so is not considered a mode.

To summarise, by creating scales using the intervals from different starting and ending points of a major scale (we used C as an example), we create seven different modes. The ones of interest to the folk fiddle player are the Dorian mode (a minor scale with a raised sixth, common in English and Celtic folk tunes), the Lydian (a rare but interesting scale found in Norway, Poland, and any centre of devil worship), and the Mixolydian (a major scale with a flattened seventh, common in Scottish tunes, old-time, and bluegrass).

Understanding and recognising modes will help you sight-read a tune (where the key signature may be confusing), to memorise a tune, to compose authentic-sounding folk tunes, and to work out suitable accompanying chords.

Scottish tune types

Scotland has a distinctive repertoire, including a number of different types of tune. Many of these tune types are shared with neighbouring England and Ireland, whilst some are uniquely Scottish.

The strathspey developed in Scotland, the first being written around 1749. They were originally called strathspey reels. They have a similar tempo to reels, and can be used for the same dances, but have a distinctive phrasing based on two kinds of dotted rhythm. Some strathspeys are designed not for dancing but for listening, and are played at a much slower tempo (they are known as slow strathspeys). The name suggests that these tunes either originated in, or became associated with, the area around the 'strath', or valley, of the river Spey in the Highlands.

Similar to the strathspey, but brisker and with more of a 2/4 marching feel, is the schottische.

Reels are widespread in England and Ireland, but have a particular place in Scottish dancing, where the reel is a specific dance figure. Scott Skinner states in his 'Guide To Bowing' that reels should be played briskly, like a well-oiled wheel: "crisp and birly like a weel-gaun wheelie". Reels in Ireland are often played with a swinging rhythm, but in Scotland they are usually played even (with all the quavers/eighth-notes the same length). Hornpipes are similar to reels, but have a distinctive phrase of three crotchets/quarter-notes and a rest at the end of most lines. Some hornpipes are played even, but since the 19th century many are played dotted, with a distinctly uneven rhythm.

Jigs are less common in Scotland than in Ireland, but are still often used in dance music. There is a tendency to play them with a heavier accent on the first of each three quavers/eighth-notes.

Marches, at a medium tempo, reflect the importance of the military in Scottish history and music. Many of the marches played on fiddle were originally played on the pipes.

Slow tunes for listening include laments (usual written in memory of a dear departed), pastorals, and slow airs. Such tunes are sometimes very complex, with the extra space allowed by the slow tempo being filled with florid runs, chords, and arpeggios.

Polkas were a latecomer to Scottish music, originating in Bohemia in the 1830s. Since Jimmy Shand had a big hit with 'The Bluebell Polka' in the 1950s, such tunes have had a place at the high table in Scottish country dance circles.

It is customary, both for dancing or for performance pieces, to play a set or medley that combines several tune types. Thus a slow air or a march might be followed by a strathspey and then a reel. For the dancing of the Gay Gordons a reel may be followed by a jig, and then back into the reel.

Scottish fiddle techniques

Let's get down to business. We've already seen a strathspey in the form of 'I Prefer The Kilt'. It has two distinctive phrases:

EXAMPLE 2.10

CD 1 TRACK 31i

EXAMPLE 2.11

CD 1 TRACK 31ii

In a strathspey these can occur in any order in the tune. This makes reading a strathspey quite challenging; unlike jigs or hornpipes, where the rhythm is steady and predictable, in a strathspey every bar could be phrased differently.

The Scotch snap

The key to playing these phrases is to play the short note as short as possible, and to separate it slightly from the adjoining note. This 'Scotch snap' or snap bowing is one of the most important characteristics of Scottish fiddling and it occurs not only in strathspeys, but sometimes in reels, jigs, and airs. It is easiest to control in the upper half of the bow. Here's an exercise to practise. Try it first with separate bows:

EXAMPLE 2.12

CD 1 TRACK 32i

Now try it with slurs:

EXAMPLE 2.13

CD 1 TRACK 32ii

Drones

Due to the influence of pipes, drones are an important feature of Scottish fiddling. These can take the form of a doubled note, an open string and fourth finger played at the same time, or a third-finger note with an open string an octave below:

EXAMPLE 2.14

CD 1 TRACK 33i

Droned notes are often preceded by a grace-note a semitone below; in classical terms this is known as an acciaccatura; it's the equivalent of the 'cut' we saw in Irish music.

The note and its preceding grace-note are slurred into one bow:

EXAMPLE 2.15

CD 1 TRACK 33ii

Drones may also run through a phrase or a whole bar, with an open string either above or below the melody:

EXAMPLE 2.16

CD 1 TRACK 33iii

EXAMPLE 2.17

CD 1 TRACK 34

Here's a strathspey by Scott Skinner which incorporates these different ideas.

The Laird O' Drumblair

J. Scott Skinner

Double-stops

Double-stops are an important feature of many Scottish tunes, strengthening or emphasising a chord. Usually the melody note will be at the top, with the lower note at an interval of a sixth below. Thus in the key of G you might play:

EXAMPLE 2.18

CD 1 TRACK 35i

Or in D you might play:

EXAMPLE 2.19

CD 1 TRACK 35ii

The sixth harmony shown above is extremely useful in many other branches of fiddle music, including Gypsy, Eastern European and all the American styles. Learning scales like this one in A will be time well spent.

EXAMPLE 2.20

CD 1 TRACK 36

Triple-stops

Triple-stops are also often used to create a chord, particularly at the end of a tune. The lower two notes are first played together, followed by the upper two, with a flourish of the bow:

EXAMPLE 2.21

CD 1 TRACK 37

Here's another Scott Skinner tune that uses grace notes, drones, a double-stopped scale in sixths, the same scale but broken, and triple-stopped chords. Fortunately it goes at a very sedate pace. By the way, he's no relation.

EXAMPLE 2.22

CD 1 TRACK 38

Earl Haig (The Laird O' Bemersyde)

J. Scott Skinner

The birl

Another important ornament, usually associated with reels, is the 'birl' or 'shiver'. This is three of the same notes played very rapidly with a flick of the wrist. The faster and shorter you can make the first two notes, the better the effect. Play it near the point of the bow.

EXAMPLE 2.23

CD 1 TRACK 39

It would probably be more accurate to write it as:

EXAMPLE 2.24

CD 1 TRACK 39

Practise this exercise:

EXAMPLE 2.25

CD 1 TRACK 40

With typical distain, Scott Skinner, in his *Guide To Bowing*, referred to this oft-used ornament as a doodle, a "quaint but senseless feature of the past ages … lacking in dignity and showing poverty of invention".

The birl is an ornament that, once mastered, can be used to great effect (I don't care what Skinner has to say on the matter!) on any appropriate crotchet in a reel. It's also widely used in Irish playing, particularly in the northern counties such as Donegal, where it is called the 'treble'. Here's a well-known Scottish tune, the Fairy Dance.

The Fairy Dance

EXAMPLE 2.26

CD 1 TRACK 41

The 'ringing strings'

Finally, here's a Shetland reel that we can use to demonstrate the 'ringing strings'. It will work in conventional tuning, but you'll get the best effect by tuning up the G-string a tone to A. The bottom string will ring on its own and bring the whole fiddle alive.

EXAMPLE 2.27

CD 1 TRACK 42

Da Ferry Reel

tuning ADAE

english fiddle

THE FIDDLE HANDBOOK

english fiddle

I t's a chilly Sunday afternoon in February, 1998, and the London Fiddle Convention has taken up residence in Cecil Sharp House. The House, as it is affectionately known to its users, is home to the EFDSS, the English Folk Dance and Song Society, and its library holds, among many other treasures, the collections of English folk music made by Cecil Sharp at the start of the 20th century. The cream of English fiddledom is gathering to play, listen, learn, compete, gossip, buy strings, and celebrate its fiddle heritage, and the ghost of Mr Sharp is 'in the House'. Striding eagerly and translucently down the echoing corridors, he has observed the fliers advertising the convention, and is looking forward to hearing a new crop of Staffordshire hornpipes, morris jigs, and Dorset four-hand reels. His passion in life had been to travel the leafy highways and byways of rural England, recording and preserving the declining ancient traditions of music and dance. Notebook and pencil in hand, he is now poised and ready to transcribe the first tune he hears, nodding approvingly as the fiddlers troop into the building.

Downstairs in the bar the first session strikes up, and a frown creases the old gentleman's brow. The fiddlers have launched into a set of Donegal reels. Sighing, he helps himself to a cup of tea and sits down to observe the assembled musicians rattle out an endless stream of Irish, Scottish, and American tunes. A young woman, wearing trousers, dammit, even leads off on a Macedonian 'horo'. What has become of the great heritage of centuries-old English fiddle tunes that he had so lovingly collected and preserved in this very building? Hours later he has still not heard a single English tune. Even the Staffordshire stalwart, Pete Cooper, of whom he had such high hopes, is playing 'horas' and 'freylechs'. As he drifts sadly out into the night, a curly-haired, bearded, and bespectacled fiddler on the stage is blissfully delivering the final insult: a blues in the key of C-sharp.

What the unfortunate Cecil Sharp observed that day was no flash in the pan. A whole generation of English fiddle players has grown up learning an eclectic repertoire of Celtic and American music, following idols like Aly Bain, Martin Hayes, Tommy Peoples, John Cunningham, Mark O'Connor, and Vassar Clements. Living mostly in an urban environment, with no apparent indigenous folk music, people have felt free to adopt whatever traditional influences seem most accessible, exciting, and appealing, which generally meant almost anything except English traditional fiddling. True, since the folk revival of the 60s, singers such as Martin Carthy had been successfully championing traditional English songs, but the instrumentals played by folk-rock bands such as Fairport Convention and Steeleye Span owed far more to Irish than English fiddle style. If anyone in the 60s, 70s, or 80s was asked "What is English fiddle and what do you think of it?" the answer would most likely be "morris dance music" and "Not a lot." Morris dancers themselves would be the first to admit that they have suffered more than their share of mockery and derision, and the stereotype of the morris fiddler is someone who plays loudly and clumpily, with single scraping bow strokes, with lots of droning (and I mean droning!), without ornamentation, and slightly out of tune. Is this a fair description? Why do all our Celtic neighbours have such sexy and vibrant fiddle styles while ours is so boring? Was this always the same in the past? And is anything happening today to amend this sorry state? No doubt you, like I, have spent many sleepless nights pondering these questions, and the shocking truth can finally be revealed.

The English Dancing Master

As is the case in Ireland and Scotland, fiddle music has been a part of life in England since before the violin shouldered out the rebec and vielle in the 16th century. Along with begging and thieving, fiddling was the chosen profession of many a landless peasant. Taverns, fairs, markets, and street corners rang to the scrape of the fiddle, as did the kitchens and grand halls of the big houses. Dancing was a popular pastime for rich and poor alike, and along with the pipe and tabor, the fiddle was the key instrument for accompaniment. In the 1500s there would have been a big difference between the dances found in barns and those in ballrooms. Dances for the poor and unwashed were simple, but lively and fun; for the upper classes, dancing was elegant and refined, but tedious. Wouldn't it be delightful, thought the begowned and bewigged, to pretend to be lowly country folk? Let's forget all this difficult formal dancing and go native. This was the start of centuries of country dancing, enjoyed by everyone from pauper to prince.

Dancing masters soon became much in demand, travelling the country and giving instructions on the dance steps, either accompanied by a fiddler or playing fiddle themselves. By the mid 17th century, such was the popularity of country dancing that Thomas Playford published the first of a long-running series of manuals, entitled *The English Dancing Master*; these books contained instructions on the dance steps, along with the tunes in manuscript form. It is a good measure of the success of these publications that they sold well despite highly unfortunate timing; 1651, when the first volume came out, was three years after the execution of Charles I. Oliver Cromwell led the new republic, fired by puritan zeal. Such frippery and frivolity as dancing, while not actually banned, was certainly worthy of a black mark against your name. Nevertheless, dancing must have gone on behind closed doors, for Playford continued in business, releasing new volumes at regular intervals. By 1658 Cromwell was dead, the republican revolution was history and soon Charles II, the Merry Monarch, was on the throne, bringing with him a band of 24 violinists. Once more the good people of England could eat, drink, and make fools of themselves on the dancefloor. Let the good times roll!

Style and repertoire in pre-Victorian fiddling

So what was English fiddle-playing really like in its pre-Victorian heyday? Research suggests that the English tradition then was as rich as anything we find today elsewhere in the British Isles and America.

Improvisation

Playford's 1685 volume gives us a first hint that the fiddlers were not churning out the artless, wooden, and unadorned tunes of the modern stereotype. The volume is entitled 'The Division Violin' and consists of a set of 26 tunes. For each there is a simple core melody, followed by a series of increasingly complex 'variation sets', and a 'ground bass' part, a simple bass riff that could be played repeatedly (on the bass viol). These divisions or variations could be read or learned, but were only intended as examples. Proficient players would be expected to create their own improvised parts, using the ground bass as a bedrock on which they could lay their own creative flights of fancy. The written variations also demonstrate various techniques such as cross tuning (scordatura), fingered double stops and athletic leaps across the strings.

The fiddlers who played this music were clearly musically literate, skilled, and creative players. The musicologist Paul Roberts has done a great deal of work on analysing and recreating early English fiddle styles, using sources including published collections, such as those of Playford, and unpublished notebooks and manuscripts of individual fiddlers. He concludes that improvisation was widespread: not only the variations but the basic melody itself could be created spontaneously. In the words of Roberts: "two or more fiddlers would sometimes improvise together Dixieland-style, or take breaks in swing style". Just as jazz players call out "fours", and then take four bar solos split between the band, so English dance players would call out "breve" or "semibreve" and then take a solo of the appropriate length. Descriptive pieces such as the fox chase, which would include the elements of a galloping rhythm, simulated dogs barking, and horns blowing, were often played by English fiddlers, along with their Celtic and American contemporaries. Such tunes would also have been largely improvised, and required considerable technique.

Ornamentation

What of the criticism routinely levelled against English fiddlers, that they use little or no ornamentation? To many, the beauty and thrill of Irish fiddle stems largely from the elaborate rolls and cuts which are such an intrinsic feature; English players, by contrast, seem to make a virtue of leaving their tunes plain and unadorned. By a miracle of pre-Victorian science we are able to listen to a 'recording' of a fiddle, cello, and tambourine trio playing a couple of reels and a march. The performance of these musicians was captured on the roll of a mechanical barrel organ, and taken on board ship by an Arctic explorer, Admiral William Parry, early in the 19th century. Presumably the organ was cheaper, consumed less rations, and complained less than an actual fiddle player; at any rate the 'recording' shows elaborate decoration, including many rolls and frequent semiquaver (16th-note) runs linking melody notes. The 'cut' – a single grace note slipped in ahead of a melody note – is today very much associated with Irish playing, but it seems likely that English fiddlers also made extensive use of it, as they also did with the 'birl', the rapid bowed ornament beloved of Scottish fiddlers.

Keys

Manuscript collections and fiddlers' notebooks indicate that a wide range of keys was used; not only the easy keys like G, D, and A major, and the minor keys of E, D, A and B, but also more interesting and challenging keys such as C, F, B-flat and E-flat. The keys would often be selected to make best use of drone notes for a particular melody, or to facilitate fingering of difficult passages. Hornpipes were often danced to bagpipes (hence the origin of the name); these were common in pre-Victorian England and still survive in Northumbria. The flat keys used by the pipes were naturally passed on to the fiddle.

Cross-tunings, or 'scordatura', nowadays mostly found in old-time American fiddling, were common in old English fiddling. Most often used were AEAE, ADAE and AEAC♯. This was another inheritance from the medieval fiddle; it added volume, made some fingerings easier, and added some harmonic colour. On the downside it was restrictive and would have become less frequently used by more advanced players.

Rhythms, tune types, and tempos

Rhythms and time signatures were also rich and varied in pre-Victorian times. Jigs could be in 6/4, 9/4, 6/8, 9/8, or 12/8. A type of jig called the 'joak' became very popular in the early 1730s; curiously, these tunes were all named after colours: 'Black Joak', 'White Joak', 'Yellow Joak', and so on. Many also had a peculiar structure; a six-bar repeated A section and a ten-bar repeated B section. This made the standard total of 32 bars, but with a very unstandard division between the sections.

Reels, nowadays associated mainly with Scottish and Irish fiddling, were a standard part of the English repertoire, and contrary to current English practice, they were often played fast.

After the battle of Waterloo in 1815, the waltz swept across Europe, much as Napoleon had done but with less bloodshed; these quickly entered the country dance repertoire. Another new-fangled craze to conquer Europe was the polka, in around 1848. This quickly became the most popular social dance until ragtime arrived in the early 20th century. Like the waltz, it quickly found its way into English fiddling and dancing, with many new tunes being written in this form.

Hornpipes were the tunes on which many fiddlers invested most time and effort; they were the showcase tunes on which the fiddler's technique could best be displayed, and on which they were likely to be judged. They were, indeed, the tunes most likely to be played for fiddle competitions. They tend to be more intricate harmonically and melodically than jigs or reels, often including accidentals and non-diatonic chords. The hornpipe is thought to have originated in England, and was known in the time of Henry VIII. It is used for both step-dancing (a solo display dance, often done with clogs) and for set-dancing (ie, dancing in sets or groups, as in country dancing). It was as a solo step-dance that the hornpipe was most exciting. Because the dance could be done on a single spot it was ideal for dancing aboard ship or in a crowded pub; the dancer used it as an opportunity to show off. Stephen Baldwin (1873-1955) was one of the few English fiddlers to have been part of an unbroken tradition of hornpipe playing. In an article in *FiddleOn Magazine*, Philip Heath-Coleman describes how Baldwin played for a Gypsy wedding in the Forest of Dean, Gloucestershire: "Arriving at three o'clock in the afternoon, he stayed until two o'clock in the morning, perched on a tree stump and playing, in his own words, 'nothing but hornpipes' to which the Gypsies danced 'with great vigour – the sweat simply rolled off them. They never seemed to get tired.'"

Whereas hornpipes today are usually in 4/4, many of those from the 18th century are in 3/2 or 9/4 time, often referred to as triple hornpipes. These have a fascinating rhythm quite unfamiliar to anyone brought up on the standard Celtic or American repertoire; some, such as 'Lads And Lasses', have a distinct syncopation. From the early or mid 18th century, 4/4 hornpipes became popular. These were originally played with an even beat (like polkas or reels); but, possibly as a result of the introduction of the schottishe around 1850, the even rhythm gave way to a dotted rhythm (as played for example on 'Harvest Home'). This uneven rhythm is the one most commonly associated with hornpipes today; they are still used for country dancing, where the dancers do a 'step-hop'. It is sometimes referred to as the Newcastle hornpipe style. Many dotted hornpipes were exported to America but eventually got straightened out, as for example with 'Fisher's Hornpipe'.

With all these different possible rhythms you might well ask how on earth you're supposed to recognise a hornpipe. The answer lies at the end of each line, which will almost always end with three even crotchets (quarter-notes); think of the 'Sailor's Hornpipe', for example.

Bowing technique

The common perception of English fiddling is that the bowing is a simple scraping, one bow per note, with little or no slurring. Analysis of early recordings and of annotated notebooks and manuscripts shows that this was not always the case.

Paul Roberts identifies the most common bowing pattern for 2/4 and 4/4 tunes as that which Americans call the Nashville shuffle; in a group of four quavers (eighth-notes) the first two are slurred while the next two are bowed separately. This gives a flow to the tune with a distinct offbeat accent to provide drive and lift. The other common American shuffle pattern, the Georgia bow, is also sometimes used, with the first quaver (eighth-note) separate and the subsequent three slurred. Jigs were usually played single-bowed, with only occasional slurs. Roberts concludes that good English fiddle players used a variety of bowing patterns and techniques to suit the phrasing of any particular tune.

Double-stops and drones

The English fiddle style grew directly out of the playing of medieval fiddles, which were designed very much with drones in mind (or rather, had not yet been given the capability to play easily without drones). While the more advanced players would undoubtedly have wanted to acquire the new single-string sonata style coming over from Italy along with the first violins, many others would have stuck with the open-string drones with which they were familiar. For a dance fiddler, drones always give the advantage of increased volume and, in the absence of any accompaniment, the possibility of some harmonic interest.

Hornpipes, with their more advanced melodies, chromatic passages, and sometimes flat keys, were often unsuitable for drones; the ability to play these tunes cleanly with single notes would mark out the more technically advanced players.

To summarise: today there is a big difference between English, Irish, Scottish and American styles of fiddling, with English losing out in almost every stylistic field. It would seem that in pre-Victorian times the situation was very different, with English fiddling sharing most of their rich and varied ornamentation, bowing patterns, and rhythms, along with a broad and diverse repertoire.

The decline of English fiddling

There are many possible reasons for the decline of the lively English tradition during the 19th century.

Rural depopulation

The English fiddle tradition was passed from father to son and friend to neighbour in the tight-knit communities of rural England, and it was tied up with local folk customs associated with the annual farming calendar. England was the first country to undergo agricultural and industrial revolution, emptying the villages and destroying rural traditions. Once in the towns, cut off from their village roots, many fiddlers may simply have given up playing.

The demise of the west gallery tradition

Many of the best features of English fiddling were tied up with the west gallery tradition, whereby village churches would support a choir, accompanied by a band. The church would pay for the instruments, and give regular practice to a rag-tag group of musicians, in which fiddlers would rub shoulders with cellos, bassoons, clarinets, and serpents. The bands performed every Sunday in the west gallery of the church, and took great pride in their work there; on Saturday nights the same musicians would be the dance band in the local pub. This tradition grew and developed from the mid 18th century until 1833, when the Oxford Movement emerged in the church, dedicated to a more formal style of worship; one target was to remove the often unruly village musicians and replace them with a church organ. By the 1860s this had been accomplished, often accompanied by the actual demolition of the gallery, and the church bands had virtually disappeared. Deprived of the regular practice and financial support of the church, many would also have ceased to function as pub bands as well.

Changes in dance fashion

English fiddling tradition was tied to country dancing and step-dancing, both of which went out of fashion in Victorian times. Jigs, reels, and particularly hornpipes were the backbone of the repertoire, but in the 19th century a series of new dances – quadrilles, waltzes, and polkas – gradually displaced the old tunes. True, fiddlers could play all these new tunes, but for the ballrooms of the rich a more modern and refined sound was demanded. If violins were used they would be more in the style of a string quartet; trained musicians reading parts, not rustic fiddlers ornamenting and improvising.

The rise of music hall

The first of the music halls, The Canterbury, opened near London's Westminster Bridge in 1852, and soon they were everywhere, providing a richly varied professional bill of humorous and sentimental songs, comedy sketches, and a bizarre mix of speciality acts including escapologists, fire eaters, magicians, knife-throwers, and mind readers. This was the Saturday night prime-time television of Victorian England. Even where fiddlers did still find jobs at a dance or a party, the audience would expect to hear music hall songs like 'Down At The Old Bull And Bush', rather than an old jig or hornpipe.

The failings of the first folk music revival

The revival came too late, and was too selective. When Cecil Sharp began to record and revive the rural dance tradition, he was already a couple of generations too late, and even what little was left was only partially preserved. His collecting ignored what was left of the step-dance tradition, and failed to reflect the diversity of repertoire of many players. He had no interest in the Newcastle hornpipe fiddle tradition, probably the most exciting and vibrant survival of English fiddling.

The poor quality of sound recordings

By the time sound recordings were made, there were very few players left to choose from. The majority of these were morris players who were not required to do much more than keep good time and rhythm, and had in many cases learned their tunes not from another fiddler but from a piper. Bertie Clark was a fiddler for the original Bampton Morris in the 1920s. He initially learned the tunes from Cecil Sharp's published manuscripts. Recordings of his playing, made in 1958, appear on *Rig-A-Jig Jig: Dance Music Of The South Of England* from Topic Records' *Voice Of The People* collection. A listen to his playing is very instructive. At the time he would have been 81 years old, was quite likely well out of practice, and was possibly arthritic. Nevertheless, there must have been some of the Emperor's New Clothes about both the recording session and the decision to include these tracks on the compilation. Let's not beat about the bush: this is quite simply the worst fiddle playing I have ever heard.

Competition from melodeon and concertina

The melodeon and concertina, both invented in the early 19th century, quickly began to compete with the fiddle; they were easier to play, and didn't come with the same problems of tone and intonation. Though it pains me to say it, on early recordings of morris musicians, the free reed instruments almost invariably sound better than the fiddles. Where fiddle and melodeon or concertina played together, many subtleties and eccentricities of fiddle technique would have been 'ironed out'; the melodeon was very limited in the keys it could play, had no possibility of sliding or playing in the grey area between notes, and had fewer possibilities for ornamentation.

The lack of fiddle contests

Unlike Ireland, Scotland, and the US, England had no tradition of fiddle contests, which undoubtedly did much to maintain a high standard of playing in those countries.

The poor image of the revival

The first folk revival of the early 20th century had an aspect of remoteness and paternalism. Sharp and his associates were from the upper classes, while most traditional musicians were working class. Even to this day the EFDSS is frequently accused of being aloof and living in a world of its own. Early attempts to popularise traditional song and dance in the school curriculum inevitably had the opposite effect to that intended. Elderly 'maiden aunts' were not the ideal medium for passing on folk culture.

The effects of empire

As the head of an empire and very much the dominant part of the British Isles, England never felt itself an underdog. While the oppressed nations of Scotland and Ireland clung to their traditional music as a badge of resistance and nationalist fervour, the English were happy to sit in the music hall singing along to 'Hello, Hello, Who's Your Lady Friend?' If only we had lost the Battle of Waterloo, things might have been so different!

A combination of all of these factors has left English fiddle a shadow of its former self, and much of what did survive was associated with the morris dancing tradition.

Morris dancing

To many people today, morris dancing was and is the heart of a tradition of music and dance that has been with us since medieval times, a symbol of a distant, unspoilt rural idyll. The name is thought to derive from 'Moorish', and the dances have probably been around since the 15th century. They were very much a local tradition; a village would have its own morris 'side', with its own set of dances, costumes, tunes, and traditions. They would perform mostly at seasonal festivities such as Boxing Day or May Day. Music was provided primarily by a pipe and tabor (a kind of drum), but, particularly in the 19th century, when cheap factory-made instruments became available, the fiddle gradually came to the fore. (It is reported that some dancers were so horrified by this newfangled idea that they quit rather than dance to the fiddle.) The music in morris was specifically tailored to the dancing; rhythm, tempo, and structure were the overriding factors in determining style. A particular challenge of morris fiddling came with matching the music to the steps; if the dancers leap into the air, there may have to be a carefully-judged millisecond pause so that the beat coincides with the dancers' feet hitting the ground.

Among the best known morris fiddlers was Jinky Wells (1868-1953). He was from Bampton-in-the-Bush in Oxfordshire, home of the Bampton Morris, which had a 600-year unbroken morris tradition. Wells was from a family which had been in the morris for many generations. He made his first fiddle himself from a corned beef tin and an old rifle butt. He joined the side as 'fool' (a sort of jester figure found in all morris traditions) in 1887, and took the job of fiddler in 1899. He both played and danced, and was so enthusiastic that he also travelled around performing solo, playing and dancing simultaneously. He would also sing while playing. He and his team met Cecil Sharp in Gloucestershire in 1909 and were invited to perform in London by Mary Neal in 1913. Recordings of him made in 1936 show that he was a fine and energetic player, using some ornamentation, and finely judged stress and accent. In contrast to the majority of morris fiddlers recorded around the same time, he had finesse and quite a sweet tone. The majority of his contemporaries, by contrast, displayed a rough and ready approach to both tone and intonation.

The post-war folk revival

Let's fast forward to 1956. In the US, a folk revival was well under way, influenced by Woody Guthrie, left-wing politics and memories of the Great Depression. Students and intellectuals in New York had started learning to play banjo, fiddle, and guitar, just like real hillbillies, and the Newport Folk Festival was already pulling in thousands.

CECIL SHARP

Cecil Sharp (1859-1924) was the very model of a modern English gentleman, educated at private school and Cambridge University. He was a music teacher and composer with an interest in folk songs and music. This interest was greatly increased in 1899 when, at Headington Quarry near Oxford, he chanced on a performance by the local morris dancers. At this time, due in large part to rural depopulation, morris dancing was almost extinct; Headington side was one of only a handful still in existence. Today it's not unusual to see a troop of jangling morris men dancing in an urban shopping centre or car park anywhere in England, but to Cecil Sharp this was like discovering the last of Robin Hood's Merrie Men. This was the time of Romantic Nationalism, when poets, artists, musicians, and dreamers all over Europe were looking for the souls of their respective nations, finding them in whatever traditions seemed ancient, pure, and untainted by commercialism. Sharp began recording and annotating the dance steps and tunes and, with the help of Mary Neal, who ran a Girl's Club in London, he set about teaching the dances to a new generation. Unfortunately, though he was keen to collect the tunes which went with the dances, he had no interest in the style of musical performance; he would even ask the musicians to sing or hum the tune in preference to playing their instruments. He formed the English Folk Dance Society in 1911, which became the focus of what was ultimately a very successful revival. After his death in 1924 his collections were housed in Cecil Sharp House near Regents Park in London; the EFDS merged with the English Folk Song Society, forming the EFDSS (English Folk Dance and Song Society). The House also became the home for the papers of other important collectors, notably Ralph Vaughan Williams (1872-1958). One of England's most influential composers, he began collecting folk songs in 1904 and incorporating traditional modes and melodic phrases into his pastoral compositions. *The Lark Ascending* is one of his most enduring works, encapsulating his dream of a lost rural idyll. The library of Cecil Sharp house is now named after him.

Cecil Sharp

London, already awash with American jazz and rock'n'roll, was suddenly hit by the skiffle craze. Skiffle was the poor man's jazz, a simple form of American folk/jazz/blues that anyone could play. Virtually overnight, guitar sales went through the roof. Those who couldn't afford a guitar could play washboard, jug, or make their own tea-chest bass. Coffee bars sprang up all over London, spreading out from Soho like the Great Plague, and within a year they were filled with skiffle bands; there were said to be more than 600 bands in London alone. The decline was as dramatic as the rise, and after just two years the bubble had burst. Lonnie Donegan, whose hit 'Rock Island Line' made him the undisputed king of skiffle, was suddenly without a kingdom. However, 600 untrained but enthusiastic bands were suddenly stuck with the question of what to do next. The ones who saw dollar signs chose rock'n'roll (including an unknown, no-hope band called The Quarrymen); the intellectuals, with their goatee beards, chose jazz; the disgruntled left-wingers, fed up with American musical imperialism, decided it was time for a second English folk revival.

Chief among the standard bearers of the post-war folk revival was Ewan MacColl, communist, actor, singer, dramatist, and writer of the mega-selling songs 'The First Time Ever I Saw Your Face' and 'Dirty Old Town'. As early as the 1940s, MacColl had begun collecting English sea shanties and industrial workers' songs, which had been largely ignored by previous collectors. Between 1958 and 1964 he was instrumental in creating the 'Radio Ballads', a set of BBC radio broadcasts linking songs with social issues and tales of the lives of ordinary working people. In 1953 he founded the Ballad And Blues Club, later to become the Singers' Club. This was one of the very first folk clubs; within a decade they would exist in their hundreds all across Britain.

MacColl championed English songs; he wanted to use the revival to counter the domineering effect of American culture on Britain. He was also very focused on authenticity, and he instituted a policy, still controversial today, that singers should only use their own accents, and only sing songs from the area where they were born and bred. He was also keen on unaccompanied song; he considered that if accompaniment was used it should be something like fiddle or melodeon. Guitars were definitely frowned upon.

These dogmatic policies were naturally unpopular with the army of ex-skiffle musicians, with their shiny new guitars, suspect American accents, and repertoire of railroad and cowboy songs. A split was created in the folk world that has still not entirely healed. It's easy to criticise MacColl for being old fashioned, restrictive, and even a musical dictator, but we must remember three things. Firstly, he regarded folk music not just as a form of entertainment (as most of us do today) but as a political vehicle for social change. Secondly, he had great respect for the meaning and integrity of the music; he was aware for example that folk songs and tunes had largely been created and sung without chordal accompaniment in the past. Adding clumsy guitar chords would inevitably change the songs, most likely for the worse. And thirdly he took the ethnomusicological view that a folk song is only a folk song as long as it is passed orally down the generations, preferably in situ. A song that is learned from a record, and performed completely out of context, loses its original meaning.

The new English folk fiddlers

It is significant that the English folk revival of the 50s and 60s was very much focused on song and to a smaller extent on dance, with tunes coming at the bottom of the heap. There were large collections of songs readily available, thanks to Cecil Sharp House. One of the most significant sources of old songs was the 'Child Ballads', a collection made by the Harvard professor James Francis Child and published in the 1880's. Child had been keen to trace the origins of American folk songs back to their British roots. Singers such as Martin Carthy, one of the earliest English folk singers (and still prominent today), had a huge pool of material to draw on whenever they liked. Tune collections did exist, but for reasons we've already discussed, these were smaller in number and poorer in quality.

One of the first fiddlers to make an impact on the English folk scene was Dave Swarbrick. He was born in London, but grew up in Birmingham. In his teens he was one of the temporary foot-soldiers of the skiffle horde, moving quickly over to folk when the bubble burst. He came to the attention of Ewan MacColl, and in 1959 was on his way down to London on the train to perform at a concert organised by MacColl. Also on the train, getting in some frantic last-minute rehearsal, were the Ian Campbell Folk Group. They were also skiffle refugees and were by coincidence on their way to MacColl's concert.

With the immortal words "Is this a private session or can anyone join in?", Swarbrick gatecrashed the rehearsal. The band were so delighted by his fiddle playing that he joined them on stage that night, and without any debate was accepted as a member. Until this point few, if any, folk song groups had a fiddle player; it added a whole new dimension to the songs, and added the possibility of playing instrumental as well as well as vocal numbers. He had a playful, jazzy, irreverent style and a repertoire that covered England, Ireland, Scotland, and America. His performances and subsequent recordings of such tunes as 'Devil Among The Tailors' and 'The Mason's Apron' made these tunes a must-have for a whole generation of fiddlers. He was also a pioneer of the use of fiddle as a melodic accompaniment to traditional song, weaving in and out of the singer's lines.

Dave Swarbrick went on to play with many of the luminaries of the folk scene, including pianist Beryl Marriott, singer Martin Carthy, and in recent years Whippersnapper. But perhaps his most important connection was with Fairport Convention, which he joined in 1969. This band was among the first to play electric folk. With a line-up including electric guitar and drums, Fairport were able to cross the boundary into popular music, in a scene closely allied to experimental and progressive rock. Steeleye Span, with their fiddler Peter Knight, followed hard on the heels of Fairport Convention, fusing rock rhythms and structures with traditional English songs. The two bands spearheaded a scene in which folk music briefly entered the popular mainstream, with gigs in colleges, rock venues, and festivals. Fairport's 1969 album *Liege & Lief*, released on Island Records, was one of their most successful and influential, while 'All Around My Hat' was a hit single for Steeleye Span in 1975. It is significant that although these bands used carefully researched traditional songs, often from the Child ballad collections, there was little in the way of traditional English instrumental tunes within their repertoire. The opportunity for folk musicians to sample rock stardom was a brief one, and by the late 70s public taste, fickle thing that it is, had moved on. The folk scene survived, but for the next 20 years or so remained almost entirely outside the commercial sector, relying on an extensive network of folk clubs and festivals, small record labels (most notably Topic Records), and a small but loyal fan base.

Dave Swarbrick

Within this scene, what was there for a fiddle player to do? A player with almost as long a pedigree as Dave Swarbrick is Barry Dransfield, who became a professional musician and singer in 1965. He was a self-taught fiddler, learning in Irish pub sessions and from American old-time music. He was introduced to the American fiddler John Hartford, who inspired him to play the fiddle down on his chest, allowing him to sing simultaneously, a common technique in old-time circles. He toured extensively on the folk circuit, initially with his brother Robin, and later solo. While he sang many English songs, his tunes were mostly Irish, Scottish, sometimes American, but rarely English. He quickly realised that if you want to shine as a performer in the English folk world you have two choices: you either become a singer, possibly using your fiddle for accompaniment, or else you play tunes, in which case you'd better make them Irish. Dransfield did both, and among his many successes, he scored one of the best jobs ever landed by a folk fiddler. In 1984 he went to Tahiti to appear as a blind fiddler in the film *The Bounty*, with Mel Gibson and Anthony Hopkins. A tough job but someone had to do it.

English fiddle today

Since the 1990s, English fiddling, along with the folk scene in general, has taken a considerable upturn. One reason is that folk music education in England has finally got into gear, some decades after its Celtic counterparts. Organizations like Folkworks, based in Newcastle, provide classes for young instrumentalists, and a folk degree course has recently been established at Newcastle University. Since 1997 BBC radio has hosted the Young Folk Awards. A quick listen to any of the finalists, let alone winners, will show that the general standard of playing has taken great leaps forward. Furthermore, for decades now many English fiddlers have been acutely conscious of the relative poverty of their national fiddle tradition; recently they have made great efforts to study old recordings and manuscripts to see if there isn't, after all, something exciting and challenging for a fiddler to do within it. Many old tune collections have been re-published, either from the repertoires of individual players or in general collections such as Pete Cooper's *English Fiddle Tunes*.

Eliza Carthy

The result of all this hard work at the grassroots is that the folk scene has produced a new set of talented young star performers whom the media have finally noticed. Foremost among these is currently Eliza Carthy, daughter of singers Martin Carthy and Norma Waterson. She started out with her parents in the family band Waterson:Carthy, but quickly became established as an artist in her own right. She has twice been nominated for the Mercury music prize and has carried off numerous BBC folk awards. Her fiddling is in the southern English style, with lots of double stopping and an emphasis on rhythm rather than melody; an ideal style for the self-accompaniment of singing, which is her chief use of the instrument. Another fast-rising star is Seth Lakeman, a fiddler and powerful singer from Dartmoor in Devon. He was part of the young folk supergroup Equation, which landed a major record deal in the 1990s. Despite high hopes and an inordinate amount of record company money, the band failed to make an impact. Lakeman left the band in 2001, and recorded his own album *Kitty Jay* in his own kitchen, with an outrageous budget of £300 ($450). While standing beside the road pondering the uncertain fate of his broken-down car, he received a call out of the blue telling him that the

Northumbrian fiddle

While the fiddle in southern England seems to have had a rapid decline from Victorian times onwards, it seems to have survived and even thrived in some of the more remote northern areas, and none more so than in the north-eastern region called Northumbria. Several factors may have contributed to this. Like the Scots and Irish, the Geordies, as they are known, have always had a sense of regional pride distinct from the mainstream of English culture and less desire to follow the latest music and dance fads coming from the south. Social dance, both step-dancing (solo or dancing in pairs) and set-dancing (for larger groups) remained popular, and the demand for reels and hornpipes never disappeared.

The closeness to Scotland undoubtedly had an effect; strathspeys and pipe marches were commonly played, and migrant workers from Ireland also had a positive influence. The Northumbrian pipes, the only true survivor of what was once a country-wide piping tradition, provided a healthy element of competition to the fiddle; the pipers were always well organised and highly respected. The earliest records of Northumbrian repertoire come from the 1690's, when Henry Atkinson published a tune-book, showing a large and diverse repertoire.

Industrialisation, coal mining and the growth of towns such as Newcastle and Gateshead did not disrupt the musical traditions, and in the 1840s we know that there was a thriving culture of professional pub fiddling. Master of all he surveyed at this time was James Hill (c1815-c1860), publican, fiddler, and prolific composer; you may know him from such tunes as 'Beeswing', 'The High Level Bridge', and 'The Hawk'. He was considered "the Paganini of the Hornpipe". Many of his tunes are complex and challenging; 'The High Level Bridge' is today widely used as a contest tune. Tunes in this style are often in flat keys, with frequent string crossing, accidentals, and chromatic passages.

Willie Taylor (1916-2000) was one of the finest players of the modern era. A shepherd, fiddler, and composer, he was also a major inspiration to Kathryn Tickell. Though primarily a player of the Northumbrian pipes, she is also a fine fiddler, and has done perhaps more than anyone to ensure a healthy future for the traditional music of her local area.

Kathryn Tickell

album had been nominated for a Mercury prize. There's a lesson for the record companies there somewhere! This was the start of a renewed and highly successful solo career. Lakeman, like Eliza Carthy, frequently sings and fiddles simultaneously, using the fiddle as a rhythm instrument, and it is interesting that this now seems to have become a tradition. Whereas you'd be hard pushed to find a single notable Irish fiddler who does this, consider this list of English singer/fiddlers: Eliza Carthy; Seth Lakeman; Robin Dransfield; Peter Knight; Chris Wood; Pete Cooper; Roger Wilson; Bella Hardy; Nancy Kerr; Jon Boden; Tom McConville; Fi Fraser; Jackie Oates; Lisa Knapp; Phil Beer.

As we said before, the main reason why so many English fiddle players are also singers seems to be the relative poverty of technique and repertoire in the instrumental tradition. An Irish fiddler has no question as to where his fiddle will take him; there is a lifetime's worth of jigs and reels to play, either in sessions, in bands, or as a soloist. In the absence of a clearly defined role within the English folk scene, an ambitious fiddle player who wants to get noticed and develop a career has to be a singer as well.

The future, however, is more hopeful. In the past decade, perhaps partly as a result of the establishment of devolved Welsh and Scottish parliaments, there has been a noticeable trend towards rediscovering a sense of Englishness, which has carried over into the arts. The Imagined Village is a fascinating project which perhaps shows a way forward, drawing together strands both of past and present, the old white working class and the new multicultural England, centuries-old folk song and modern sounds and rhythms. Along with popular artists such as Billy Bragg, Benjamin Zephania, Paul Weller, and Transglobal Underground are folk stalwarts such as Martin Carthy and singer/fiddlers Eliza Carthy and Chris Wood. This is a fine example of folk breaking out of its self-imposed ghetto.

Recent research has shown that English fiddling was once as rich and diverse as that of its Celtic neighbours. Once we stop focusing on the distinctly dodgy playing that survived along with the morris dance, we can start to rebuild some of the ambition, commitment and excitement of the old hornpipe and west gallery musicians. Despite a hiatus of some 150 years, if it can find a new role in modern English society there is no reason why the English fiddle shouldn't once more hold its head high.

PLAYING ENGLISH FIDDLE

At this point one would hope for a detailed and fascinating analysis of current trends in the ornamentation and bowing patterns of English fiddle playing. However, we've spent the last 300 years explaining why that won't be necessary. Instead here are a few tunes to give you a taste of the repertoire.

To start with, here's one of the best-known morris tunes, 'Shepherd's Hey'. It was collected by Cecil Sharp from the fiddler of the Bidford Morris in 1906, though it is used throughout the Cotswolds and beyond. It was popularised through the orchestration of composer/folklorist Percy Grainger, and also recorded by Ashley Hutchings and Dave Swarbrick. The tune's simplicity is typical of morris tunes. I've written in a couple of drones; some fiddlers would put in a lot more of the open D drone, particularly under the first line. The last three beats of each section are accented; in some versions of the dance, these beats coincide with the clapping of hands, the beating of sticks or the occasional breaking of bones.

Shepherd's Hey

EXAMPLE 3.1

CD 1 TRACK 43

'Sir Roger de Coverley' was a tune first published by John Playford in 1695. It was originally in two parts, and written in 9/4 time. Both the dance and the tune were widely used, and both evolved rapidly so that numerous versions exist. The tune inspired Sir Richard Steele and Joseph Addison to create a fictional character of the same name in their periodical The Spectator in 1711. He was a jovial country squire, "cheerful, gay and hearty" who "keeps a good house in both town and country". His great-grandfather is supposed to have invented the dance. Sir Roger de Coverley is also mentioned as a popular dance in George Eliot's *Silas Marner*, and Charles Dickens's *Christmas Carol*.

The tune is nowadays normally written in 9/8 time, and played much like an Irish slip jig.

EXAMPLE 3.2

CD 1 TRACK 44

Sir Roger de Coverley

'Hod The Lass Till I Run At Her' is a wonderfully eccentric reel from the north of England; the first record of it is from the 1830s in the Lake District. As regards the title, I think it's one of those things best left unexplored. The tune has a syncopation rarely found in the more widely known English repertoire. The last C note in the first bar of each section can be either natural or sharp, or possibly even something in between. The piece is a leftover from an innocent age when they didn't give a damn.

EXAMPLE 3.3

CD 1 TRACK 45

Hod The Lass Till I Run At Her

Hornpipes are perhaps the most characteristically English type of tune, and much beloved by fiddlers and dancers alike, especially in the 18th century. While today's hornpipes are almost exclusively in 4/4 time, there was once a huge repertoire of tunes in 3/2 or 9/4. This one was first published in 1713 by Daniel Wright in his *Extraordinary Collection Of Pleasant And Merry Humours*. More recently John Offord has

EXAMPLE 3.4

CD 1 TRACK 46

John Of The Green, The Cheshire Way

published an extensive set of hornpipes from Lancashire, of which this is one. To people unfamiliar with 3/2 hornpipes this sounds almost Balkan in its sense of rhythmic surprise, and the first bar of the last line with its tumbling three-note phrases sounds like something out of *Riverdance*.

Here's a more standard 4/4 hornpipe, but played with even notes rather than dotted notes. It was first written down by the poet, fiddler, and tune collector John Clare (1793-1864). The title, *The Savage Hornpipe*, may refer to Richard Savage; he was also a poet and, perhaps appropriately, a convicted murderer.

EXAMPLE 3.5

CD 1 TRACK 47

The Savage Hornpipe

Finally a hornpipe in the modern dotted or 'step hop' rhythm. This one was written by the great Newcastle fiddler James Hill, to commemorate the famous twin road and rail bridge built across the Tyne in 1848. The tune has made its way into the Scottish, Irish, and American repertoires, often under the title 'The High Level Hornpipe'.

The High Level Bridge

James Hill

EXAMPLE 3.6

CD 1 TRACK 48

klezmer fiddle

klezmer fiddle

Klezmer is powerful stuff. I first became aware of this some time in the 80s when I was asked to play some jazz at a Jewish function. Sandwiched somewhere between 'Autumn Leaves' and 'Ain't Misbehavin'', we slipped in 'Khoson Kale Mazeltov', a tune I'd learned from a book some days before. The assembled diners, who had hitherto treated us with polite indifference, suddenly rose en masse and joyfully whirled around the dance floor. Even in my inexperienced hands, this tune, for my purposes labelled 'exotic' alongside a ragbag of Italian, Cajun, Russian, Balkan, and French tunes, had suddenly become a thing of potency.

Some years later, with considerably more experience and a heap of Jewish weddings under my belt, I was giving a klezmer workshop, playing a slow 'zhok'. Afterwards an old lady came up to me and told me that when I played the tune, she had unexpectedly burst into tears. My playing doesn't normally have that effect, honest! I was reminded yet again that this music has a rare poignancy and an uncanny ability to touch people's emotions. So what is it about klezmer that is so special?

A little bit of research will quickly reveal that it's surrounded by a good deal of confusion, myth, and misunderstanding. For example, is it Eastern European music, or American, or for that matter Israeli? Is it primarily secular or religious? Is it happy or sad? Deeply old-fashioned or up-to-the-minute hip? And what does the name klezmer actually mean, and does it refer to the music or the musicians? To answer these questions we have to go way back to the Jewish 'Old World'.

The word klezmer derives from the Hebrew words 'kley' and 'zemer', meaning musical instrument. In Europe the use of the term klezmer (plural 'klezmorim') eventually became attached to the musician rather than the instrument, and it's only in recent years that klezmer has been used as a description of a style or genre of music. In this book I will make cavalier use of both meanings of the term.

The history of klezmer fiddle

The origins of klezmer lie in the heart of Eastern Europe. From the 14th century on, Jews had been gravitating in that direction, attracted by the tolerance and sometimes even welcome of some Russian and

Polish noblemen. In 1791 Catherine the Great of Russian established the Pale Of Settlement, an area bordering the Russian Empire, and including parts of present-day Poland, Lithuania, Belarus, Moldova, Ukraine, and some of western Russia. Here Jews were allowed to live and work, valued for their skills and industry but viewed always with suspicion and kept at arms length. At its height the Pale was home to five million Jews, a population that must have supported thousands of klezmorim.

From the 15th century onwards there are many written accounts of klezmer bands operating both in the 'shtetls' (small rural communities) and in large towns and cities such as Kiev, Kishiniev, and Odessa. The profession of musician was generally hereditary, and they were organised into guilds, the first of which was founded in Prague in 1558 with the 'fidl' (fiddle) as its emblem. A 'kapelye' (band or orchestra) would usually be led by a fiddler; there would also be a second ('sukund', or 'tweyster') and possibly third fiddle, a bass or cello, several wind instruments, a drum, and a cymbalom (a type of hammered dulcimer). The second and third fiddles would play the melody an octave down, or add rhythm.

The wedding was an essential part of Jewish community life and culture, and was the bread and butter of the klezmorim. It was an elaborate event, often lasting several days or even weeks. Ceremony developed around every aspect of the wedding, with music to suit every aspect of the ritual. Different tunes were required for every part of the wedding. A 'Tsu Der Khupe', for example, is a slow processional tune played as the bride makes her stately approach to the 'khupe' (wedding canopy), whilst a 'Mazltov Dobriden' (congratulations and greeting) is used to welcome the guests as they arrive at the wedding. The 'Broyges Tants' (dance of anger and reconciliation) was played for the mothers of the bride and groom, who were assumed to view one another with suspicion if not loathing. The first section is slow and menacing, where the two circle each other in a threatening manner, while the second half speeds up as the tension lifts, the two mothers join in a joyful dance, and the frank exchange of views regarding the cost of the flowers, the choice of venue, and the inebriated state of the groom is temporarily forgotten. Whilst much of the repertoire is for dancing, the 'Doina' is a listening piece. It is a semi-improvised rubato tune led by the fiddle or clarinet, and is the opportunity for the soloist to display his virtuosity and justify his fee.

Whilst klezmer is distinctly secular, it has many ties with the religious music of the synagogue. Since the destruction of the Second Temple in Jerusalem by the Romans, in 70AD, music for normal ceremonies in the synagogue had been vocal, sung a capella by cantors or 'khasonim', sometimes accompanied by a choir. The melodies and modes used for these sung prayers often formed the basis for the tunes played by the klezmorim. The vocal inflections of the cantors were also a key influence on the style of the klezmer players. There are two essential ornaments used by klezmer instrumentalists; the laughing/crying/sighing sound as a note is bent downwards, and the sob or broken note (the 'krekhts'). Both of these are directly inherited from the cantor, as are the scales and manner of phrasing of the melodies.

Perennial wars between Russia and the Ottoman Empire, from the 17th century on, ensured that many Jews were called up for military service. For klezmorim this often meant joining a military band; playing waltzes and quadrilles in the officers' mess was a lot more attractive than carting a rifle up to the front. This military experience had a positive effect on klezmer as a whole, introducing musicians to modern manufactured instruments such as brass and woodwind, teaching them a wider popular repertoire, and instilling discipline and rigour in their playing. The insistent, snare-heavy drum style still heard in modern klezmer bands can be traced back to this period, as can the rise of the clarinet and the decline of the fiddle. The clarinet has a similar voice, range, and expressiveness to the fiddle but is louder and can easily dominate a band. The days when the fiddler was automatically the bandleader were numbered.

The relatively liberal period for the Jews of the Russian Pale came to an end in 1881, with the assassination of Tsar Alexander II. Under the reign of his son, Alexander III, there was a brutal clampdown on civil liberties, with the Jews a particular target. Arrests, murders, and widespread pogroms soon overwhelmed the Jewish population, and this was the start of a massive period of emigration to the United States. It would last until 1924, when the doors finally slammed shut. Some 2,500,000 Eastern European Jews made the trip to Ellis Island.

Klezmer in the United States

Klezmer thrived in the USA, with emigré bandleaders like Dave Tarras and Naftule Brandwein (both clarinettists) becoming recording and performing stars within the rapidly growing American Jewish community. Bandleader Abe Schwartz, himself a violinist and pianist, pioneered the idea of having a single lead instrument to play either melody or improvised solos. This had parallels in the jazz world, where soloists like Louis Armstrong and Sydney Bechet began to emerge from what had previously been more anonymous collective ensembles.

Chief among the record companies signing klezmer musicians were Victor and Columbia, with nostalgia for the Old World being the chief marketing strategy. These early recordings had an important effect on the transmission of style and repertoire. For the first time, individual tunes became codified and standardised. Whereas before there may have been dozens of different versions of every tune, now the first successful recording would be seen by many as the 'right way' to play it.

A recording industry was already active in Europe. Victor had sent Fred Gaisberg to London as early as 1899, from where he travelled through much of eastern Europe including St Petersburg, Warsaw, Bucharest, and Budapest, making field recordings of Jewish musicians. There were also independent, European-based companies chasing the same market, including most notably Syrena in Warsaw. Among the artists on this label was the somewhat mysterious V. Belf's Romanian Orchestra, recorded between 1911 and 1914. Belf was actually from the Ukraine; the use of the word Romanian was probably more of a marketing ploy than anything else. Around 30 tracks were recorded, including many (such as 'Odessa Bulgar') that are still staples of the repertoire, possibly because of these recordings. The ensemble consists of clarinet, two violins, and cello. There is also piano, possibly introduced for the first time for the purpose of this recording. As with the early recordings of Irish traditional music, the sudden inclusion of chords to what had previously been largely melodic music was somewhat ham-fisted. The recording quality is poor, and the clarinet dominates the sound, so that little can be gleaned in terms of style or ornamentation from the rather ghostly-sounding violins. Nevertheless these recordings offer one of the chief surviving insights into the repertoire and style of Old World klezmorim. They have been widely used as source material in the late 20th-century klezmer revival, changing hands mostly in the form of hand-copied cassettes. As far as I'm aware they are still not available on CD.

Offshoots of klezmer, such as Yiddish theatre music and klezmer jazz, became popular in America, but assimilation and secularization within the Jewish community as a whole meant that klezmer began to decline. The repertoire, previously rich and diverse, was rapidly narrowing as demand for it decreased at weddings. The style was by now referred to simply as 'the bulgars'; by the 50s and 60s the Jewish wedding scene had declined to just a few veteran musicians playing in the so-called Borscht Belt, the faded hotels of the Catskill Mountains in New York State.

The klezmer revival
The rebirth of klezmer began, strangely enough, among the ranks of American 'old-time' revival musicians. Urban, middle class, educated Americans started a process of re-evaluation and rediscovery of old-

time music, the fiddle and banjo music inherited from the early British and Irish pioneers. This had survived in rural and mountainous areas such as the Appalachians, and by the early 60s there was a new breed of 'citybillies' learning the old tunes at festivals and folk camps and forming new bands. They were part of a counterculture, a rejection of the shallow values of popular music in favour of something older, purer, and more meaningful. Among the ranks of the new old-timers was Harry 'Hank' Sapoznik, born-again banjo player with the Delaware Water Gap String Band. It slowly dawned on him that a large proportion, indeed a majority, of the new breed of pickers, scrapers, and strummers were, like himself, Jewish. In the absence of roots music of their own they had attached themselves, like ducklings to a surrogate mother, to the nearest available musical tradition.

Sapoznik famously describes his conversation with old time fiddler (and genuine old-timer) Tommy Jarrell. Having ascertained over breakfast, following a bacon-sandwich-related incident, that Sapoznik was in fact Jewish, Jarrell enquired drily, "Hank, don't your people got none of your own music?" The question struck a chord, and Sapoznik went home determined to find a satisfactory answer. Like most of his generation, he had grown up with the certainty that his parents, whatever their many qualities, were deeply old-fashioned, and that any music they might enjoy was something to be avoided at all cost. The Jewish dancing to klezmer at his own bar mitzvah had been about as welcome as the aforementioned bacon sandwich, and until this moment he had not considered klezmer as being in the same category as his beloved old-time music, something with deep, solid roots, rich in cultural symbolism.

His grandfather pointed him in the direction of YIVO, the New York Yiddish research institute. Here he was in turn directed to a dusty basement, where amid piles of decaying newspapers he found cabinets full of old 78s. These were klezmer recordings that had been accepted by the institute more from a sense of duty than enthusiasm, and that had not been touched since they had been laid to rest. In the virtual absence of any working klezmer musicians in New York, or anywhere else for that matter, these forgotten treasures and others like them represented the last chance to bring klezmer back to life. Good fortune and good contacts landed Sapoznik a Federal grant to continue the study of his new-found passion, the most significant part of his task being to listen to, catalogue, and finally re-release some of the YIVO collection. He also began to seek out firstly the few old musicians still in circulation who could show him how klezmer used to be played, and secondly the small but rapidly growing group of his contemporaries who were engaging in the same voyage of discovery.

Among those in the first category was the fiddler Leon Schwartz (1901-1989), from the Romanian/Ukranian area of Bukovina; though never a big star, he had played klezmer all his life, both at home in Europe and, since 1921, in New York. In the latter category, Sapoznik discovered that Andy Statman, a fine New York Jewish bluegrass mandolin player, was in the process of reinventing himself as a klezmer clarinettist, taking lessons from none other than Dave Tarras, who was still alive and playing like a demon.

Revival bands

Possibly the first 'new' klezmer band to form in America was not in New York but over in California. Led by Lev Liberman, The Klezmorim released their first album, *East Side Wedding*, in 1976 on Arhoolie Records. Though serious students of the music, theirs was certainly not a dry, scholarly reconstruction. They took a wacky, vaudeville approach to their performances, as you might guess from the fact that one of their members, Rick Elmore, had formerly been street performer Professor Gizmo the one-man band, whilst Brian Wishnefsky had been Hairy James, the trumpet-playing gorilla. In the words of Liberman, they had a "Barbary Coast/Haight-Ashbury recycled thrift store 1920s novelty- music aesthetic".

Andy Statman took a very different approach. Along with musicologist Zev Feldman, he produced an album in 1979, *Jewish Klezmer Music*, with a meditative and distinctly old-world feel. He has remained at the forefront of the klezmer revival, but has moved further and further towards the Hasidic ethos of music not as commercial entertainment but as a serious path to spiritual enlightenment.

By the time The Klezmatics formed in 1986 there was already a fully-fledged revival in progress, albeit a rather disparate and confusing one. It had been demonstrated clearly that there was a large and enthusiastic audience for the music, among both Jews and Gentiles. To some it was a welcome source of cultural affirmation, a symbol of Jewish pride. To others it was something exotic, new, and exciting, and it didn't really matter where it came from. To some it was the next best thing to prayer, whilst to others it was great dance music to get wrecked to. Due in no small part to the success of Klezcamp, an intensive festival of teaching and learning of klezmer and all thing Yiddish, there was now a large and growing supply of eager young musicians.

An interesting feature of the klezmer revival is that almost everyone joining a klezmer band since the 70s has come to it from some other musical place. We've already seen the move from old-time, bluegrass, and street music. The Klezmatics were no exception to this trend, many of them being jazz musicians. The band's Alicia Svigals brought the violin back into high profile as a lead instrument for the first time. She had been heavily into Greek music, which gave her a flying start with much of the authentic klezmer feel.

We've already seen how klezmer was developing on a very broad front; The Klezmatics entered the fray on the far left wing, as "the planet's radical Jewish roots band". They actively celebrate the homosexuality of some of their members, whilst their tune 'Mizmor Shir Lehanef' is written in praise of the path to enlightenment, not through the Torah, but through cannabis. Here was a band that could fill rock clubs and out-hip the hippest audience, whilst at the same time being a serious and highly respected klezmer band. It also provided inspiration for the legions of new bands worldwide who were scratching their heads in search of the perfect name. The names Klezmernauts, Klezical, Klezmechaye!, Klezmos, Klezmotones, Klezmeydlech, Klezmokum, Klezamir, Klezmorim, Los Klezmeros, Kleztraphobix, Klezmic Noiz, Klezcetera, Klezmocracy, and Klezgoyim are already taken. For my money the prize has to go to the New York lesbian band Isle Of Klezbos. I drew the short straw when I came up with the blindingly original Klezmania for my band in London. This being in the days before Google, I was blissfully unaware of Klezmania (Australia), Klezmania (San Francisco), and Klezmania (Boston). Doh!

Alicia Svigals

Among the more imaginative names relinquishing the K word are The Mazeltones, The Shtetl Blasters, Shir Fun, Take The Oy Train, The Red Sea Pedestrians, and The Vulgar Bulgars. Yid Vicious has among his track listings such gems as 'Anarchy In The Ukraine' and 'Never Mind The Cossacks'. Clearly an ethos of fun, cosmopolitanism, and secularism is the order of the day for the majority of new klezmer outfits.

There are now hundreds of bands, not only in the US, but throughout Europe and elsewhere, playing klezmer in a bewildering variety of forms and drawing on a huge range of influences. Some concentrate on reproducing Old World klezmer, such as Budowitz and Joel Rubin. Others, like The Klezmer Conservatory Band and The Maxwell Street Klezmer Band, go for the classic American sound. Many bands go for the jazz klezmer sound, including The Klezmorim and The Flying Bulgar Klezmer Band, while the more daring have ventured into the fields of avant-garde (John Zorn), electro (Zohar), or shtetl metal (Naftule's Dream).

Clearly klezmer is in an extremely healthy state, bursting with

What tunes do I need for a Jewish wedding?

Today's wedding repertoire is quite different from what was expected in the heyday of klezmer. The band may be asked to provide some music for before and after the ceremony, which could include any of the klezmer standards. For the bride's approach to the khupe and walking seven times round the groom, a specific slow, stately tune may be asked for. 'Echet Chayil' ('Woman Of Valour') is a favourite; another is 'Erev Shel Shoshanim'. 'Sunrise, Sunset' is also popular, though many clients won't pay you if you play anything from *Fiddler On The Roof*. My favourite is Andy Statman's 'Flatbush Waltz'. There may be some music during the ceremony, but that is usually down to the cantor and pianist. After the glass is broken at the end of the ceremony, 'Simen Tov Mazel Tov' is almost universal, followed by a string of similar tunes. When you get to the reception, some klezmer may be asked for, but jazz, Latin, and light classical are often the perfect accompaniment to the smoked salmon and champagne. If you've got any klezmer jazz or Yiddish theatre tunes (eg, 'Bei Mir Bist Du Sheyn' or 'And The Angels Sing'), now's the time to do them. During dinner, the same mix is called for, but there'll often be Jewish dancing between courses. Here's the big surprise. The chances are they won't want klezmer for this. The repertoire for Jewish dancing nowadays is made up almost entirely of Hasidic melodies and 20th-century Israeli tunes. These mostly have Hebrew words and titles, though they may be performed instrumentally. They mostly have religious and/or Zionist connotations, which in itself makes them at odds with the generally secular ethos of klezmer. Popular numbers include 'Od Yishama', 'Tzadik Katamar' and 'Tzion, Tzion'. Since so many of these tunes are in a minor key, the odd major tune ('Ufaratsa' or 'Tzena Tzena') is worth its weight in gold. These tunes may sound superficially like klezmer, and can be played with the same style and ornamentation. However they are shorter and simpler, usually just with two lines. They are less complex and demanding than klezmer tunes (which frequently have three or more sections, and a variety of mode changes). However, they are very convenient for stringing together. In my music pad I have around 20 in a row that can, if need be, run from one to the next in a continuous string. Once they start dancing, they're not going to stop in a hurry! There may also be some specialist dances such as 'Yesh!' (which looks suspiciously like a barn dance), or 'Yid'n' for a rather bizarre hopping dance. On a really bad night you might have to do some Israeli pop and disco numbers like the Israeli Eurovision winner 'Hallelujah', or the Eurotrash 'Masiach' (once described to me as the worst song in the world). Actually, I quite like it.

imagination, confidence and eclecticism; and, unlike at any time in its history, the music is now as likely to be heard on the concert stage as it is at a wedding. Perhaps the single biggest boost for the klezmer revival came when the classical violin superstar Yitzhak Perlman began to take an interest. His project began with a TV documentary featuring a visit by to his ancestral home Krakow in Poland, in search of his musical roots. He was accompanied on the trip by musicians from The Klezmatics and Brave Old World, and tried his hand at playing along with some klezmer. The programme concluded with an all-star concert at the Lincoln Centre in New York. Such was the interest generated that an album followed, called *In the Fiddler's House*, with Perlman again accompanied by musicians from Brave Old World and The Klezmatics, plus Andy Statman and The Klezmer Conservatory Band. In the same way that Stéphane Grappelli's TV pairing with Yehudi Menuhin in the 70s introduced a whole new audience to the jazz violin, so Perlman's klezmer extravaganza provided the perfect showcase to bring klezmer into the mainstream. The album sold more than a quarter of a million copies, making it the biggest klezmer album ever, and was followed up with a video, concert tour, and a further live album.

Yitzhak Perlman

PLAYING KLEZMER FIDDLE

Probably the most striking and attractive feature for the fiddler approaching klezmer for the first time is the unusual scales, most of which will be totally unfamiliar to someone brought up on a diet of British, Celtic, or American music. Just as the blues scale has a mysterious way of tugging at the emotions, so the klezmer scales seem to exercise a powerful effect on the psyche.

Klezmer modes

The three principal scales or modes are derived from, and named after, those used by cantors in the sung prayers of the synagogue.

1. Ahava Raba. Also known as the 'Freygish', and equivalent to the commonly-used Arab mode 'hijaz', this is a type of major scale but with a flattened second; there is a wide three semitones/half-steps interval between the second and third notes. The sixth and seventh notes are also lowered.

EXAMPLE 4.1

CD 1 TRACK 49I

Because the key has both flats and sharps, there is a choice of how a tune in this mode could be written out. The common practice is for a tune in D major to be written with a key signature of B-flat, with accidentals written for the F-sharp note.

Sometimes you will see a key signature written with two flats plus the F-sharp, thereby eliminating the accidentals. Here, for example is the opening of 'Hava Nagila', not strictly a klezmer tune, but perhaps

EXAMPLE 4.2

CD 1 TRACK 49II

the best known Israeli dance tune. You will also hear this mode in such tunes as 'Nigun Atik', 'Kandel's Hora' and 'Tanz, Tanz, Yidelech'.

2. Mi Sheberakh. This is a minor scale with a raised fourth, again producing a wide interval, this time between the third and fourth note.

EXAMPLE 4.3

CD 1 TRACK 50

This scale is thought to have been used most in Romania and the Ukraine; it is sometimes called the 'Ukrainian Dorian', though it is also found all the way down the Balkans and into Asia Minor. You can hear it used in 'Odessa Bulgar' or 'Khoson Kale Mazeltov'.

The key of D minor, usually in this Mi Sheberakh form, is so common in klezmer that clarinettist Sid Beckerman said "to you, D minor is a key. To me it's a living".

D minor is a very convenient key for the fiddler, as it is easy to transpose the melody up an octave, whilst staying within third position. It is good practice to frequently move up an octave on the repeat of a section, giving more variety, and allowing a different set of ornaments with the different fingering.

EXAMPLE 4.4

CD 1 TRACK 51

3. Adonoy Molokh. This is a normal major scale, but with a flattened seventh; it's the equivalent of the Mixolydian mode, and as such much more familiar to non-klezmer fiddle players.

It is rarely used for the opening part of a tune, but makes a useful modulation from a straight major tune, for example in 'Der Shtiller Bulgar' or 'Kishiniever Bulgar'.

In addition to these three modes, the standard major and harmonic minor scales may also occur. It is common for klezmer tunes to have at least two and sometimes three or four sections, and the mode usually changes from one part to the next. Here for example is 'Tantz, Tantz, Yidelekh' ('Dance, Dance, Little Jews'). Sections A and C are in Ahava Raba, with the B section modulating to the relative major.

EXAMPLE 4.5

CD 1 TRACK 52

Tantz, Tantz, Yidelekh

This appeared on the Belf recordings as 'Ma Yofus', and under its new title on a 1917 recording by the Abe Schwartz orchestra. It was a popular hit, quickly becoming established as *the* Jewish dance tune of the early 20th century. The record company Columbia, not wishing to leave a cow unmilked, released a Latin American version under the grand title 'Continua Bailando – Baile Nupcial Hebreo', and Ukrainian-American fiddle star Pawlo Humeniuk recorded it in 1927 as 'Oj, Pidu Ja Szicher Wicher'.

Ornamentation

There are a number of stylistic ornaments essential to klezmer fiddle playing, and there's no better place to hear how it should be done than on *Fidl*, the showcase solo album by Klezmatics violinist Alicia Svigals. To quote Zev Feldman, she is "the first American-born violinist to develop a mature contemporary version of the klezmer fiddle style". Her album is full of rich, dark ornamentation, with almost every note given a heavy klezmer accent; to someone not familiar with the style, you would almost think you were listening to a different instrument. Also well worth hearing, for a slightly different take on ornamentation, is violinist Steven Greenman. He has a duo with cymbalom player and klezmer expert Zev Feldman, and their album *Khevrisa* is full of old world melancholy, and a very intimate violin sound.

The 'krekhts'

The most important ornament is the 'krekhts'. This is a sound derived from the emotionally charged vocal delivery of the cantor, variously described as a sob, a sigh, or a moan – a sort of musical "oy vey"! The sound is achieved by a flick of the third or fourth finger, interrupting a melody note, but not actually sounding a separate note.

Here it is used on a D Ahava Raba scale; it only falls conveniently on first and second finger notes, though at a pinch you could do it on open string and third finger notes as well.

EXAMPLE 4.6

CD 1 TRACK 53

By its nature, it is best used on a note played with a first or second finger. It's most effective on slow tunes; on faster tunes – bulgars or frylechs – there isn't really time to fit in the krekhts.

The 'kvetch'

The laugh/cry/slide/kvetch is another technique borrowed from cantorial singing, and widely appropriated by the clarinet. Basically it involves playing a melody note, and bending it downwards as the note trails off. Depending on the context it can sound like laughing, crying, or chirping. The term 'kvetch' is a Yiddish word for complaining ("enough of the kvetching already!"). It is indicated here by an arrow.

EXAMPLE 4.7

CD 1 TRACK 54i

The bent note

If a single long note is held, it will often be bent downwards in the middle, and then back up again, finishing back on pitch. This is another effect you will hear from many clarinet players. If a melody doesn't have a sufficiently long note, a little improvisation will soon provide one:

EXAMPLE 4.8

CD 1 TRACK 54ii

The trill/vibrato

Long notes may also be decorated with a trill. This may be a close trill, played with a higher finger pressed right up against the melody note. It is an effect widely found in Rumanian and other East European fiddle styles, where it is more akin to a wide vibrato than a trill. The Yiddish term 'dreydlekh' is sometimes used for trills; others use the term more generally, for all klezmer ornamentation. (For three opinions on Yiddish klezmer nomenclature, ask any two fiddle players!)

EXAMPLE 4.9

CD 1 TRACK 55

False harmonics

A particularly effective technique on slow tunes, where the fiddle is well exposed, is the false harmonic. These are very easy to produce once you get the hang of it. Simply reduce the amount of downward pressure on the bow, whilst maintaining a good amount of lateral bow movement. The effect will be one of the very first mistakes you made when you started learning the fiddle: a ghostly, whispering sound with an indistinct note. Trust me, in the right context the effect is mysterious and poignant. Again, Alicia Svigals' album *Fidl* is an excellent showcase for this effect.

EXAMPLE 4.10

CD 1 TRACK 56

EXAMPLE 4.11

CD 1 TRACK 57

Finally here's a slow 'hora', a circle dance, with some of the possible ornamentation written in.

Bessarabian Hora

eastern european fiddle

Russia ▪ Poland ▪

Ukraine ▪ Romania ▪

Hungary ▪ Bulgaria ▪

THE FIDDLE HANDBOOK

eastern european fiddle

Russia

The world of Russian folk music is a world of smoke and mirrors. Nothing is quite as it seems.

Things began well enough. In villages across Russia, music, song, and dance were performed by peasants in an informal setting, marking family and seasonal celebrations. In early medieval times there developed a tradition of professional performers called 'skomorokhs'. They combined the talents of singer, actor, comedian, and musician, giving dramatic and satirical performances, costumed, masked, and accompanying themselves on a variety of musical instruments. Among these was the 'gudok', a bowed instrument related to the English rebec or the Bulgarian 'gadulka'. Like many primitive fiddles it was played upright, on the lap. It had three strings which, because of the flat bridge, could be played together. Two were tuned the same, and one a fifth higher. The gudok gets a walk-on part in Borodin's opera *Prince Igor*, but by and large it disappeared with the arrival of the modern fiddle in the 16th century.

Trouble for the skomorokhs was on the way. Angered by their bawdy and irreverent antics, the church persuaded Tsar Alexis to ban them in 1648, along with all instrumental music. The ordnance 'On Improvement Of Morality And The Elimination Of False Beliefs' instructed that "There shall be no skomorokhs. Their lutes, domras, flutes, whistles, and all similar Satanic things, and masks, shall be confiscated. Break and burn all of them." For the next couple of centuries, at a time when most European countries were developing large and complex repertoires of instrumental dance music, all that Russians were officially allowed was choral music.

The 19th century was a time of nation-building throughout Europe, and Russia was no exception. Napoleon had been turned back from the gates of Moscow, the borders were expanding to the south, and national pride had never been greater. A group of classical composers known as The Five or The Mighty Handful, including Borodin, Mussorgsky, and Rimsky-Korsakov, wanted to create a distinctively Russian music, and began to include traditional folk tunes in their compositions. It became fashionable for wealthy landlords to organise their serfs into choirs, which would sing traditional songs and put on tableaux of village life for the amusement and entertainment of guests.

At the end of the 19th century, a salon violinist named Vasily Andreyev, capitalizing on the love of the growing middle class for all things Russian, realised that whilst it was all very well to have concert orchestras and choirs performing Russian music, there was little or nothing in the way of instrumental 'folk' music being performed. He took it upon himself to reinvent what was virtually a dead tradition. He rediscovered and reinvented two plucked stringed instruments, the balalaika and domra, and created large ensembles playing complex arrangements of simple folk melodies. Nothing like this had been seen before in Russia, most certainly not in the villages that the music claimed to represent.

Whatever the authenticity of his new creations, within a short time there were 'folk orchestras', both professional and amateur, playing to enthusiastic audiences throughout the country.

Alongside these new ensembles, there was a growth in the popularity of Gypsy performers, mostly singers, dancers, and violinists, belonging to family dynasties of professionals. The first Gypsies had arrived in Russia around the year 1500, living mostly around villages in the south of the country. Following the invitation of a Gypsy band to play for the birthday of Catherine the Great in St Petersburg, the Russian gentry developed an endless fascination with the image of the romantic, carefree Gypsy life. Violinists such as the legendary Loyko Zabar became famous for their fabulous technique and passionate delivery; along with the 'noble' peasant, the Gypsy became an icon central to Russian music.

The Revolution of 1917 brought the Bolshevik party to power, and with it a new phase in the development of folk music in Russia. Folk orchestras and choirs as an entertainment for the bourgoisie were clearly no longer an option, but the idea of music "of the people, for the people" was a concept that would prove irresistible to a government increasingly obsessed with social manipulation. Stalin ordered the creation of official Soviet folklore ensembles, run and conducted by trained, professional composers and musicians. They presented a carefully sanitised version of folk song, music, and dancing, purged of the elements of bawdy innuendo, rough-and-ready dissonance, and religious fervor that represented what little was left of real village music.

Performers wore immaculate ethnic costume, played improved, factory-made instruments in polished, carefully arranged, and choreographed sets. Their performances demonstrated the virtues of order, discipline, and friendship among peoples. Alongside well-known 'traditional' songs such as 'Kalinka' (actually written in 1860 by the composer and folklorist Ivan Petrovich Larianov) were songs with an overt political message, about tractors, collective farms, and national exports. Quotas were established: the ensembles' directors had to guarantee that 30 per cent of their output would be not folklore but 'fakelore', songs specially composed for their propaganda message. During the Great Patriotic War (World War II to the rest of us) the patriotic song came into its own, with stirring anthems such as *Katyusha*, written in 1938 about a girl longing for her man, who has gone off to war. The song later lent its name to the fearsome multiple rocket launchers which howled out of the Russian forests.

Following the war, the concept of state folk orchestras was exported to all the other Warsaw Pact countries. There was a delicate balancing act to perform; folk music from individual regions had the potential to be a potent force in inflaming nationalist political ambitions, which were to be repressed at all costs. The ideal was for the beaming performers to reinforce the impression of a satisfied, healthy, and enthusiastic proletariat, free to express joyfully their national pride.

In practice the result, with a few notable exceptions, was music that was bland, homogenised, and totally inauthentic. With the collapse of the Soviet Union in the late 80s, most of the state ensembles were disbanded. Folk music, naturally, was not left in a healthy state. The terrible events of the 20th century, including the forced collectivisation of farms, the destruction of the war, and mass deportations of ethnic peoples, had left village life, where the last vestiges of real traditional music might have survived, in tatters.

What's a poor fiddler to make of this situation if he or she wants to learn a few Russian fiddle tunes? Fortunately, not all is lost. There may be an absence of a genuine tradition of instrumental village music-making, but Russia does have one powerful hand to play. The tunes for which Russia is best known, although mostly vocal in origin, translate wonderfully to the violin. 'Ochi Chyornye' ('Dark Eyes'), 'Two Guitars', 'Deep Sorrow', and 'Moscow Nights' are all passionate, stirring melodies, dark, soulful, and magical. And how to play them? Again, there may not be a Russian fiddle style, but the Gypsies have made this music their own and theirs is assuredly the style to use. Double stops, glissandos, wide vibrato, dramatic changes of tempo, improvisation: these are the techniques that make it possible to play the same simple 16-bar melody every day for a decade without ever exhausting the possibilities. One of the best Russian Gypsy bands playing in this style is Loyko, featuring two violinists, cousins Sergei Erdenko and Oleg Ponomarev. They are from a Russian Gypsy musical dynasty and have named their band after Loyko Zabar. If you're looking for sizzling violin Russian pyrotechnics, look no further!

Here's a 19th century Russian folk song made unexpectedly famous when it was used in the GameBoy game Tetris, and subsequently covered by various dance and techno bands.

The song 'Korobushka' is based on a poem by Nikolai Nekrasov, written in 1861, about a peddler and his bag of wonderful wares. Like most Russian folk tunes it is in a minor key, and has a very simple chord sequence, allowing for lots of variations.

EXAMPLE 5.1

CD 1 TRACK 58

Korobushka

Russian

Ukraine

One common theme that emerges from studying the history of different folk cultures is that there's nothing quite like a few centuries of invasion, oppression, and emigration to ensure the vigorous survival of a country's traditional music.

While in Russia we've seen a sorry tale of the virtual elimination of authentic village instrumental music, in neighbouring Ukraine an exciting tradition of fiddling is alive and well. In the West there is a tendency to think of Ukraine as simply a part of Russia, but in fact it has a very distinctive culture and history. Although it was incorporated as one of the Soviet Union's 16 Republics, it has since 1991 been once more an independent country, lying on Russia's south-western border. As the breadbasket of Europe, this has always been attractive territory for predatory neighbours, and in the 19th century it was split between the Russian and Austro-Hungarian empires; Moscow referred to their portion rather condescendingly as 'Little Russia'.

The majority of the population was rural, and numerous episodes of agrarian resettlement in the 19th century forced workers off the land with no choice but to emigrate. The majority went to America, where many found work in the mining and construction industries. They took with them a large body of traditional music and dance which, as is typical of expatriate communities, they clung on to for all it was worth. By the time of the Russian revolution, there were around 750,000 Ukrainians in the US and a further 250,000 in Canada. In their new communities many bands were formed or re-formed, creating the typical village music of their homeland. Recordings made in the 20s and 30s give us an excellent record of what that music sounded like. The typical band was a 'troyista muzyka' (musical trio), usually led by a fiddle, along with instruments such as a 'buben' (two-sided drum), 'tsymbaly' (cymbalom) or 'sopilka' (flute). In medieval times the 'bandura', a type of lute, was distinctive of Ukraine, being the favourite mode of accompaniment for the 'kobzars', travelling minstrels not unlike the skomorokhs of Russia. The three-stringed rebec-like fiddle, the 'gudok', was also common until it was replaced by the violin.

There are various tune and dance types peculiar to Ukraine:

Kolomyjka

This can be a combination of tune, song, and dance; some recordings have a line of singing alternating with a line of instrumental melody, whilst some are purely instrumental. The text, in rhyming couplets, is usually a humorous commentary on everyday life. It is believed to originate in the town of Kolomyja, in the Carpathian foothills in western Ukraine. Its simple 2/4 rhythm and structure makes the kolomyjka very adaptable, and the texts and melodies of literally thousands of different versions have been annotated. One collection alone, by Volodymyr Shukhevych in 1905, contains more than 8,000. Although centuries old, the form remains very popular today. The melodies are fast and exciting, sometimes with syncopation, and can be in major or minor keys. They make great fiddle tunes.

Kozachok

The name derives from 'kozak' or Cossack. The Cossacks were Ukranian peasants who, from the 17th century, refused to accept serfdom, instead becoming warriors, often acting as mercenaries, and sometimes gaining a degree of independence. They became a symbol of military skill and heroism, and the kozachok celebrates their exploits. The melody is usually in a major key. The rhythm, like that of the kolomyjka, is in 2/4, often accelerating after a slow introduction.

Hopak

Similar to the kozachok, this is a lively dance in a major key, used by dancers to show off their flashiest kicks and leaps, and to demonstrate strength and speed. The name comes from the word 'hopaty' (to jump). It was originally only danced by male Cossack soldiers, but was eventually adopted by villagers in Cossack areas as a mixed dance. Composers such as Mussorgsky, Rimsky-Korsakov, and Tchaikovsky incorporated hopak melodies into operatic compositions.

Melodically, Ukrainian music tends to be more varied than Russian. Whilst in Russia the great majority of tunes are minor keys, in Ukraine there is a majority of major key tunes. There is also more use of the oriental-sounding augmented second, rarely found in Russian music.

Early Ukrainian-American recordings

The staple diet of Ukrainian instrumental music is most often heard these days as accompaniment for dance ensembles; whilst the melodies are shown off to good advantage, the arrangements are frequently rather orchestral. The best place to hear them played with an honest, raw fiddle style is on the recordings made by musicians who emigrated to the US in the late 19th and early 20th centuries.

One such recording now widely available is *Ukrainian-American Fiddle Music; First Recordings 1926-36*, released in 1977 by Arhoolie Records. It features a variety of different instrumental and vocal combinations. The playing is lively, passionate and, in the words of the liner notes, "full of piss, fire, and vinegar". The fiddle leads most of the ensembles, along with second fiddle, bowed bass and cimbalom.

One of the best known Ukrainian Americans was fiddler Pawlo Humeniuk (1884-1965). He emigrated in about 1902, and in 1926 released a record, *Ukrainske Wesilie* (Ukrainian Wedding), which recreated the various traditions and ceremonies, along with much humour and chatter from cameo characters including the gruff father and weeping bride. Though pitched perfectly for the homesick Ukrainian, it sold well even to non-Ukrainian speakers, shifting in total almost 150,000 copies. Humeniuk was a hard worker, playing weddings, concerts, and vaudeville, and by 1940 he had made more than 100 records. His playing is sturdy and vigorous, ornamented with trills, drones, and occasional slides. He uses little or no vibrato, even on the slow sentimental numbers; this is very different from the Gypsy style that best represents Russian fiddling.

A selection of his recordings was re-released by Arhoolie in 1993, under the title *Pawlo Humeniuk: King Of The Ukrainian Fiddlers*.

Since the mid 20th century, Ukrainian traditional music has been absorbed to some extent into the melting pot of polka and two-step playing that is so popular in rural America. The kolomyjkas, hopaks, and kozachoks, particularly those in the major keys, sit happily alongside old-time 'American' fiddle tunes; it has even been pointed out that the hoedown tune 'Flop-Eared Mule' bears an uncanny resemblance to the Ukrainian 'Dowbush Kozak'.

In recent years the conservatory-trained Ukrainian Gypsy fiddler Vassyl Popadiuk (known as Papa Duke), who emigrated to Canada, has achieved crossover success with his band. He plays 'Gypsy world fusion', and is equally popular with émigré Ukrainians and in the mainstream market, though his playing, to my ear, owes more to the Gypsy tradition than the Ukrainian.

Ukraine was not immune to the concept of 'fakelore' we have already seen in Russia. There was a tradition of choral music sung by trainee priests, going back to the year 1600. They composed their own songs, both sacred and secular, and many of these were absorbed into the general village folk repertoire. In 1902, in Kharkiv in north-eastern Ukraine, someone came up with the idea of combining this choral tradition with the bandura-playing kobzar troubadour tradition, and an ensemble of 14 singers and bandurists was formed. The combination seemed to capture the essence of Ukraine history and culture, and quickly caught on. By 1930 there were around 900 of these 'Bandurist Capellas' in the Ukraine.

EXAMPLE 5.2

CD 1 TRACK 59

Kolomyjka Lubka

Ukraine

PLAY A,B,A,B,C,A

State-run folklore ensembles were also formed in Soviet times; the macho Cossack dancing and the lively hopaks lent themselves to large-scale stage performance. Indeed, it is this Ukrainian tradition that largely dominates what we in the West think of today as 'Russian' folk music and dance.

'Kolomyjka Lubka' ('Sweetheart Kolomyjka'), is from the Ukrainska Selska Orchestra recording from New Jersey in 1930, on another Arhoolie album, *Ukrainian Village Music*.

Hungary

When the Hungarian pianist and composer Franz Liszt published his book, *The Gypsies And Their Music In Hungary*, in 1859, he opened a can of worms. He was already well known for his appreciation of Gypsy music, and the publication in 1853 of his Hungarian Rhapsodies. What caused such ire among his fellow countrymen was his assertion that whilst traditional village music in Hungary was "modest and imperfect", and worthy of little respect, the instrumental music of the Hungarian Gypsy orchestras was "capable of competition with anything in the sublimity and daring of its emotion and in the perfection of its form". This was not a subject to be treated lightly. There is no nation more intensely patriotic than the Hungarians, and the mid 19th century was a period of great national emotion as the country tried, and failed, to free itself from the Habsburg Empire. Music had become the focus of this flowering of nationalism and, since the 1760s, Hungarian music had largely been in the hands of Gypsy orchestras. What Liszt was claiming was that without the Gypsies, Hungarian music would amount to very little. His detractors, however, would claim that, while no-one doubted the contribution made by the "new Hungarians", as they were euphemistically known, what they were playing was fundamentally Hungarian music, not Gypsy music.

The Gypsies had been around in Hungary since the 15th century. The King gave them freedom of movement in 1423. The 17th century saw the departure of the Turks and the opening up of the country to Western and church influences, which were particularly important for introducing the concept of harmony. For native Hungarian village musicians, the Reformation of the church, as in many parts of western Europe, saw a hardening of attitudes towards music, dance, and general sinful enjoyment. Fiddlers got top billing on the Wanted posters; one preacher in 1681 railed that "I would have all the violins found in every town, in every village, and, cutting them in two, hang them up on willow trees, and the violinists who play the dances would be hung up by their legs beside them." Whilst this threat may have been a considerable deterrence to God-fearing Hungarians, the Gypsies, seen by themselves and others as outsiders, would have taken little notice, and they gradually began to replace the natives as providers of musical entertainment.

The first renowned Gypsy violinist and band-leader that we know of was Mihály Barna, who, in the mid 18th century, led a quartet, backed by second violin, harp, and bass. It soon became fashionable for aristocrats to employ their own Gypsy orchestras. By this time the violin had become the principal instrument in Hungary, largely displacing the bagpipe, which had hitherto been a popular dance instrument.

From the 1760s onwards, Hungarians experienced a great upsurge of nationalist feeling and the Gypsy orchestras were able to capitalise on this, performing sentimental old folk songs as well as composing new ones. Within a short time it seemed there were Gypsy musicians everywhere. A new genre of music sprang up to accompany army recruitment drives. Experienced soldiers would travel around the villages and, accompanied by the inevitable Gypsy band, perform athletic dances designed to show off their strength and virility. The young men of the village, carried away by the heady mix of patriotic music, alcohol, and testosterone, would find themselves signed up for a spell in the army. The new musical style which went with these occasions was called 'verbunkos'. The tunes included elements from many sources – Hungarian, Turkish, and Viennese – but one common feature to all verbunkos tunes is that they start off 'lassú' (slow), and end up 'friss' (fast). This feature is said to represent either the two sides of the Hungarian character (gloomy and carefree) or the two emotions induced by joining up (the tearful farewell and the excitement of battle). Other musical characteristics included a high degree of ornamentation, the use of a type of phrase called a 'bokazo' (representing a clicking of heels), and the use of the 'Hungarian Gypsy scale' (a harmonic minor with a raised fourth, giving two spicy augmented second intervals).

EXAMPLE 5.3

CD 1 TRACK 60

The interval of a fourth, representing the military signals of a trumpet, is another common motif.

Verbunkos quickly came to be seen as a symbol of romanticism, national rebirth, and all things Hungarian, and was wildly popular with everyone from the peasantry to the aristocracy. During this period, Hungarian Gypsy ensembles started to perform with great success in other European capitals. It is reported that at one ball they were alternating with a group of German musicians who, seeing the Gypsies playing to great applause for almost two hours, entirely by memory, "almost chewed up their music in rage".

Among the leading writers and performers of verbunkos was the Gypsy bandleader János Bihari (1764-1824), "the Napoleon of the fiddle". He is credited with more than 80 compositions in the verbunkos style, including the 'Rákóczi March', which was subsequently incorporated into classical works by composers such as Liszt and Berlioz. Liszt was such an admirer of Bihari that he wrote "like drops of some fiery spirit essence, the notes of this magic violin came to our ears". Another notable composer and performer was Márk Rózsavölgyi, a virtuoso violinist, He is said to have composed the first 'czardas', a new slow/fast tune form which grew out of verbunkos, in 1835. He was also at the forefront of another new musical movement, popular Hungarian song known as 'Magyar Nota'. Interestingly, although known as a famous Gypsy violinist, he was in fact born Mordchele Rosenthal: he and his entire ensemble were not Gypsies but Jews.

Nota was the equivalent of today's pop song, defined by the 20th century composer and ethnomusicologist Kodály, somewhat loftily, as being intended for "a transitional type of man: one who had already outgrown folk culture, but had not yet reached a higher cultural level". The melodies of nota songs owed a lot to western art music, were easily harmonised, and usually came from the outset with piano accompaniment. Whilst verbunkos had often turned songs into instrumentals, nota did the opposite, using established tunes to make songs. 'Quietly Flows The River Maros', for example, is a nota based on a czardas originally written by Miska Borzo. One of the first successful Gypsy musicians to write nota was Pista Danko (1858-1903). Among his compositions was 'One Kitten, Two Kittens' (see below), a song so popular in its day that when the band first introduced it, at the Hungaria Restaurant in Szeged, they were made to play it continuously for two days. Now that's a gig I'm glad I missed.

By now a standard repertoire was becoming established for the urban Gypsy ensembles, which has not changed greatly in a century. Many of the nota songs were turned back into instrumentals, usually sweet, sentimental numbers with titles like 'My Violin Is Broken', 'A Bird Sings Gaily On The Leafy Branch', 'My Little Thatched Cottage' and 'Whom Is The Swallow Mourning?'. Verbunkos and czardas tunes, mostly written by Gypsies, remained popular, and the works of art-music composers including Hungarian themes, such as Brahms' *Hungarian Dances* and Liszt's *Hungarian Rhapsody*, were quickly adopted (a strange twist indeed – Gypsy folk into art music into Gypsy folk). Extracts from light operas, such as Lehar's *The Merry Widow* or Kálmán's *The Gypsy Princess*, were often played. The Italian composer Vittorio Monti in 1904 wrote his czardas: it was his only famous composition, but so successful that it is today by far the best known czardas. The Romanian composer Dinicu contributed two numbers that quickly became Gypsy standards; the 'Hora Staccato', and 'Ciocarlia' ('The Lark'), famous for its extended section of bird noises played at the very top end of the fiddle.

With the increasing sophistication of the urban repertoire, a wide gulf was beginning to open up between this and the simpler, earthier, and more rustic rural repertoire. Inevitably, some intellectuals began to regard the urban repertoire as too slick, schmaltzy, and sentimental, considering it had lost touch with its source, the true music of the Hungarian peasants. Thus it was that, struck by the chance hearing of a "genuine peasant folk song" in 1904, composer Béla Bartók developed a fascination with the primitive music of the Hungarian countryside and began a quest to collect as much of it as he could. "In the so-called cultured urban circles," observed Bartók, "the unbelievably rich treasure of folk music was entirely unknown. No one even suspected that this kind of music existed." Using an Edison cylinder recording machine, he began in 1906 a series of expeditions, recording and transcribing a staggering total of 10,000 tunes. Many of the tunes were collected in Hungarian-speaking areas beyond the country's borders, for instance Transylvania in Romania. Bartók, along with his fellow composer Kodály, incorporated many of the themes, forms and modes into his compositions, successfully creating music which was both very modern and at the same time suffused with what was seen as the true spirit of ancient Hungary. They also reopened the Liszt controversy, rejecting the idea that Gypsy and Hungarian music were inextricably linked.

The postwar communist takeover led to the inevitable state folk ensembles, but unlike in some Iron Curtain countries, the Gypsies were valued for their music and were allowed to continue working in city restaurants and hotels. Support was given for special schooling for Gypsy children, through the Young Communist League. The most successful of these enterprises, still thriving, is the Rajco School in Budapest, founded in 1952 by Gyla Farcas. Today, in addition to the school, there is a Rajco Ensemble, a professional performing group made up of its graduates. Also still operating is the Hungarian State Folk Ensemble. Recognising the split between urban and rural music, it has two bands that alternate during a show, one playing romantic Gypsy music, and the other playing village music.

GYPSY VIOLIN STYLE

From a fiddler's point of view, the style of the urban Gypsy ensembles of Eastern Europe provides an exciting and challenging approach to playing. It is one of the few areas of folk music in which a sound classical technique is a great advantage instead of a disadvantage. Techniques used by the Gypsy fiddler include:

- Use of higher positions, up to the very top of the neck.
- Use of harmonics, either 'true' or 'false'.
- Pizzicato with the left hand, sometimes simultaneous with bowing.
- Spicatto and détaché bowing techniques.
- Wide vibrato, used in a controlled fashion to display emotion.
- Frequent use of double-stops and arpeggios to emphasise chords.
- Frequent changes of tempo, shifting gear often from very slow, rubato sections to dizzying speeds.
- Improvisation using all the above techniques.

The heritage of János Bihari is maintained through the dynasty of the Lakatos family. Sándor Lakatos (1924-94), an educated Gypsy based in Budapest, was a fifth generation descendant of Bihari, and led one of the finest traditional urban Gypsy orchestras. Today his nephew Roby Lakatos, born in 1965, brings Gypsy music into the 21st century, bringing together a fabulous classical technique, a repertoire including many of the old czardas, a superb clean and modern jazz style, a touch of Latin flair, and the best moustache in Eastern Europe.

Roby Lakatos

The Dance House movement

During the 1970s, traditional music entered a new era with a revival known as the 'Táncház' or 'Dance House' movement. This was in large part a reaction to a perception among a group of intellectuals that folk music, originally the property and birthright of the Hungarian people, had been appropriated by the state, from which people were feeling increasingly estranged. Effectively, the music was now being played only by classically trained musicians or by Gypsies. When Sándor Timár, choreographer of the Bartok Dance Ensemble, wanted some authentic live music for an avant-garde production, he was not satisfied with either of these alternatives. Instead he turned to the young, long-haired duo of Béla Halmos and Ferenc Szabó who, on a variety of instruments, were prepared to experiment and improvise within a peasant music context. Encouraged by the results, the duo, along with Timar, established a dance house where young people could come along, listen to Hungarian village music, and learn traditional dances. The idea caught on like wildfire, and soon young people in their droves were scouring the countryside in search of villagers who could teach them authentic tunes or dances. Táncház, and bands to play at them, soon sprang up everywhere. The key to this success was that this new approach stressed involvement and ownership of the music by everyone involved; this was no longer something controlled by the state. The most successful of the new bands was Muzsikás who have, since their formation in 1972, built a solid international reputation for their faithful recreation of authentic village music. The band consists of Mihály Sipos and László Porteleki on violins, Péter Éri on kontra, and Dániel Hamar on bass, along with Marta Sebestyen on vocals. One of their most interesting projects to date is *The Bartók Album*, which presents some of Bartók's original field

EXAMPLE 5.4

CD 1 TRACK 61

One Kitten, Two Kittens

Hungarian

recordings alongside his art compositions based on these themes, plus contemporary recordings in traditional village style.

'One Kitten, Two Kittens' is a tune written by the Hungarian 'King of Nota', Pista Dankó (1858-1903), a Gypsy composer and bandleader who rose from poverty to achieve national fame. The tune uses alternating sections of arco (bowing) and pizzicato (plucking).

Poland

Surrounded as it is by the exciting, exotic, and flamboyant fiddle music of Russia, Ukraine, Hungary, and the Balkans, Polish fiddling can seem a little tame. The music matches the countryside: wide, flat plains, neatly cultivated farms, and tidy villages. The music is mostly in major keys, the tempos steady, the time signatures straightforward, the melodies stately and elegant.

There are five 'national' dances of Poland: the krakowiak, polonaise, mazurka, oberek and kujawiak.

Krakowiak

The krakowiak originates in the region of Krakow, the country's former capital. It is a fast dance in 2/4 time; a characteristic rhythmic phrase – eighth-note quarter-note eighth-note – frequently appears in the melody, and the tune is often arranged in repeated two-bar phrases.

EXAMPLE 5.5

CD 1 TRACK 62

Originally a two-part form, the krakowiak has become more complex under the influence of 'art music' composers, with a contrasting third part and modulating link sections.

Polonaise

The polonaise is a medium-tempo dance – you can think of it either as a slow 3/4 or a fast 6/4. It is danced by couples walking in a stately fashion around the dance hall. The dance originated in a folk setting in the 16th century, as a type of song. Then it was used as a wedding processional. As it became increasingly popular with the upper classes, it became exclusively instrumental. It was already popular in the 18th century, when a collection of 62 polonaises was published by Joseph Sychra; it eventually became "the most highbred expression of the Polish national spirit and became in the process the most representative of Polish dances throughout Europe," according to the *New Grove Dictionary of Music*.

The polonaise can often be recognised by a characteristic rhythmic pattern at the start; one quarter-note, two eighth-notes, and four quarter-notes.

EXAMPLE 5.6

CD 1 TRACK 63

Polonaises were frequently included in works by great composers, both Polish (notably Chopin) and non-Polish (Bach, Telemann, Mozart). The form was exported to Sweden, where, as the polska, it became the national folk dance.

The next three dance forms are all superficially similar; they are all in 3/4 time, with the strong accent on the second or third beat. They are best differentiated by tempo: the oberek is fast; the mazurka is mid-tempo; and the kujawiak is fairly slow. The general mazurka rhythm, common to all three, has a typical phrasing of two short (either two eight-notes or a dotted pair) and two long notes.

Mazurka

The mazurka or mazur is a term that is sometimes used to include the oberek and kujawiak as well. It originates from the flat Mazovia area around Warsaw; men from this region are known as Mazurs. The mazurka, a couple dance with much heel-clicking and foot-stamping, originated at least as early as the 16th century, and by the 17th had spread throughout the country. In the 18th century the King of Poland and Elector of Saxony, Augustus II, introduced the dance into German society, and in 1797 a traditional mazurka ('Dabrowski Mazurka') was adopted as Poland's national anthem. By 1830 the mazurka was popular throughout western Europe, where to some extent it came to symbolise solidarity with Poland's struggle to regain independence.

Oberek

The oberek or obertas originates from the central Polish region of Mazowsze; the name derives from 'obracec sie', to spin. It is an energetic dance, often played at weddings, in which couples spin or twirl acrobatically around the room. The accompaniment is typically provided by a 'kapela' or small village band, typically led by the fiddle. Performance by such bands always includes singing; the leader will open a tune with a mocking introduction, telling the band to play but teasing them for their poverty and lack of accomplishment. The other musicians might join in good-naturedly with the chorus.

The basic melody of an oberek is played repeatedly (and the whole dance may last up to an hour!), but the lead fiddle will show off his skill with complex variations and by driving the tempo faster and faster. It is easy to recognise an oberek by the characteristic rhythm of the four-bar introduction (which usually occurs on every repeat of the tune) and the way every eight-bar phrase ends with an accented second beat of the bar.

EXAMPLE 5.7

CD 1 TRACK 64

Kujawiak

The kujawiak comes from the central Polish region of Kujawy. Like the oberek it is a spinning dance, but more dignified and stately; the movement of the dancers is said to be reminiscent of tall grain stalks in the field gently swaying in the breeze. Like most of Poland's national dances, it has peasant origins, but was adopted by the nobility, undergoing various changes in the process.

Two other dance/tune types are also widely played in Poland, the waltz and the polka. Both are relatively recent inventions from abroad. The polka is said to have been a hybrid dance invented near Prague, in nearby Bohemia, in the 1830s. The name polka (which can mean 'Polish woman') is often misinterpreted to imply that the dance originated in Poland. Whatever their origins, both the polka and waltz, because of their rhythm and tempo, fit very naturally into the Polish repertoire.

Tatra Mountains fiddle

Having described how calm, civilised, and frankly unexciting Polish music can be, there is one major exception. In most of Poland the music and dance has become very formalised, with the original village origins largely obscured by gentrified ballroom influences, but there is one part of the country where the old peasant folk culture has remained relatively untouched. This is the region known as the Podhale, in the foothills of the Tatra Mountains to the south of the country, where the people are called the Gorale. This beautiful and remote area has long had a special place in the hearts of Poles as the cradle of Polishness itself, an inspiration to writers, poets, and composers alike. Here the music is altogether more wild and unrefined, not having been modified to suit the requirements of the nobility. Indeed, this is traditionally the haunt of bandits and outlaws, whose exploits are the source of many legends and songs.

The typical band from this region is a string band with lead violin ('prym'), several second violins ('sekund') playing lower harmonies or two-string chords, and a three-stringed cello ('basy').

Various eccentricities to the music survive, including the very unusual Lydian mode. This is a major scale which includes a sharpened fourth, giving three whole-tone/whole-step intervals in a row. It is sometimes called the Polish mode or, in Poland, the mountaineers' scale.

EXAMPLE 5.8

CD 1 TRACK 65

Also unusual is the five-bar melodic structure to tunes such as the 'Ozwodna'. This and other tunes from the mountains are in 2/4 rather than the 3/4 more commonly found in the plains.

Dances in the Podhale are often started by the lead dancer, who will sing a line of tune to the band, who will then pick up and continue the melody as the dance proceeds. Singing, either solo or with several male and female voices, is an important part of the band's performance, and, remarkably, a song will often be superimposed over a completely different instrumental melody. Where an instrumental melody is taken over by singing of the same melody, there will often be a lurch of tempo (typically the fiddles will be playing faster than the singers want to sing). The Gorale music is simple, emotional, powerful and with a large element of improvisation.

One of the best representatives of Gorale fiddle music is The Trebunia Family Band, led by fiddler Wladislaw Trebunia; their excellent 1995 album, *Music Of The Tatra Mountains*, gives a faithful recreation of a village typical dance, with much stamping, shouting, singing, eating, and drinking going on during the all-night recording session. The band had already achieved international fame in 1991 due to their unlikely and remarkable collaboration with the Jamaican reggae group The Twinkle Brothers. Now, 23 albums later, the band is known as the Trebunie-Tutki band and led by Wladislaw's son Krzystof. The polka 'Ozwodna' is typical of their playing.

Another young band, and one determined to rid Polish music of its stuffy image, is The Warsaw Village Band. They reach both forwards, incorporating elements of hip-hop and techno, and backwards, using

Ozwodna (Goralski Polka)

POLISH

various archaic Polish instruments including a unique Polish fiddle variant, the 'suka', played in the band by Sylwia Swiatkowska.

The suka, like the Bulgarian gadulka, is played vertically, on the knee or hanging from a strap, and the strings are stopped at the side with the fingernails. The body of the instrument is very similar to the modern violin, but the neck is very wide, and the pegbox is crude. This is thought to be a 'missing link' between the upside-down or 'knee chordophone' instruments, and the modern violin. It died out, and was known only from drawings of a single specimen displayed at an exhibition in 1888. A century later the instrument was reconstructed by Andrzej Kuczkowski, and is today also being popularised by string specialist Maria Pomianowska.

Romania

Romania is the seventh largest country in Europe, both in terms of size and population, and it is famous all over the world for its fiddle music. The country has three main regions; Wallachia to the south, where it borders Bulgaria; Moldavia to the north-east, where it borders Moldova and Ukraine; and Transylvania to the north-west, bordering Serbia and Hungary. Moldavia and Wallachia show a strong Ottoman influence, both on scales and instrumentation, whilst the mountainous region of Transylvania has been influenced by the Austro-Hungarian Empire, and indeed has a large Hungarian-speaking population, with musical

EXAMPLE 5.9

CD 1 TRACK 66

influences to match.

As is the case in Hungary, the majority of the professional musicians in Romania, both urban and rural, are Gypsies. Since the mid 19th century they have been settled throughout the country, have learned the local repertoire of songs, dances, and tunes, and performed in bands or 'tarafs' at weddings and parties. Whilst by no means all Gypsies are musicians, it is a tradition passed down through families, the children learning from an early age and achieving a level of skill and breadth of repertoire that would not be possible if, like the local population, they were also working on a farm or at some other job. The violin dominates the Gypsy folk tradition in Romania to the extent that the word 'lauta' (violin) is extended to include all Gypsy musicians ('lautari').

Prior to the 18th century most of the bowed stringed instruments heard in Romania were foreign imports such as the Serbian 'gusle' or the Turkish 'kemence'. The violin proper arrived some time in the 18th century, and it was not until the mid 19th century that Gypsies started to settle in large numbers. They quickly took on the mantle of entertainers to peasant and aristocrat alike, and, as in neighbouring Hungary, the Gypsy ensemble soon dominated the music scene.

Taraf de Haïdouks

The typical Gypsy band consisted of a lead violin (the 'primas'), a second violin and/or viola, called a 'contra', a 'cymbalom' (a type of hammered dulcimer), and a bowed bass. Also sometimes heard was a 'taragot' (sometimes described as a primitive wooden saxophone); a 'nai' or panpipe, and a 'cobza' (a type of lute). The bagpipe was common among peasant musicians until the arrival of the violin. From the 19th century the clarinet and accordion also gradually made an appearance.

The primas took the main melody, enhancing it with chromatic runs, double-stops, arpeggios, pizzicato, harmonics and the like, all performance tricks that could be improvised on the spot to enhance the performance. He would conduct the rest of the band with an imperious nod of the head, a scowl or a flourish of the bow, directing dramatic changes of tempo and mood. One of the most impressive and characteristic techniques of the Romanian fiddler is the use of a single bow-hair. The hair, well rosined, is tied in a loop around the G-string. Instead of holding the bow, the right hand slowly pulls the hair, producing an eerie rasping sound. You can hear this to good effect on the opening track ('Dance Of The Firemen') of Taraf de Haïdouks' album *Band Of Gypsies*, in the famous 1992 documentary film *Lacho Drom*, and in a magnificent scene in the film *Train De Vie,* where a duel takes place between a Gypsy band and a klezmer band.

Another interesting technique, perhaps borrowed from Turkey, is the 'two strings'. The A string is taken from its notch in the bridge, and placed right next to the E string, either in the same, slightly enlarged notch, or in a separate notch very close to the E. The A string is then tuned down to a low E, so that the two strings can be played simultaneously and in octaves, giving the effect of two violins playing in unison. Some old klezmer players also adopted this technique.

In the Transylvanian area of Bihor, bordering Hungary, a strange 'horn violin' is used. This is identical to the Stroh violin invented in England in the late 19th century. Its purpose was to increase the volume of the violin for the purposes of recording, then in its infancy. In a recording studio a single violin could not compete with other, louder instruments such as the clarinet, so a horn (like that found on an old-fashioned gramophone) and resonator of mica were used to amplify the violin mechanically. It does not have the usual hollow body, and only the top three strings (D, A, and E) are used; although louder than a standard fiddle it is therefore more limited, and the tone is thin and scratchy. Quite how this came to be adopted as a 'traditional' folk instrument in Transylvania remains something of a mystery.

The second violin or contra (sometimes also called 'braci' or 'secunda') is used to provide both harmony and rhythm. It has three strings, tuned to G, D, and A, and a flattened bridge allows easy double and triple stopping, creating simple chords. The contra is held not under the chin, but low down on the chest, tilted perpendicular, allowing for very economical use of the bow. A typical bow stroke has a slight pause in the middle, separating an on- and off-beat, giving a sort of 'ooh-ah, ooh-ah' sound.

Tune types

The principal vehicle for the primas to strut his stuff is the 'doina', a lyrical rubato improvisation; it can be either slow or fast. A typical format for a doina would be to have an extended single chord, perhaps a D minor, played low but fast by the cymbalom with an 'um-chah' rhythm. Over this the violin is free to play slow or fast, high or low, for as long as he likes. The whole thing moves up a minor third to G minor, then up to a dizzying A-flat diminished (the diminished chord is very typical of Romanian music), finally to A (the dominant) and

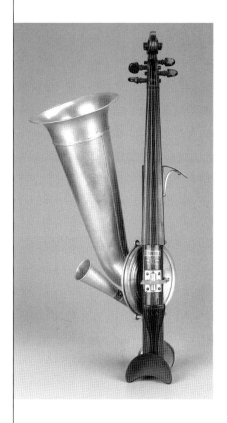

A Stroh violin made in England in the early 20th century.

then back to D minor. The whole performance might have no set melody at all, and all the changes are directed by the leader.

A slow doina, which is for listening only, is often followed immediately by a fast dance tune called a 'sirba', in 2/4 time. The most common dance is the 'hora' (a circle dance) which can be either fast or slow. There are also various dances in asymmetric time signatures, particularly in the south of the country where there is a strong Bulgarian influence. The 'invirtita', for example, can be in 7/8 time. It is worth noting that, being originally folk dances which were never written down, and being played by musicians with plenty of skill but no formal training in the classical sense, the concept of a strict time signature may be somewhat arbitrary and misleading. The slow hora, for example, has basically two beats to the bar, a long one and a short one. I've written this in 3/4, but try and avoid making it too much like a waltz. In the *Balkan Dance Music Book* (Eliznik) these tunes are written in 5/8, but described as "between 5/8 and 3/4". The only way to really get to grips with such rhythms is to listen to plenty of original recordings. My favourite tune in this style is the 'Hora Femeilor', a particularly haunting version of which was used as the theme music for the 1980s BBC TV series of Olivia Manning's *Fortunes Of War*. Play it with close trills on as many notes as possible.

EXAMPLE 5.10

CD 1 TRACK 67

Hora Femeilor

Romanian

During the communist era, many of the urban Gypsy bands which had been playing in hotels and restaurants in the capital, Bucharest, were expanded to form state folk ensembles on the Soviet model. The Institutuli do Folklor din Romania, for example, was an 80-piece folk orchestra formed in 1948, with a classically trained arranger and conductor, Victor Predescu. With state support such groups were able to make commercial recordings and tour internationally. Inevitably, they were simultaneously cleaned up and watered down, giving an artificially sanitised version of what was really raw, dirty music with its feet firmly in the soil.

The dictator Ceausescu had a policy of deliberately cutting off many inconveniently placed rural villages from the modern conveniences of electricity and piped water, with a view to eventually eliminating them entirely. Ironically, this had the effect of helping to preserve the music and traditions of many of them, cut off as they were from outside musical influences. Thus it was that in the village of Clejani, south of Bucharest, there were around 200 Gypsy musicians living amid squalor and poverty, surviving by playing weddings in the local area. Among them were lautari of incredible virtuosity, little touched by outside influences. In 1989, immediately after the fall of Ceausescu, two Belgian musicians, Stephane Karo and Michael Winter, visited the village and selected 11 musicians, including violinists, singers, accordion, cymbalom, and bass. With this group, named the Taraf de Haïdouks ('band of brigands'), they made recordings and arranged a tour in western Europe. Their music was a huge success; in contrast to the state folklore ensembles, the Taraf come over as extremely spontaneous, undiluted, and unprocessed. Numerous CDs, tours and media triumphs have followed, and they have deservedly built an international reputation as simply the best Gypsy band in the world.

Bulgaria

The state folk ensembles of communist Eastern Europe earned themselves a reputation, richly deserved, for blandness, homogeneity, and inauthenticity. The exception to this was so startling that, when its recordings appeared in the West in the mid 80s, they quickly gained cult status, arousing feelings of awe, wonder, and incomprehension in equal measure. I speak of *Le Mystère des Voix Bulgares*, the work of a female choir led by Philip Koutev, founder of the State Ensemble for Folk Songs and Dances. Bulgaria was one of the most impenetrable, hardline states of the Warsaw Pact, often used by Russia to do the dirty work that even the KGB didn't want to get involved in, such as the attempted assassination of the Polish Pope. All the more surprising that it should produce music of such beauty and originality.

Philip Koutev was born in 1903, and graduated from the Conservatory of Sofia in 1929. He was both a contemporary composer and a serious collector of Bulgarian village music, so when in 1949 orders came from on high to create a state folk ensemble, he was the natural choice to lead it. He took inspiration from the Russian

Piatnitsky Choir, a pre-revolutionary workers' choir which allowed the singers to use their own natural voices and repertoire. In Bulgarian villages it was women who did the singing. They used powerful, piercing voices, a technique often described as 'open throat' singing, completely free of vibrato. In the villages they would sing throughout the working day, often with a melody voice being sung over another drone voice. One of the features so striking to a western listener was the frequent dissonance, the voices sometimes coming within a semitone (half-step) or even a quarter-tone of each other for long, held notes. With classically trained voices laden with vibrato it would have sounded horrible. Even with pure Bulgarian voices it should have been painful. Instead, it was mysteriously and unmistakably beautiful. Koutev, while respecting the tradition, form, and meaning of the original songs, expanded the harmony to include modern polyphonic textures. It was avant garde and individualistic, and there were no songs about tractors. It was everything that a state folk ensemble should not be, and yet, somehow, he got away with it.

Along with the women's voices, Koutev also used Bulgaria's wonderful instrumental tradition. The three principal instruments are the 'gaida' (bagpipe), the 'kaval' (an end-blown flute) and the 'gadulka'.

The gadulka

The gadulka is a type of fiddle, played vertically either resting on the knee or held by a sling around the neck. The body is pear-shaped, quite similar to a Greek 'lyra'. There is no fingerboard, and the strings are stopped with the fingertips or back of the fingernails, allowing for smooth sliding between notes, but making it extremely difficult for a violinist to master. The three melody strings are usually tuned AEA. There are also a number of sympathetic strings (between 10 and 12), which lie underneath the melody strings. These are not fingered, but ring on their own as the instrument is being played. They are tuned chromatically between A and E. There are two round or oval sound holes on either side of the bridge called 'ochi' (eyes).

The gadulka is used either as a melody instrument or as part of the accompaniment for singing. Originally all village instrumentalists would have been amateurs, but in communist times many of the best players were given jobs as full-time musicians, either in the state radio orchestra, in Koutev's group, or in a similar ensemble. One of the first Bulgarian instrumental groups to visit the west was Balkana, a five-piece group with a line-up of gadulka, gaida, 'tambura' (a long-necked lute, a bit like a Greek bazouki) and 'tapan' (a two-sided drum). The group toured with Trio Bulgarka, three of the singers who had featured in Koutev's choir. Mihail Marinov was the gadulka player. I was lucky enough to see them on their first tour in England, and was amazed by the dexterity of the gadulka playing. As a violinist you are taught that accuracy and position changing absolutely requires the fiddle to be firmly under the chin, and that folk players who play down on the chest do so at the expense of any advanced left-hand technique. To see a fiddler effectively playing with the instrument upside down, yet with amazing agility, is quite an eye-opener.

Another star of the gadulka is Nikola Parov, who formed the group Zsaratnok in the 80s. He began collaborating with Andy Irvine, the Irish folk musician and founder member of Planxty, who in his youth had spent some time travelling in Bulgaria, soaking up the wine and the music in equal measure. Parov and Irvine, along with writer and keyboard player Bill Whelan, recorded a crossover album called *East Wind*. This in turn led to Parov being included in Whelan's successful scheme for world domination, *Riverdance*.

The state's promotion and modernisation of traditional Bulgarian music was not confined to the elite folk choirs and orchestras in Sofia, the capital. In the villages too, musicians and singers were encouraged to indulge in 'artistic amateurism', performing for local events and celebrations. Instruments such as the gadulka, gaida, and kaval were manufactured to new high standards, giving more regularity of pitch and intonation. In 1965 a national festival was established at Koprivshtitsa, in the Sredna Gora mountains. Held every five years, this is a spectacular all-singing, all-dancing event at which groups from all regions of Bulgaria perform and compete.

Playing Bulgarian music

For the westerner, there is one feature above all that makes Bulgarian music, along with that of neighbouring Macedonia, so fascinating. Most European folk music has time signatures of 2/4, 3/4, 4/4, or 6/8. The Dave Brubeck Quartet's 1959 jazz hit 'Take Five' was considered revolutionary in the West, and had a generation of young hip intellectuals congratulating themselves when they finally got the hang of counting five beats to the bar. In the Balkans, 5/4 was absolute child's play; real men (and women) danced, sang, and played effortlessly in 7/8, 11/8, 13/8, and 15/8.

The key to getting on top of these rhythms is to break them down into groups of two and three beats. A 7/8 tune, for example, is usually counted 123, 12, 12 (which you could also write as 3, 2, 2). It could also be 12, 12, 123, depending on how the melody is phrased. Fortunately most tunes keep a single rhythmic pattern, though some might change unexpectedly. Traditional musicians tend to think of these beats as combinations of quick (12) and slow (123) beats. The bad news is that this sometimes means the rhythm as actually played may not fall into any of the neat and exact patterns demanded by classically trained musicians.

Here's a quick tour of some of the main rhythms. In most cases the accent will come on every 1, with the strongest accents on the 1 of every 3. Most of the rhythms are used for circle dances called 'horos' or 'oros'. A typical tune title will therefore be 'Paidushko Oro', meaning 'dance in the paidushko rhythm'.

5/8: The 'paidushko', also known as "the Old Man's hobble" or "the lame one". Phrased 12, 123. Traditionally a men's dance, it is named after a village in north-east Bulgaria.

6/8: The 'pravo'. This is one of the most basic wedding dances, usually written in 2/4 with triplets.

EXAMPLE 5.11

CD 1 TRACK 68

Madro

Bulgaria

12,12,123

7/8: If split 12, 12, 123 this is a 'ruchenitsa', a couple dance named after the village of the same name in south-east Bulgaria. If 123,12,12 it's a 'cetvorno'. 7/8 is possibly the most common of the asymmetric time signatures; if you're going to try and master just one of them, this is it. 'Madro' is a four-part ruchenitsa.

4/4 or 8/8: The 'cocek', a very popular dance associated with Gypsy wedding bands, is split 123, 123, 12, reflecting a strong Turkish influence. In Albania and Bosnia it is called 'usul derveshi', and was once used in the rituals of the 'whirling' dervishes.

9/8: Variously called the 'gruncarsco', 'svornato' or 'daicovo'. This rhythm, 12, 12, 12, 123 was almost certainly introduced from Turkey, where it is called 'usul kusten', and is widely used in both folk and classical music.

10/8: Also introduced from Turkey, this rhythm, 123, 12, 12, 123, the 'aramaska cocuk', is danced only by women.

11/8: The 'kopanica', or 'jedenaistvo' ("the 11-beat one"), is 12, 12, 123, 12, 12. A line dance.

13/8: The 'postupano', from central Macedonia: 12, 12, 12, 123, 12, 12. I find it helpful to create a mnemonic: a spoken phrase that makes it easy to remember the rhythm. This one could be "eating through piles of biscuits", where the stress of the rhythm comes on the 1 of each pair, or the 1 and 3 of a triplet.

15/8: The 'bucimis': 12, 12, 12, 12, 123, 12,12.

25/16: The 'sedi donka': 123, 12, 12, 123, 12, 12, 12, 12, 123, 12, 12. Two questions loom large: How? and Why? This rhythm qualifies as an extreme sport, alongside naked bungee-jumping and freestyle bear-wrestling.

american old-time fiddle

The roots of old-time fiddle ■

Old-time in the 20th century ■

The old-time revival ■

Competition fiddling ■

Playing old-time fiddle ■

american old-time fiddle

What was so special about John Utie? Way back in the year of 1620, on board the Francis Bonaventure, he sailed up the James River into the new British colony of Virginia. He was perhaps little different from his fellow settlers, escaping the religious strife and persecution back home or looking for adventure. What made him special from our point of view is that he was possibly America's first fiddle player. He had been "a fidler in England" and had no doubt earned a few extra rations on board ship by playing "upon a Violl at sea". Working as a planter in the tobacco plantations, he got himself into hot water, accused of being a "fidlinge rogue and rascall" for stealing his employer's tobacco (finding himself unable to make a "livinge by fidlinge").

He was certainly among the first of many settlers who arrived along the eastern seaboard, mostly at first from Britain, bringing with them their fiddles, songs, folk tales, and generations of cultural baggage that would make them feel at least a little at home in this strange and fierce new world.

The roots of old-time fiddle

One of the largest groups of early settlers came from Northern Ireland. The so-called 'Scots Irish' had been encouraged in the period 1690-1715 to move from Scotland to the province of Ulster, given generous leases on rich farmland as an encouragement. When these leases finally expired, many of the settlers were uprooted and opted to head west to the new colonies. By this time much of the east coast was already settled, so the Scots Irish were among the first to venture up into the Appalachian Mountains in search of land.

Here, in the southern states of Virginia, West Virginia, North Carolina, Kentucky, and Tennessee, they founded many small farming communities, which, isolated by distance, forest, and mountain, saw little change for centuries to come. It was this region that became the heartland of old-time fiddling in the United States.

Life in the backwoods was a world away from what we know today.

In the 21st century we hear music from morning till night, from the alarm clock to the radio to the car to the office, at the garage, in the shops, on the mobile phone, on the television, in the bar; even a birthday card will play you a tune. And, like as not, there is never a musician in sight. How different it was before the 20th century, when music, as valuable then as it is now to the easing of the day's stresses and strains, depended on having a musician right there.

From the start the fiddler was the life and soul of any party. Whether it was at the end of an ordinary day's work, or some community task – a barn raising, corn husking, peanut shelling, log rolling, or a wedding or christening – you couldn't have a decent party without some drink, some dancing, and a real live fiddle player. Often he would act not just as fiddler but also as dance caller. Fire and brimstone preachers did what they could to tarnish the fiddler's reputation, accusing him of leading the flock to hell in a handcart, but cold knees on a chapel floor found it hard to compete with dancing feet, sawing fiddles, and hard liquor.

Little wonder that children would sit enraptured at the edge of the gathering, memorising the tunes and wishing they could have a go on the fiddle themselves and be the one who, as if by some primitive magic, could make people sing, dance, and come alive. Many an old fiddler recalls how, when daddy was out working, he secretly pulled the fiddle off the wall where it was hung for safety, and tried to scrape out his first tune. It might earn them a beating, but like as not daddy would be delighted to see the young'uns following in his footsteps.

If there wasn't a fiddle in the house, and not enough money to buy one, it wasn't beyond the wit of child or man to knock together their own instrument. The simplest of fiddles could be made from cornstalks and a shoelace. By comparison with this, a construction made from a dried gourd with a fingerboard was high tech, and more than enough to get many of them started. Anyone who had the know-how and the tools to make a decent instrument would have plenty of takers if he wanted to do it for a living.

Alabama fiddler Tom Freeman was typical. He is quoted in Joyce Cauthen's book *With Fiddle And Well-Rosined Bow*: "I can remember when I'd go to old-time breakdown dances, when the fiddler would lay his fiddle down, I'd grab it and he'd have to choke me loose from it: I dearly loved a fiddle. So when I was only nine years of age I decided to make me a fiddle out of a gourd, and I did so. … I cut the hair out of a horse tail and bent a hickory stick and tied a hair to each end and that was my bow for my gourd fiddle. The first tune I ever learned was 'Carry Me Back To Georgia To Eat Corn Bread And 'Lasses.'"

An interesting variation on the normal style of fiddle playing was 'beating straws'. While the fiddler played normally, an assistant standing behind him would tap rhythmically on the available strings with straws, knitting needles, or light sticks (fiddlesticks), creating an extra element of rhythm. This would only work well if the fiddle was being played in a cross tuning. It was common for fiddlers to use non-standard tunings, allowing easier use of drones on certain melodies. A common key for straw beating was AEAE, achieved by tuning both the G and D strings up by a tone (whole step).

By the end of the 19th century, even the remote communities of the Appalachians had access to the Sears, Roebuck catalogue. For a few dollars you could have a fiddle delivered to your doorstep – in 1900, it would have cost you $3.95, case and bow included – along with guitars, mandolins, and banjos. The five-string banjo in particular proved a good partner to the fiddle, able to play much of the same melody line (though in a lower register) and providing a high drone with the instrument's fifth short string. The banjo style used in old-time music is frailing or clawhammer, with a more relaxed feel than the frenzied and machine-like bluegrass style that developed later.

Fiddle music was by no means confined to the home or farm. Wherever there was an event that needed to attract a crowd, there would be a need for live music. Fairs, circuses, and travelling medicine shows would provide employment for a fiddler, and political rallies would often vie for the services of the best musicians. There are many examples of politicians using fiddlers for their own ends, not least in the Coen Brothers film *O Brother Where Art Thou?*, where the Soggy Bottom Boys play a key role in the re-election of the state governor. Sometimes the politician himself was a fiddler. 'Fiddlin' Bob' Taylor of Tennessee, lacking either money or influential friends in his 1878 bid to join the House of Representatives, relied on his fiddling to win votes. His tactic was successful. To quote Chief Francis O'Neill: "Music proved more persuasive than oratory, for it entered the hearts of his audience, while eloquence passed over their heads."

Such was the popularity of fiddle music that, as early as the 19th century, fiddle conventions were being held all across America. Here fiddlers would compete for a championship title and a money prize, and huge crowds would attend the events. Such was the number of these contests that many musicians would be tempted into going professional with the help of the prize money and the adulation of the crowds.

The repertoire of American fiddlers would have started off entirely European; mostly Scots-Irish, or English, with elements here and there of German, French, Polish, and Scandinavian. Collectors such as Cecil Sharp, who toured the Appalachians between 1916 and 1918, were able to identify British roots in hundreds of songs, tunes, and dances. Some tunes, such as 'Fisher's Hornpipe', 'Soldier's Joy', or 'Moneymusk' have changed little from their originals. Inevitably tunes had already developed a plethora of new names, many of them very distinctively American. Many titles are still familiar today ('Billy In The Lowground', 'Golden Slippers', 'Tom And Jerry', etc. Others have less familiar but highly entertaining titles: 'Monkey Wrapped His Tail Around A Flagpole', 'Rabbit In The Pea Patch', 'I'll Never Drink Anymore', 'Johnny Will Your Dog Bite?', 'Dance All Night With A Bottle In Your Hand', and so on.

The repertoire and style of playing was by no means static, and was gradually evolving its own direction. One of the biggest influences was that of the black population. The slaves transported from Africa to work in the plantations brought with them some very distinctive musical ideas that were to help shape the course of American music. The banjo, originally made from a gourd, was an African innovation. Many slaves were encouraged by their masters to play music, either to keep their fellows happy, or to entertain the master and his guests. They quickly took to the fiddle, playing for the white folks a sedate repertoire of church music or European dance tunes, suitable for a proper 'soirée'. For their own dances and Saturday night frolics they would play something more akin to the Appalachian hoedown, usually with a distinctive driving, rhythmic, syncopated twist. By the time of emancipation, when there would have been more genuine mixing of the ethnic populations, there were hundreds of black fiddle players as well as banjo players, singers, and guitarists. Deliberate imitation of black styles of singing and playing occurred in the minstrel shows of the 19th century, when blacked-up white showmen would perform such songs as 'Jump Jim Crow' and 'Possum Up A Gum Stump'. The use of sliding notes, and scales with a flattened third and seventh, are considered to owe much to this influence.

The evolving repertoire included many reels (often referred to as hoedowns or breakdowns), and some hornpipes. Simple dance tunes were given words, often funny, nonsensical, rude, or scurrilous. To the well-known tune 'Turkey In The Straw' (formerly known as 'Old Zip Coon') was sung:

> Oh, I had a little chicken and she wouldn't lay an egg,
> So I poured some hot water on her left-hand leg,
> Then I poured some hot water on her right-hand leg,
> Now my little chicken laid a hard-boiled egg!

Waltzes were popular; being more melodic and lyrical, these would often have a sentimental reference to a place or person. Ragtime, which grew out of the cake-walk tunes of black musicians, became increasingly influential from the beginning of the 20th century, as did blues, a development of Negro spirituals.

Old-time fiddle in the 20th century

Great changes to American fiddling came about in the early years of the 20th century with the advent of recording and radio broadcasting. The first American fiddler to make it big with a record was Georgia's 'Fiddlin' John' Carson. He inherited his title from Governor 'Fiddlin' Bob' Taylor, who for many years was virtually unbeatable at fiddle contests. However, when the unknown hillbilly Carson showed up at one such event, a thrilling duel was fought, and Taylor was finally beaten. Perhaps with a politician's eye for the main chance, he magnanimously admitted defeat, and, to the delight of the crowd, bestowed his fiddle on the newcomer. Fiddlin' John, as he was henceforth known, recorded 'The Old Hen Cackled And The Rooster's Gonna Crow' and 'The Little Old Cabin In The Lane' in June 1923. His singing was described privately by record boss Ralph Peer as "pluperfect awful", but it tapped into a huge new market for the industry, and was an immediate hit. He cut many more sides in the following years, including a recording with another fiddler, 'Bully' Brewer (Okeh 45448), which includes the following exchange:

Bully: I'm the best fiddler that ever wobbled a bow.
Carson: I don't give a durn; I'm the best fiddler that ever jerked the hairs of a horse's tail across the belly of a cat.
Bully: Well, I'll play 'Old Hen Cackle'.
Carson: Turn your dog loose.
[Bully plays]
Bully: Well, what're you gonna play, John?
Carson: I'm gonna play the fiddle. … That's a durn sight more than you've done!

Significantly, the record label, Okeh (pronounced OK) had to find a marketing term to describe this rough-and-ready, down-home mountain music. It might previously have been referred to as 'hillbilly' music, a derogatory term suggesting tobacco chewing, slack-jawed yokels. The *New York Journal* in 1900 defined a "Hill-Billie" as "A free and untrammelled white citizen of Alabama, who lives in the hills, has no means to speak of, talks as he pleases, drinks whiskey when he gets it, and fires off his revolver as the fancy takes him."

Negro music was already being marketed as 'race' music. The

euphemism for Carson's style of fiddling and fooling would be 'old-time music'. This choice of label had a subtle and significant effect. What had for centuries been simply the most popular music available for common folk was suddenly just one of a plethora of styles newly available to a mass audience. And it was seen as representing old-fashioned, wholesome American family values, a symbol of continuity with the old pioneer days. From this point on, old-time music would have an element of self-consciousness that had not existed before, and would always be looking backwards instead of forwards. Not that this was a bad thing; in fact it virtually guaranteed that in a perpetually conservative society like America, old-time music would always have a future. Alan Lomax, the ethnomusicologist and song collector, put it this way: "[Old-time music] gives the listener a feeling of security, for it symbolises the place where he was born, his earliest childhood satisfactions, his religious experience, his pleasure in community doings, his courtship and his work – any or all of these personality-shaping experiences."

The success of John Carson's first release was quickly followed by a flood of new recordings. Fiddlers and string bands throughout the country were offered the chance of a trip to New York or some other city to cut a few sides of their best tunes, with the offer of maybe $25 a tune up-front, or a royalty of one cent per record sold. Eck Robertson was among these; his early recordings of 'Sally Goodin', 'Ragtime Annie', and 'Done Gone' are considered well ahead of their time, showing a precision, cleanness, and articulation rare in fiddle playing of the time.

The power and influence of the recording industry was demonstrated by Columbia's A&R man Frank Walker. Rather than auditioning and accepting whatever acts came his way, he created his own studio group, Gid Tanner & The Skillet Lickers, featuring an unprecedented three fiddle players. Their first release sold more than 200,000 copies. In common with most old-time music of the day, the Skillet Lickers were long on entertainment value. Gideon Tanner, who fronted the band, was a buffoon and expert trick fiddler, and "could turn his head all the way round, like an owl" whilst playing.

Fiddlers who had built a reputation through personal appearances up and down their own states suddenly had a national audience and could become big stars. Radio stations began to spring up, and live broadcasts by musicians were another way in which fame could suddenly spread. Although less well paid than making records, regular appearances on state-wide radio would enable fiddlers to command much better fees for dances. So popular were the radio appearances of old-time musicians that it was reported in the *Birmingham News* in

1925 that, in contrast to the luke-warm response to normal 'light' music routinely broadcast, "right in the middle of one of these high class programs let someone step up to the microphone, play 'Arkansas Traveler' or 'Yankee Doodle' on the fiddle – not a violin – and the cheering comes thundering in from all over the United States".

With the new mass circulation media of radio and phonograph, it became possible for fiddlers to learn new tunes and new styles of playing that would have hitherto been unavailable.

Coinciding with the increasing popularity of old-time music, and its new-found conservative associations, the car magnate Henry Ford saw a way to combine his love of fiddle music with a bit of social engineering. In 1926, in an attempt to stave off the twin evils of jazz and communism, he began promoting fiddle championships at his dealerships around the country, making big stars out of some of the winners. His executives were expected to take dancing classes and to attend barn dances that he promoted.

Old-time music continued to find an audience through the Great Depression and World War II, but the 50s saw a sudden and dramatic decline in its fortunes. This is probably down to two factors. Firstly, the post-war generation had a new mood of forward-looking optimism, with science, the economy, and the availability of consumer goods powering ahead. Country music and jazz had already made inroads into the potential audience, and rock'n'roll swept away much of what was left. The self-sufficiency of small, isolated communities was disappearing, and with it the need and opportunity for home-made, local entertainment. People travelled much more, and television and cinema were grabbing ever larger slices of the leisure market. The small schools and courthouses that had been the venue for so many fiddle conventions were being closed down and amalgamated, and the few hoe-downs that still took place now had the cheaper option of recorded music instead of a live band. Old-time music had never looked more old and out of time.

The old-time revival

The late 60s saw a reversal in this decline. Coinciding with a new radical politics, environmentalism, and the development of a counterculture, the old days of wholesome food, a life on the land, and a banjo on the back porch suddenly started to look attractive, whether you were a dyed-in the wool Republican or a pot-smoking long-haired Democrat. Artists such as Mike Seeger, Pete Seeger, and the New Lost City Ramblers pioneered an active revival of old-time music, capturing a young, dedicated, and largely urban new audience. For the first time, old-time music festivals began to spread across the country. These were usually outdoor, family-friendly events, combined with endless barbecues, handicraft stalls, line dances, square dances, and rodeos, not to mention the fiddling contests. A large community of old-time fans started to meet not just to consume the product, but to participate in countless pickin' and grinnin' sessions. Among the key attractions at festivals and conventions are the star old-time fiddlers of today, such as Brad Leftwich, Bruce Molsky and Dirk Powell.

Competition fiddling

Fiddle contests (a term more or less synonymous with fiddle conventions) were hugely popular all across the States for more than two centuries. The earliest recorded American fiddle contest was in 1736, held in Hanover County, Virginia, the prize offered being "a fine Cremona fiddle to be plaid for, by any number of country fiddlers". With fiddling being such a valued skill, there would always have been an element of competition between fiddlers, who would be vying for the best jobs and the highest fees, and also between the fans, who wanted their local hero to be seen as the best.

Most contests were small, local affairs in schoolhouses or courthouses, but many were huge, attracting dozens of fiddlers and thousands of eager fans. It was possible for a fiddler who was prepared to travel to attend three or four contests a week, earning cash prizes or produce of some kind; these prizes would have been particularly welcome when the conventions reached their peak, which was in the gloomy years of the Great Depression. The poster for a typical contest, held in DeKalb County, Alabama in 1933, boasted "The Biggest, the Funniest, the most Soul-inspiring Event in the history of the Fiddle and the Bow. The old time tunes will rekindle the smouldering fires of youth, retouch the golden heartstrings or a broken chord, rejuvenate and transplant the soul to the green fields of memory's ecstatic joys and pleasures of the LONG AGO."

Some of the contests were mobile; a promoter would arrive in a town square and announce the open contest and the cash prize. The local fiddlers would all know one another, but would be wary of a stranger – he might be a travelling 'gunslinger' of a fiddler who would win wherever he went, or might even be a 'ringer', in league with the promoter.

The concept of the 'brag fiddler' developed, someone who fancied his own skill and was happy to take on all comers to prove it. In such a competitive atmosphere, showmanship was at a premium. Fiddlers would develop a patter and stage show, and 'trick fiddling' started to evolve. This involved finding ever more bizarre ways to play the instrument: tossing the fiddle in the air, playing behind the head, one arm under one leg, fiddle upside down, bow held between the knees and fiddle held with both hands, and so on. Certain tunes became associated with trick fiddling; using 'Pop Goes The Weasel', a fiddler would play each section of the tune in a different contorted position. Expert trick fiddlers could do all these antics whilst playing accurately and in time. Alabama fiddler E.D. 'Monkey' Brown was one such fiddle wrestler. He got his nickname when it was said of him at a Tuscaloosa fiddle convention, "that boy can do more with a fiddle than a monkey can with goobers [peanuts]".

Less athletic but equally demanding tricks developed along more conventional lines; the double shuffle or 'hokum bowing' is a flashy pattern of triplets carrying across two bars; this was popularised by jazz fiddler Joe Venuti in the late 1920s, incorporated into 'The Beaumont Rag', and reached its apogee in the tune 'Orange Blossom Special' in the 1940's.

In the early days, tricks were one sure-fire way to walk off with the prize. It was a case of almost anything goes, whether it was trilling like a mockingbird, braying like a mule, hollerin', jokin' or dressing as a rooster to play the 'Chicken Reel'. Practically the only thing not allowed was a player who had formal training; the old-timers saw a big difference between themselves and the purveyors of more highfalutin classical music, and wanted to maintain that difference. If a player "trembled his fingers" (ie, used vibrato), he would be viewed with deep suspicion.

The contests were always highly entertaining, and the larger ones may have been combined with other attractions such as hog calling, cracker eating, husband calling, buck dancing, lying contests, ugliest fiddler contests, and so on.

More recently, as contests have become more formalised, trick fiddling, cross tuning, hokum bowing, and the tunes most associated with them are explicitly banned in most competitions. Typically a contest will be divided into three age groups, and in each round you will play three tunes; a breakdown, a waltz, and a 'tune of choice', such as a rag, polka, or hornpipe. There'll be a time limit of around five minutes. The judges are normally professional musicians, and they will be looking for clarity, intonation, rhythm, and creativity. After a considerable lull in the post-war years, fiddle contests have once more become very popular, and hundreds of them attract large audiences across the USA and Canada. The National Oldtime Fiddlers' Contest at Weiser, Idaho, has been held annually since 1953.

A typical set of rules will include a paragraph such as this: "No cross-tuned fiddles, five string fiddles or plucking on strings allowed. TRICK FIDDLING tunes such as 'Orange Blossom Special', 'Listen To

MARK O'CONNOR

No fiddle book would be complete without a mention of Mark O'Connor, but which chapter he belongs in is an open question. In the fiddling world there are many players who deserve the title Jack Of All Trades, but, uniquely, Mark O'Connor seems to be master of them all.

Born in Seattle in 1961, he started out as a guitarist. Then, on seeing fiddler Doug Kershaw's appearance on the first Johnny Cash Show, in 1969, he decided that was the instrument for him. With remarkable speed he mastered the fiddle, and with lessons from Texas contest supremo Benny Thomasson he was soon winning contests wherever he entered, adopting with ease the slick, clean, swinging Texas style. At the age of 12 he released his first album on Rounder Records, and by 14 he had three national championships under his belt.

Mark O'Connor

Ever restless, he experimented with hot club jazz, and on leaving school in 1979 landed a job playing guitar with "Dawg Jazz" mandolinist David Grisman. This led to a meeting with legendary French fiddler Stéphane Grappelli, who was guesting with the group. Learning that O'Connor was also a violinist, Grappelli encouraged him to play twin fiddles in their concerts, and offered him lessons.

His impeccable technique and remarkable adaptability made him an ideal session player, and O'Connor then spent six years in Nashville, becoming the first-call fiddler and recording with hundreds of artists. He continued with his own projects, including two outstanding albums, *New Nashville Cats* (1991) (featuring a veritable army of the finest Nashville session players), and *Heroes* (1993) on which he duetted with all of his childhood fiddle heroes. The diversity of styles he covers on this album is breathtaking, from jazz-rock (with Jean-Luc Ponty) to Indian (L. Shankar), cajun (Doug Kershaw), bluegrass (Kenny Baker), hot club (Grappelli), and country-rock (Charlie Daniels).

Not content with being top of the tree as a fiddler, Mark O'Connor has developed into a highly respected concert violinist, writing and performing his own symphony, concertos, and string quartets. Much of his work in recent years has included cellist Yo-Yo Ma and double bassist Edgar Meyer. With Yo-Yo he performed his 'Appalachia Waltz' for President Clinton at the White House. The *New York Times* was not exaggerating when it described his as "one of the most spectacular journeys in recent American music".

O BROTHER, WHERE ART THOU?

Old-time music got a huge shot in the arm when, in 1990, the Cohn Brothers released their quirky comedy *O Brother, Where art Thou?* Set during the Depression era in the South, it has a plot loosely based on that of Homer's *Odyssey*. The story centres around a group of escaped convicts (led by George Clooney), who form an impromptu old-time band, play "for ten dollar apiece, singin' into a can!", and become an overnight success, helping to re-elect Tennessee governor Pappy O'Daniel and earning a pardon. Though full of humour, the film beautifully captures the gritty reality of the period, and the music, unusually for Hollywood, is fully authentic. Along with a few vintage recordings, most of the tracks are recreations by the cream of bluegrass and old-time musicians. Bluegrass star Alison Krauss is one of the lead vocalists, and fiddle playing comes from old-time fiddle guru John Hartford and bluegrass session king Stuart Duncan.

The key song on the multi Grammy-award winning soundtrack is 'Man Of Constant Sorrow', written by the blind Kentucky fiddler Dick Burnett around 1913. Made famous by The Stanley Brothers, the song also appeared on the debut albums of Peter Paul & Mary, Judy Collins, Rod Stewart, and Bob Dylan. Five million copies of the soundtrack were sold, and many of the musicians went on to perform songs from the film on a live tour and DVD release, entitled *Down From The Mountain.*

The Mockingbird', 'Black Mountain Rag', and 'Lee Highway Blues' WILL NOT BE ALLOWED during competition!"

Old-time fiddling has as much diversity within it as any other type of fiddling, but in the contest environment, one sub-species has, by a process of natural selection, come to dominate. This is the Texas style, now so common that the term 'Texas fiddling' is synonymous with 'contest fiddling'. Benny Thomasson was the player who brought this style to the forefront, possibly learning the basics from blind Kentucky fiddle player Ed Haley. Mark O'Connor, before branching out in every direction possible, took it to its peak.

Whereas the old hillbilly style of bowing was largely an aggressive saw-stroke action, with one bow per note, Texas fiddling uses the 'long bow method', a smooth, flowing action with several notes slurred into one bow. Melodic and harmonic variations have developed to an almost baroque extent, and an element of improvisation is also used. Breakdowns are commonly played with swing rather than straight, and are often at a slower tempo than in Appalachian style. Double-stops and higher positions are common, a warm clear tone and perfect intonation are required. It is a style far more suited to the concert platform than the dance hall. In short, Texas fiddling, though the direct progeny of old-time, is a modern young thing which its grandparents would hardly recognise.

PLAYING OLD-TIME FIDDLE

The roots of old-time are in the solo fiddler playing for dancing. A strong, driving rhythm was the most fundamental element of this style of playing, and the starting point for this is the simple saw stroke.

EXAMPLE 6.1

CD 1 TRACK 69i

The pattern consists of one long and two short bows; the long bow alternates between down- and up-strokes. There's a temptation to play this with the accent on the long bows, but that's not the effect we're looking for. If there was a guitarist, he would be 'chopping' on the second and fourth beats of the bar, not the first and third. In the absence of an accompanist, the old-time fiddler had to cover both jobs, giving a 'dig' to the bow on the second of each three notes in the pattern. The accent comes both from extra downward pressure on the bow, and also extra speed of movement.

EXAMPLE 6.2

CD 1 TRACK 69ii

Some tunes are simple enough to allow you to play this pattern all the way through. Here's an old-time tune still widely played. I love playing 'Old Joe Clark'; because it's so simple it allows you lots of freedom to add your own ideas to it.

Old Joe Clark

There are many versions of words for this tune, none of them complimentary to the aforementioned Mr Clark, such as:

I went down to Old Joe's house
He was sick in bed.
Stuck my finger down Old Joe's throat
Pulled out a chicken head.

Old Joe Clark he'd taken sick
What do you reckon ailed him?
He drank six gallons of buttermilk
Then his stomach failed him.

Notice that this is a modal tune; although it's clearly in the key of A, all the G's are natural, not sharp. This is common in old-time tunes.

The Nashville shuffle

The bowing pattern we've been looking at is sometimes called the single shuffle, or the Nashville shuffle. If you listen to some playing from a real old-timer, who learned in an actual log cabin (as opposed to those of us who learn from CDs and books in our city apartments), there isn't actually a whole lot of shuffle going on. When the recording industry kicked off, and fiddlers started getting jobs as backing musicians for singers, or playing in a band situation, the shuffle started

EXAMPLE 6.3

CD 1 TRACK 70

to become a separate entity, a simple technique that would fit almost anywhere and make anything sound old-time. This is perhaps the origin of the term Nashville shuffle, since Nashville quickly became the centre for the recording industry for old-time, bluegrass, and country music.

Even if it's not completely authentic, it's a good idea to learn how to create a shuffle for any tune or song. Here, for example, is a Nashville shuffle version of that great old mountain tune 'Twinkle Twinkle Little Star':

EXAMPLE 6.4

CD 1 TRACK 71

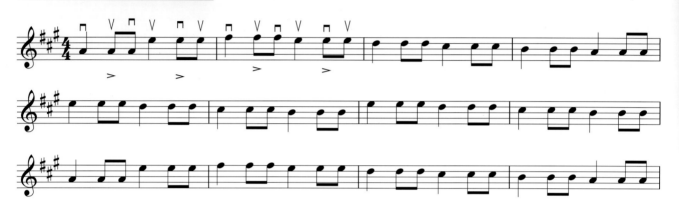

If you're playing fast tunes, this sawing action can start to seem like hard work, and you might be tempted to throw in a few slurs. In addition, the majority of Irish and Scottish-based reels do not have the pattern like this:

EXAMPLE 6.5

CD 1 TRACK 72i

Instead they have something more like this, with eight quavers (eighth-notes) to the bar:

EXAMPLE 6.6

CD 1 TRACK 72ii

For these reasons a variation developed on the Nashville shuffle, where the long notes are split into two slurred notes. The effect is both smoother and more economical:

EXAMPLE 6.7

CD 1 TRACK 73i

The splitting of the first note in the pattern gives us some interesting options. In the above example we've used C as the 'target note', and put a clean B note before it. As an alternative you could slide up to the note using the same second finger:

EXAMPLE 6.8

CD 1 TRACK 73ii

Or, if it's an open D, A, or E string you're shuffling on, you can double it by sliding up on the string below, starting a semitone (half-step) below and ending on the same note as the open string:

EXAMPLE 6.9

CD 1 TRACK 73iii

If your fourth finger isn't as accurate as you'd like it, and the note is a bit out of tune, it's not such a problem; the two pitches together will create a nice fat sound and the ear will forgive the discrepancy.

The Georgia shuffle

We'll come back to playing double strings shortly, but first here's a more evolved pattern, called the Georgia shuffle. Here all the notes are slurred except the accented one, and all the accents have the same down-bow. The effect is smoother and is a step towards the 'long bow' used in competition fiddling and bluegrass.

Try these two patterns.

EXAMPLE 6.10

CD 1 TRACK 74i

EXAMPLE 6.11

CD 1 TRACK 74ii

The Georgia shuffle will also work in reverse, with the accent on the up-bow. It's easiest to play this up near the tip of the bow:

EXAMPLE 6.12

CD 1 TRACK 75

Here's 'Fisher's Hornpipe' played with the Georgia bow:

Fisher's Hornpipe

EXAMPLE 6.13

CD 1 TRACK 76

Practise these patterns until they feel very familiar , but don't get too hung up on them. As you may already have decided, playing the same pattern all the way through a tune is very limiting and can sound pedantic and monotonous. Ideally your bowing will change to suit individual phrases rather than forcing itself onto every part of a tune. Your long term goal is to teach your bow arm to think for itself: a bit like the Stegosaurus, which is reputed to have had a separate brain in its backside to take care of its hind legs.

Drones

The other key element of old-time fiddling is the use of drones. This is achieved by bowing two strings at once; you'll be fingering on one string, whilst the other is an open string.

The drone may be above the fingered notes:

EXAMPLE 6.14

CD 1 TRACK 77i

Or below the fingered notes:

EXAMPLE 6.15

CD 1 TRACK 77ii

Where the two notes are an octave apart (for example on the first and last notes above), a slide up with the fingered note often sounds good.

Here's a phrase where the drone is both above and below the fingered melody, in different places:

EXAMPLE 6.16

CD 1 TRACK 78i

A drone section like this might include a doubled note as we encountered earlier. This can be done with a fourth finger or, if you're already a fully powered-up violinist (and this would have had you booted out of an old-time fiddle contest), by going up to third position with your second finger.

EXAMPLE 6.17

CD 1 TRACK 78ii

Writing out the drone notes makes the music appear cluttered, and makes it look a lot harder than it really is. If you're learning a tune from sheet music, it's usually something you'll add on yourself. Try playing through a few major scales, with added drones. You'll find that some notes sound great, others not so great. Here's A major:

EXAMPLE 6.18

CD 1 TRACK 79i

In the A major scale most of the notes on the A and E strings work well, but on the G and D strings it's not so good. In fact two notes, C-sharp and G-sharp sound "pluperfect awful". The G and D strings don't make for good drones in the key of A. If you want to keep that drone sound going, you have to enter the slightly more scary realm of double-stops, where you actually finger the drone note instead of using an open string.

Double-stops

Here is one (of many) possibilities for a better droned/double-stopped scale of A:

EXAMPLE 6.19

CD 1 TRACK 79ii

Double-stopping like this is used very sparingly in traditional old time playing, though it gets much more advanced in competition fiddling, bluegrass and western swing, so we'll hear more about it in future chapters.

Have a go at this great old tune, 'Granny Will Your Dog Bite?'. You may recognise the title even if you haven't heard the tune; it's one of a number of titles hidden in the lyrics of 'The Devil Went Down To Georgia'.

Granny Will Your Dog Bite?

EXAMPLE 6.20

CD 1 TRACK 80

The words for the first part are:

Granny will your dog bite, dog bite, dog bite?
Granny will your dog bite?
Law child, no.
Wolf bit her biter off, biter off, biter off,
Wolf bit her biter off, long time ago.

Granny will your hen peck, hen peck, hen peck?
Granny will your hen peck?
Law child, no.
Hog bit her pecker off, pecker off, pecker off,
Hog bit her pecker off, long time ago.

You can play G and D drones all the way through the first line. The second line has a couple of double-stops in the second bar, and you can do a G drone on the last note. Most of the tune uses the Nashville shuffle; use plenty of bite on the accented notes.

Notice how the last bar is only half the normal length. This is the kind of charming eccentricity which often gets ironed out of old tunes. You could very easily lengthen the note at the end to make a full bar. If you're that way inclined, go right ahead.

Cross tuning

We talked earlier about the problem of doing drones when the open string doesn't fit well with the key. One way round this is to retune the fiddle. This may sound a bit drastic to someone with a classical background, or you might look on it as cheating, but in the old days it was very common practice. It is called 'cross tuning' or 'open tuning', and there are numerous variations. Let's try one out. The standard tuning is GDAE (reading from low to high pitch). We're going to AEAE, so tune the G string up a tone (a whole step) to A, and the D string up to E. Try playing this scale, with drones.

EXAMPLE 6.21

CD 1 TRACK 81

At this point you may have flashing light and warning sirens in your head, telling you that what you're reading and what you're hearing are two different things. Trust me, it's easier this way. Find the fuse in your brain which operates the alarms, and pull it out. You play what you see on the music, as if you were still in standard tuning. You've now got a real old-time fiddle in your hands, with a raw, archaic sound all of its own.

Here's a traditional tune in AEAE, called 'Greenback Dollar'.

AEAE is probably the most common alternative tuning, (sometimes called 'cross-key', or 'high-bass') particularly useful for tunes in the key of A. It allows you to use the top two strings for melody, the lower two for drones, and occasionally to switch to playing the melody an octave lower, but using the same fingering. Eck Robertson's famous showpiece 'Sally Gooden', recorded in 1922, used this tuning.

DDAD ('dead man's tuning') is used for some well-known tunes including 'Bonaparte's Retreat', and 'Midnight On The Water'; the latter was written by Luke Thomasson, father of Benny, the champion contest fiddler. It is mostly used for tunes in the key of D.

Greenback Dollar

EXAMPLE 6.22

CD 1 TRACK 82

Other common tunings include:
- AEAD ('old sledge' tuning)
- GDAD ('gee-dad')
- AEAC# ('Black Mountain rag' tuning)
- GDGD
- GDBD
- ADAE

Most retunings are no more than a tone (whole step) up or down. If you go up any more than that, then you might break a string, especially if it's an E.

As well as making droning easier, these open tunings allow the open strings to ring sympathetically, in harmony with the tune, as well as making the use of fiddle-sticks more convenient. Many tunes don't make any sense unless you use the correct tunings, and it's an essential part of the authentic old-time sound. While the use of open tunings has declined across fiddle music in general, within the hard-core old-time fiddle community it's as strong as ever; people playing in jam sessions will often spend an hour or more playing within a single cross-tuning.

cajun fiddle

Early Cajun fiddlers

Cajun string bands

Post-war Cajun music

Cajun fiddle today

Playing Cajun fiddle

THE FIDDLE HANDBOOK

cajun fiddle

The deepest roots of Cajun music lie in western France. Settlers left there in the 17th century for Acadie, in what are now the Canadian provinces of Nova Scotia and New Brunswick. The seemingly endless Anglo-French wars of the time eventually led to the Acadians being given, in 1755, the blunt choice of swearing allegiance to the British crown or leaving. They left, many eventually arriving, after years of hardship, in the virtually empty territory of Attakapas, west of New Orleans, where a living could be made from trapping, fishing, and farming. They established communities throughout the south of Louisiana, having little contact with the rest of society, evolving and maintaining a distinctive culture of language, customs, food, and music. They were a tough, conservative, individualistic people. They had a strong belief in family values, they worked hard, and they played hard.

The earliest music of the Cajun people was the unaccompanied singing of what were called in French 'complaints': long, rambling tales, often improvised around themes that could be traced back to France. It is doubtful if many instruments were brought by the first settlers, though by 1780 there are the first written records of fiddles being used in Louisiana. At first, solo fiddle was used either for dancing or for the accompaniment of songs. In common with many cultures where fiddle was played solo at dances, the musicians developed techniques to maximise volume and impact. Open tunings were used that allowed use of drone strings; GDAG was common for G tunes, whilst ADAD allowed the same melody to be played with the same fingering and drones in two different octaves. Shuffle patterns provided rhythm; bowing was hard and fierce. Eventually the use of a second fiddle became common, playing lower harmonies or octaves, and providing more rhythm. This is called 'seconding' or 'bassing'.

The arrival of the accordion in the 1870s had a profound effect on Cajun music and the role of the fiddle within it. Various types of accordion were available, but it was the small diatonic ten-button accordion that rapidly gained popularity among Cajuns. It was light, durable, straightforward to play, and above all loud; in any band that had fiddle and accordion together, the accordion would be the obvious choice as lead instrument. This had an immediate effect on the style of fiddle playing. The fiddle was capable of subtle nuances of pitch and scale that rapidly went out of the window. Tunes were simplified, often cutting out bridge sections or anything involving a tricky modulation, and the choice of keys became narrowly restricted to what the accordions could handle. Fiddlers had to develop new tunings specifically for this reason. Many of the early accordions were in C. For a fiddle player this is not a good key, as there are few possibilities for open string drones, unlike D, which is perfect for this purpose. Fiddlers who had learned tunes in D would often tune all four strings down a tone (whole step) so that they could keep the same fingerings when playing in C.

The Cajun repertoire at the start of the 20th century was much more diverse than it is today, including polkas, waltzes, contradances, varsoviennes, mazurkas, and quadrilles, along with tunes they shared with Anglo-Saxon old-time fiddlers: jigs, reels and hoedowns. Music and dancing were extremely popular, taking place initially in house parties ('bals de maison') where family, friends and neighbours would gather at a someone's house, usually at weekends. Soon larger public dances – 'fais dodos' – developed in dance halls built for the purpose. By now bands had expanded further, often including the triangle ('petit fer' or 'little iron') and, from the 1920s, the guitar.

Early Cajun fiddlers

One of the earliest star performers on the Cajun fiddle was Dennis McGee (1893-1989), whose life and career encompassed virtually all the major developments in the style. He got his first fiddle from his father, also a fiddler, at the age of 14, and mastered it rapidly. He was a bold and innovative player, described as a "Cornbread Paganini" or, by Dave Greely, fiddler with Steve Riley's Mamou Playboys, as "The first Cajun-punk fiddle player". His repertoire included the full range of old continental and French material described above, as well as the waltzes and two-steps that would eventually come to dominate Cajun music. When he was bandleader he often used a second fiddler, mostly his brother-in law Sady Courville or sometimes Ernest Fruge. He made some of the earliest recordings of Cajun music, laying down numerous vocal and instrumental tracks between 1928 and 1930.

McGee had an ornate style, full of trills and ornaments. He is best known for his partnership with the black accordionist Amédé Ardoin; together they won a fiddle and accordion contest in Opelousas in 1928, which led to Ardoin being signed by Columbia. They worked extensively together, playing, unusually, at both white and black venues, sometimes both in the same night. The black French-speaking inhabitants of south Louisiana were known as Creoles. They lived in close proximity with the white Cajuns, sharing much of the culture, though not necessarily mixing freely. Ardoin paid the price for crossing the boundary. One night after a white gig he was severely beaten, following which his health severely deteriorated; he died sometime in the 40s. McGee's long life was a boon for Cajun music. Although he, like most Cajun musicians, split his time between music and farming or other jobs, and indeed gave up playing entirely for some periods, he was still in good form in the 70s. This meant he was able to pass on much of his invaluable knowledge and technique to younger players, as well as benefiting from the new opportunities for prestige concert work that opened up with the Cajun revival. There is a fine collection of his work re-released on a Yazoo album: *The Complete Early Recordings Of Dennis McGee.*

Cajun string bands

The 1930s were a time of great change in Louisiana. The discovery of a new oil field at Bosco in 1932 brought about a rapid expansion of the oil industry and an influx of workers from Texas. The long isolation of this rural backwater was coming to an end. The new workers brought with them a craving for the latest musical fads from that state, country music and western swing, and this quickly fed into the musical language of the Cajuns. Had the music been still restricted to the dance halls this would surely not have been the case, but the recording industry and regular radio broadcasts meant that Cajun bands were now competing directly on the airwaves with bands from outside. The accordion, which had been the lead instrument for decades, suddenly seemed old-fashioned, whilst the fiddle was now the height of fashion. A number of notable accordion players, including Nathan Abshire, Iry LeJeune, and Austin Pitre, saw the writing on the wall and quickly switched to playing fiddle.

A new, smoother string-band sound developed. The triangle was ditched along with the accordion, and in came the guitar, and sometimes double-bass and drums. With this sound, bands could not only maintain their audience in Louisiana, but also gain new audiences outside. One of the pioneers of the Cajun string band sound was fiddler Leo Soileau (1904-1980). His first hit, in partnership with singer/accordionist Mayuse LaFleur, came in 1928 with a song called 'Mama, Where You At?'. LaFleur was killed in a bar-room brawl only days after the recording. Soileau tried working with other accordionists, but his own speed and dexterity on the fiddle seemed to leave them standing. He eventually settled, in 1934, on a line-up of two guitars and drums as his backing band, which he called Leo

Soileau's Three Aces. The addition of the drum backbeat and the swinging guitars gave a modern sound to the familiar Cajun repertoire, and could also be used for French-language versions of American standards. Together they recorded more than 100 singles, and toured around Texas, Tennessee, and as far afield as Chicago. After World War II the band made regular radio broadcasts from various stations, always opening with their trademark song 'Under The Double Eagle'.

An obvious problem for a band led by fiddle but featuring drums was that of volume. The first band to find the solution were The Hackberry Ramblers, led by fiddler Luderin Darbonne. They began using amplification at their gigs, powered by the battery of their Model A Ford, idling on the street outside. Quite apart from allowing them to be heard clearly in a large, noisy dancehall, it allowed for greater dynamic range and subtlety. Darbonne had spent most of his youth in East Texas, where he picked up a strong dose of western swing influence on his playing. The band began singing some songs in English, which obviously helped to increase their appeal outside Louisiana. One of their most popular numbers was 'Corrine, Corrine'.

Perhaps the name most linked with the Cajun swing sound was Harry Choates. He was an outstanding fiddle player, equally at home with traditional Cajun material or western swing. He was also a wild and eccentric character, a heavy drinker who would appear on stage in a formerly white cowboy hat, which, in the words of a band member, "looked like a hundred horses had stomped on it when it had been stuck in a grease barrel". As well as being a great fiddler, he also played guitar, accordion, and steel guitar, yet probably never owned an instrument, preferring to borrow whatever he needed. His biggest hit came in 1946: 'Jolé Blon' was a rewrite of 'Jolie Blonde', known as 'the Cajun national anthem'. He is reported to have sold the rights to the song for $100 and a bottle of whiskey. He died in an alcoholic haze at the age of just 29, beating his head on the bars of a jail cell, where he had been locked up for failing to pay alimony to his estranged wife. His work fortunately lives on in re-releases such as *Harry Choates: Fiddle King Of Cajun Swing* on Arhoolie Records. A listen to this album shows the versatility of Choates. On the one hand, he can play straight-ahead Cajun numbers, albeit with a smoothness rarely seen with other fiddlers; on the other, he not merely jumps on the western swing bandwagon, he pushes the driver out of his seat and whips up the horses.

One of the finest Cajun fiddlers of this period was Doc Guidry, who was born in Lafayette in 1918; he recorded with Happy Fats & The Rayne-Bo Ramblers for Bluebird in 1936, and later under the name Sons Of The Acadians, with his cousin Ray Guidry and brother Nason. His record label for this band, Decca, gave him hillbilly songs to translate into French for the Cajun market. Guidry also worked with Jimmie Davis on his two successful campaigns for the governorship of Louisiana. Davis, as well as being a politician, was a successful singer, and would perform popular hits on the campaign trail – hillbilly numbers in the English speaking areas, and Cajun songs such as 'Jolie Blonde' in the French parts. Davis will perhaps be remembered longest for his co-authorship of 'You Are My Sunshine', once described as "the most popular and valuable song in the history of Country Music".

Post-war Cajun music

After World War II, tastes changed again, and the accordion made a comeback in the hands of players like Iry LeJeune, who had a big hit with the songs 'Lovebridge Waltz' and 'Evangeline Special'. It is possible that many Louisiana French-speakers found that the drift towards mainstream country music was a dilution not to their taste, and soldiers returning from the war wanted to hear their own down-home Cajun sound. Accordionists such as Nathan Abshire and Lawrence Walker also saw renewed success in the post-war years, but by the 50s Cajun music was into lean times. The biggest-selling Cajun song of all, 'Jambalaya (On The Bayou)', recorded by and credited to Hank Williams, was released in 1952. It was a huge mainstream hit, but Hank Williams was a country singer with no direct Cajun connections at all; although very popular among Cajun musicians, the song is regarded as something of a pastiche, and, as is so often the case with big hits, the actual source of the tune is a matter of some dispute. It is generally accepted that the tune is based on the Cajun song 'Grand Texas'. The popularity of 'Jambalaya' was based more on the song itself, and on the status of Hank Williams, than on the general popularity of Cajun music.

In common with hillbilly music, Cajun music was in a fairly short space of time beginning to look distinctly dated. Country music, now centred in Nashville, was becoming bland and homogenised. Fiddles, accordions and banjos were no longer welcome in the studios, and even Nashville country seemed under dire threat with the onset of rock'n'roll.

One of the few Cajun fiddlers to weather the storm in the 50s and 60s was Doug Kershaw. Born on a tiny island off the Gulf Coast in 1936, he moved to Lake Arthur as a child, where he took up the fiddle and guitar and was soon busking for nickels on street corners. At the tender age of eight he was accompanying his mother when she performed at clubs like The Bucket of Blood ("And that's exactly what it was!" he claims). In the early 50s he started his own band, The Continental Playboys, gaining radio play and finally a place in the

Grand Ole Opry. Critics would claim that he increasingly turned to 'Cajun Lite' – mainly country and country-rock material with little of the depth and heartache found in true Cajun music. A real showman, he sings, dances around the stage and plays fiddle simultaneously, his instrument low down on his chest.

Another fiddler crossing the Cajun/country boundary was Rufus Thibodeaux; like Kershaw he cut his teeth playing tough roadhouse gigs with the family band. He made his name in the 40s, playing with legendary steel player Papa Cairo and Opry star Jimmy C. Newman. Through Newman he got a foothold in Nashville, and by the mid 50's was established as part of the session musicians' 'A Team', appearing on a host of country hits with artists such as George Jones, Lefty Frizzell, and Jim Reeves. In the late 60s and 70s he cut a series of solo Cajun albums, and, starting in 1978, began appearing regularly on Neil Young albums. His playing is smooth, slick, and flashy, betraying influences of bluegrass, country, and western swing.

One fiddler who stuck to his Cajun roots through thick and thin was Dewey Balfa (1927-1992). Music was in his blood from the start; in the words of writer Rick Koster, "Balfa came from a virtual harvest of fiddlers." He showed his interest early on: "I would take sticks and rub them together pretending to play the fiddle, and I'd sing …" At first there was no fiddle for him to play, until "we had an old neighbour who had a fiddle that he didn't play much. So one day, my father traded him a pig for the fiddle." He started doing gigs in the 40s with the family band, gradually advancing from house parties to dance halls, and then to accompanying and recording with the accordionist Nathan Abshire. He played on through the lean rock'n'roll years, when even in south Louisiana Cajun music was seen as something to be ashamed of rather than celebrated. No one was more surprised than Balfa when, in 1964, the musicologist Ralph Rinzler asked him to play at the prestigious Newport Folk Festival.

The urban northern audience had hitherto had virtually no exposure to Cajun music. Instead of the contempt and ridicule Balfa expected, he was greeted with rapturous applause. In his own words, "I had played in house dances, family gatherings, maybe a dance hall

ABOVE: **Doug Kershaw**
BELOW: **Dewey Balfa**

where you might have seen as many as 200 people at once. In fact, I doubt I had ever seen 200 people at once. And in Newport, there were 17,000; 17,000 people who wouldn't let us get off stage." A serious and thoughtful man, he was deeply affected by the experience, quickly realising that his music, now something of an endangered species, had great value and should be vigorously promoted rather than allowed to wither. Returning to Louisiana he was soon at the heart of a movement to revive, preserve, and promote Cajun culture in all its forms. He helped to found CODOFIL (Council For The Development Of French In Louisiana), reversing a trend that had seen the deliberate discouragement of the French language in the state education system. He helped to found the Tribute To Cajun Music Festival in 1974, and took up a teaching post at the University of Louisiana Center For Acadian And Creole Folklore. Through the 70s and 80s, with his group The Balfa Brothers, he travelled widely, acting as an ambassador for Cajun culture. After his death in 1992, his daughters Christine and Nelda, both of whom played guitar but had never played professionally, formed a band along with fiddler/accordionist Dirk Powell and fiddler Kevin Wimmer. Under the name Balfa Toujours, they preserve their father's legacy and continue to promote Cajun music. Dirk Powell's background was in old-time Appalachian music. Since turning to Cajun, he has concentrated on the more archaic styles of playing, with aggressive rocking bows and lots of rich ornamentation.

Cajun fiddle today

Typical of the beneficiaries of Balfa's drive to preserve the legacy of Cajun music is the fiddler David Greely. He received a Louisiana Folklife Apprenticeship Grant in 1992, allowing him to study with Balfa, deepening his technique and extending his repertoire. Although born in Baton Rouge, and with a grandfather, Eddie Theriot, who was an amateur Cajun fiddler, Greely had come to Cajun music only indirectly. The unlikely first step was attending a Black Sabbath gig, where the support act was Richard Greene's progressive bluegrass band Seatrain. This inspired him to buy a fiddle, and in no time at all he was playing bluegrass and western swing. After several years with different bands he landed a solo gig in a restaurant in San Antonio, Texas, where all they wanted was Cajun music, which he finally began to take seriously. In 1987 he met fellow fiddler Steve Riley at a jam session in Marc Savoy's music store in Eunice, Louisiana, and they formed what was soon to be one of the foremost Cajun bands, Steve Riley & The Mamou Playboys. As frontman, vocalist, and accordionist, Riley leaves most of the fiddling up to Greely, though they occasionally do some twin-fiddle numbers. Whilst they can be very traditional, the kicking bass and drums rhythm section gives the band a modern, rocking sound verging on zydeco, and the three-part harmony vocals also add to the commercial accessibility of the sound. Speaking of the dangers of bringing too much change to the traditional sound, Greely says "Cajun music is like a tree that you plant and you water and you take care of it and you want it to grow. But you don't want it to, like, mutate, grow arms and teeth and eat the kids."

The revival of interest in Cajun music led to a new generation of talented players, including, for the first time, many who had some training in music outside of Cajun or country. I had the pleasure of hearing fiddler Ken Smith when he was on tour in England with D.L. Menard and Eddie LeJeune. I was struck by the amazing tone and cleanness of his playing, more akin to the likes of Mark O'Connor than the rough-edged playing one associates with many Cajun players. I later discovered that, though Cajun born and bred, he was also a Louisiana state fiddle champion and had mastered the Texas championship 'uberstyle' where every note is analysed for its quality and intonation.

Michael Doucet

Undoubtedly the best known of the younger fiddlers is Michael Doucet. Although he was from Lafayette, he had very much an Americanised upbringing, and was not 'born into' Cajun music. He started out with a folk trio while a college student, and his interest in his own culture didn't fully develop until a trip to France in 1974, where he heard a group of eight fiddlers playing 'Jolie Blonde'. This glimpse of the deepest roots of Cajun music, and the respect which it engendered in the French homeland, brought about a cultural awakening in Doucet. Speaking of the occasion, he recalled, "Where were we? Died and gone to heaven, you know. It was amazing. It was like speaking to people of our great-grandfathers' era who were our age. It was the turning point of my life." Returning home he studied diligently with most of the remaining fiddle masters of Louisiana, notably Dennis McGee, Dewey Balfa, and Canray Fontenot, developing a keen understanding of the nuances of the different players.

Doucet also learned about the history of his people, and was inspired to name his band after Joseph Broussard, known as Beausoleil, an Acadian resistance leader who opposed the English at the time of

CREOLE AND ZYDECO MUSIC

The Creoles are the black and mixed-race French speakers of Louisiana, descendants either of 'free people of colour' or former slaves from the time of French rule in the region. Their musical heritage is a mixture of African and the same French/American mix as the whites. Just as the Cajuns have a distinctive brand of the French language, so the Creoles have their own patois. Poor Creole and Cajun families lived in close proximity in Louisiana, and there must have been considerable cross-fertilization, as illustrated by the partnership between white fiddler Dennis McGee and Creole accordionist Amédé Ardoin.

Creole fiddler Canray Fontenot (1922-95) started out with a fiddle he constructed from a wooden cigar box, with strings of wire pulled from a screen door. His playing had a strong blues element, though it was one he had to use surreptitiously at Cajun dances. As he explained to author Michael Tisserand, "They didn't want no blues because they would dance too close to one another, they didn't want that at all. You was out of business if you played blues. So we started to slip up on them with something like the 'The Prison Bars' where you could blues it or you could waltz it." He worked with his father, mother, and grandfather, and a neighbour, Douglas Bellard, the first creole fiddler to appear on record.

With the development of amplification in the 30s and 40s, Creole music evolved into zydeco. This differs from Cajun music in several respects. The band is usually led by piano accordion (as opposed to the smaller Cajun button accordion). Fiddles are rare, and the triangle almost non-existent, but drums, bass, electric guitars, and sax are common. A distinctive instrument in many zydeco bands is the 'frottoir' or corrugated tin washboard. The music tends to be a lot louder, with more blues, rock, and funk influence. The beats tend to be fast and insistent, and waltzes, so common in Cajun music, are rare. Among the leading artists are Queen Ida, Clifton Chenier, Buckwheat Zydeco, Rockin' Dopsie and Boozoo Chavis.

Canray Fontenot

the 1755 deportation or 'Grand Dérangement', eventually settling in Louisiana. Doucet's band Beausoleil have recorded some two dozen albums and completed numerous world tours. Their 1997 album *L'Amour Ou La Folie* won a Grammy award for best traditional folk album. Though showing great respect for, and knowledge of, traditional Cajun music, Beausoleil have been consistently innovative, incorporating elements of country, blues, jazz, and tex-mex. Through his travelling, workshops, and production of teaching resources, Doucet has become probably the leading spokesman for Cajun fiddle music today. His playing is clean, precise, and rich in ornamentation, and there's no better place to start if you want to begin learning Cajun fiddling.

PLAYING CAJUN FIDDLE

Cajun fiddle has a lot in common with old-time fiddle, particularly in the use of shuffles, double-stops, and drones. In the old-time section we learned the Nashville shuffle, and we use something very similar in Cajun music.

EXAMPLE 7.1

CD 1 TRACK 83

Here's a simple phrase, without shuffle or embellishment:

We're going to superimpose this shuffle pattern on it:

EXAMPLE 7.2

CD 1 TRACK 84

The shuffle pattern has a lot of quavers (eighth-notes) that don't appear in the melody, so we're going to add a lot of extra notes. The first and fifth note of the shuffle pattern (F-sharp in the example above) is what you might call a leading note; it can be either one or two notes down in the scale from the main melody note (in this case G). Applying this pattern to the melody, we get:

EXAMPLE 7.3

CD 1 TRACK 85

You'll notice that we haven't stuck rigidly to the pattern; in some places it will fit more easily thank others. The push-and-pull between melody and rhythm is one of the variables that makes Cajun fiddle playing endlessly fascinating.

CAJUN

We're going to add some open string drones.

EXAMPLE 7.4

CD 1 TRACK 86

In bars one and two we're adding a lower open D drone. In bar three, use your fourth finger to make an A drone, doubling the open A. In bar four it's an open A drone. If your highly trained classical ear is complaining about the fruity dissonance between G and A at the end of bar four, go and have a cold shower. You'll get no sympathy from me! In the last two bars we have an open G drone under the melody.

Slides, both up and down, are an important feature of Cajun fiddling. This is easiest when moving between an open string and first finger; you slide up to the first finger, and down to the open string. (Whilst upward slides are common in lots of fiddle styles, this downward slide is very unusual.)

EXAMPLE 7.5

CD 1 TRACK 87i

You can also use an upward slide whenever you're using a fourth-finger drone:

EXAMPLE 7.6

CD 1 TRACK 87ii

EXAMPLE 7.7

CD 1 TRACK 88

Now let's change key to A, and look at the first few bars of a very well known two-step, 'Lacassine Special'. The basic melody is as follows:

174   THE FIDDLE HANDBOOK

We're going to add some ornaments. Firstly some triplets, very common in Cajun fiddling:

Now we'll break up a couple of the longer notes to make room for some slides:

EXAMPLE 7.8

CD 1 TRACK 88ii

And then put in some semi-quaver (16th-note) rolls:

EXAMPLE 7.9

CD 1 TRACK 88iii

By this time it's already getting hard to see what the original melody was. This is typical of Cajun music; the basic melodies are very simple but the ornamentation can be dense. Don't be satisfied with learning just one written version of a tune, with its ornamentation; ideally you should first learn the tune, then be able to add your own small variations as you go along.

EXAMPLE 7.10

CD 1 TRACK 88iv

All the exercises above have been in the two-step rhythm. We can apply most of the same principles to the waltz. Here's a basic melody:

EXAMPLE 7.11

CD 1 TRACK 89

The Nashville shuffle obviously isn't going to work on a waltz, but here's one possible bowing pattern that will do a similar job:

EXAMPLE 7.12

CD 1 TRACK 90

Cajun waltzes usually have a gentle swing, so the first of each pair of notes is lengthened, and the second shortened. This pattern allows you to put a clear accent on the second beat of each bar.

Whenever a bar starts with a crotchet melody note, we can break the note up, putting in a lower note which leads up to the melody note:

EXAMPLE 7.13

CD 1 TRACK 91

Now we'll put in some slides, triplets, and rolls:

EXAMPLE 7.14

CD 1 TRACK 92

There's also room for plenty of drones.

Finally, a couple of complete tunes – perhaps the two best known of all. Firstly 'Jolie Blonde', recorded by virtually every Cajun artist and regarded as the Cajun 'national anthem'. I'll put in some ornaments but no drones, to make it easier to read. If you compare any two written or recorded versions of the tune you'll find lots of small variations in the melody, rhythm, and ornamentation. In this version I've included some of the bowing pattern designed to emphasise the second beat, as we looked at above.

That is followed by 'Allons A Lafayette', a tune that appeared on the first ever Cajun recording, by Joe Falcon in the late 20s, and was also popularised by Harry Choates and Dewey Balfa.

EXAMPLE 7.15

Jolie Blonde

EXAMPLE 7.16

Allons A Lafayette

bluegrass fiddle

Bill Monroe ■

Monroe's fiddlers ■

The bluegrass revival ■

Bluegrass fiddle today ■

Playing bluegrass fiddle ■

bluegrass fiddle

When bluegrass was first 'discovered' by the folk revivalists of the late 50s and 60s it was something of a mystery. It certainly came from the South and had connections with the 'blue grass' state of Kentucky, but was it, as some claimed, music as old as the hills or was it a much more recent creation of the singer, mandolinist, and bandleader Bill Monroe? Whatever it was, it was certainly as exciting and challenging as anything a fiddler or other instrumentalist could get his hands on.

The southern Appalachian Mountains, mostly in the states of Virginia, West Virginia, North Carolina, Kentucky, and Tennessee, were, in the early years of the 20th century, the Land That Time Forgot. Settlers from the British Isles, mostly protestant 'Scots Irish', had begun arriving in the mid 18th century, had pushed up through the Cumberland Gap into the hills, cleared their patches of ground to build farms, and stayed put. The Civil War came and went, the Yankees up north industrialised and got rich, while the folk up in the mountains kept themselves to themselves and stayed poor.

What kind of music was around in the Depression years in the South? Old-time fiddle music was still going strong. Whether in the kitchen, the farm, or the schoolhouse, local fiddlers would play for dancing and for their own enjoyment. String bands were very popular, with the fiddle often joined by guitar, mandolin, and banjo. The music consisted of songs, both ancient and modern, and instrumentals – dance tunes inherited from the early settlers, modified, or newly written. Competitive fiddlers' conventions abounded and the standard of playing at the top levels was high.

The white farmers rubbed shoulders with blacks, many of whom played banjo and guitar and sang a mixture of blues, work songs, field hollers, and spirituals. Both in the church and out of it, hymns would have been sung, and many children learned to read 'shape notes', a type of notation used in church music, at singing schools in the summer holidays. The radio, increasingly common even in the backwoods, allowed people to hear professional singers and musicians, and hillbilly singers like The Carter Family and Jimmie Rodgers, performing for live broadcasts at local or regional radio stations.

Bill Monroe

This, then, was the musical backdrop to the early life of Bill Monroe, who was born in 1911 on the family farm in Rosine, Kentucky. He grew up shy and something of a loner, and when his mother died when he was only 10, he was left with a feeling of loss which perhaps never really left him. Music had been a part of family life; when Bill was old enough to pick up an instrument, the fiddle and guitar had already been claimed by his older brothers, so he had to make do with a 'potato bug' mandolin (named because of its round shape and contrasting stripes) that he found lying around the house. Despite his

Bill Monroe

shyness, he was a strong and determined boy, and he practised hard on his instrument, even though he would much have preferred to play the fiddle. He had an uncle who was a fine old-time fiddle player, and Bill liked nothing more than to listen to Uncle Pen's hoedowns. Soon Bill was good enough to accompany his uncle at local dances, and shortly after his mother's death he went to live with Pen.

The two got on well together, and the fiddle music they shared was to become a key plank of Bill's musical development. Another important influence was a local black coalminer called Arnold Shultz. He was a fine guitarist; indeed, although he was never recorded, people who heard him said later that he was a phenomenal player. Bill also attended singing school. He enjoyed the singing and developed a fine voice, but, perhaps due in part to his poor eyesight, he could not get on with the reading of shape notes, and learned purely by ear.

Eventually, like many children from the South, Bill and his brothers left the impoverished and overcrowded family farm and headed for the cities of the North. They found work in an oil refinery in east Chicago. Among their workmates were thousands of displaced rural southerners like themselves, all homesick and probably somewhat alienated by their surroundings. Anyone who could play and sing country songs that reminded them of home had a ready audience, and the three Monroe brothers, on fiddle, guitar, and mandolin, soon found themselves in demand to play for parties and dances. Sooner or later they were going to get 'discovered', but as fate would have it, it was as square dancers that they got their first break. They were spotted at a local dance by Tom Owen, who led a dance team, and invited to appear on 'National Barn Dance', a show broadcast on Chicago's WLS radio. Tempted by the glamour, not to mention the easy money (the not inconsiderable sum of $22 a week), they took up this offer, and eventually were able to quit their jobs at the refinery. Once in the showbiz world, it was a short step to getting noticed as a musical group, and soon The Monroe Brothers, Bill and Charlie (Birch had by now returned to the refinery), were performing on radio KFNF in Shenandoah, Iowa.

By 1938 they had a deal with Victor Records, and had landed their first hit, a gospel number 'What Would You Give In Exchange For Your Soul?'. Soon after, rivalries within the band led brother Charlie to quit, leaving Bill to fend for himself. Bill Monroe was neither a natural frontman, nor a good businessman. Nevertheless he was extremely determined, and he saw this as an opportunity to form his own band, free at last from the overbearing presence of any other Monroes. The first person he hired was guitarist and singer Cleo Davis, followed by fiddler Art Wooten from North Carolina. It was with this band that the name Bill Monroe And His Blue Grass Boys was first used, the 'blue grass' being a reference to his home state of Kentucky, nicknamed the Blue Grass or Bluegrass State because of the presence of the bluegrass plant in its grasslands and pastures.

As a band they rehearsed hard, with Monroe paying particular attention to Art Wooten. From the very start he regarded the fiddle as the key to the sound he wanted to achieve, and he always spent long hours demonstrating with his mandolin what he wanted to hear on the fiddle. The material they were doing at this time was a mixture of old country standards, original songs, old-time fiddle breakdowns, and gospel songs. For the latter, they had carefully worked out four-part harmony parts.

Eventually the Blue Grass Boys decided they were ready to audition for Nashville's Grand Ole Opry. In the words of Davis, "We really put on the dog. We started out with 'Foggy Mountain Top', then Bill and I did a duet tune with a duet yodel, fast as white lightning.... I think that really sewed it up." Delighted by what he heard, presenter George Hay told them "If you ever leave the Opry, it'll be because you fired yourself."

The band were a big hit with audiences. They were used to country and gospel songs, and to string bands playing hoedowns, but here was a band that for the first time successfully combined the two. The songs were fast and exciting, with a driving fiddle shuffle and startlingly nimble mandolin solos, pinned down by a steady bass.

The music was tight, demanding, and innovative. The Blue Grass Boys were the first band to move out of the 'safe' keys of C, G, and D; to pitch Monroe's high lead vocal they used B-flat, B, and E, particularly tough for a hoedown fiddle player.

In 1940 the band made a further series of recordings for Bluebird, including the fiddle tune 'Katy Hill', and the song 'Mule Skinner Blues'. With a demanding work schedule, and subsequently the risk of call-up for the war, there was a rapid turnover of musicians in the Blue Grass Boys, a pattern that was to continue throughout Monroe's career.

Monroe always considered the fiddle to be the key instrument of bluegrass; he would have learned it himself had not his brother got to it first. In a career of gigging and recording spanning more than 50 years, a host of fiddle players got the call; some for just a few shows, some for over a decade. The function of the fiddle within the band evolved gradually. At first it was only expected to play fairly standard old-time breakdowns. Howdy Forrester introduced the idea of playing variations, and Kenny Baker took the first real improvised breaks. As the years progressed, Monroe sometimes added twin and triple fiddles. An ability to do double-stops reduced the number of fiddlers required and became essential. Vassar Clements introduced a strong blues influence, which has also become a central part of the bluegrass fiddle arsenal.

Monroe's fiddlers

Here is a brief roundup of some of some of the Monroe's more notable fiddle sidemen.

Art Wooten

From North Carolina, Wooten was the first fiddler hired by Monroe after splitting with his brother Charlie. He was a relatively 'old school' fiddler. Monroe said of him, "On the old-time fiddle numbers, he was hard to beat." He introduced 'Orange Blossom Special' into the band, having learnt it from the man who was to be his successor, Tommy Magness. Wooten went on to work with both Flatt & Scruggs and The Stanley Brothers in the late 40s and 50s, and produced two solo albums in the 70s.

Tommy Magness

A champion hoedown fiddler from Tennessee, Magness was already a veteran by the time he joined The Blue Grass Boys, having worked with Reg Hall & His Blue Ridge Entertainers. With Reg he made the first recording of 'Orange Blossom Special', beating even its author Ervin T. Rouse to the count, though Rouse's publisher prevented the release. Magness was hired in 1940. Monroe said of him, "He had that fine old-time touch, rich and pure, but he was able to put a touch of blues to it." Together they recorded 'Katy Hill', a fast but clean rendition that many regard as the prototype bluegrass fiddle tune (although this recording shows the fiddle tune being played repeatedly with virtually no variation, something that would be unthinkable in later years). After leaving, Magness spent some years working with country star Roy Acuff.

Howdy Forrester

From west Tennessee, Forrester began his professional career with singer Herald Goodman, and played twin fiddles with Georgia Slim. He moved down to Texas, where he encountered the technically advanced contest style of fiddling: "Those fellows actually scared the dickens out of me because they were reaching up into the second position and getting notes I'd never seen before.... If you're in somebody's backyard, you'd better get a hoe just like he's got." He joined The Blue Grass Boys briefly in 1942, introducing some of the ideas he had picked up in Texas. Monroe said of him, "Howdy, now he's the first man who played with me that played double stop, and Howdy knows that neck all the way, and he knows how to get that tone out, give the fiddle a chance." Forrester was a prolific writer of tunes, many of which have become widely played, including 'Memory Waltz', 'Weeping Heart', and the fiddle contest standard 'Wild Fiddler's Rag'.

Chubby Wise

From Lake City, Florida, Wise was with The Blue Grass Boys from 1942 to 1948, including the 'golden years' when Flatt and Scruggs were with the band. Among the classics he recorded with Monroe were 'Footprints In The Snow' and 'Kentucky Waltz'. After leaving in 1948, he had a long and successful career. He wrote the tune 'Shenandoah Waltz', which was a hit for Clyde Moody, and appeared on the western swing classic, Bob Wills's 'Maiden's Prayer'. In 1956 he recorded 'Foggy Mountain Breakdown' with Flatt & Scruggs (even if you've never heard of bluegrass, you still know 'Foggy Mountain Breakdown'). He worked for many years with the 'Singing Ranger', Hank Snow, and appeared on the best selling live Merle Haggard album *The Fightin' Side Of Me*. Throughout his life 'Orange Blossom Special', which he claimed to have co-written, was his trademark piece.

Benny Martin

Nicknamed 'The Big Tiger' by his friend Hank Williams because of his size and ebullient personality, Martin joined Monroe in 1948. He was one of the first fiddlers to use sliding double-stops. He went on to work with Flatt & Scruggs. He remained popular due to his fine singing and extravagant showmanship; he had a trick double fiddle that he could flip on its back and still carry on playing. His 'country stomping' act was a successful opener for Elvis Presley at many shows in the 50s.

Bobby Hicks

From the 'Banjo State' of North Carolina, Hicks was with Bill Monroe from 1954-57. He was in the first of the 'triple fiddle' line-ups, though when Monroe realised that Hicks could play perfect double-stops, one of the other fiddlers was out on his ear! He returned to the band in the 80s, playing on the Grammy award-winning album *Southern Flavor*. In 2002 he was among the all-star cast of the *O Brother Where Art Thou?* tour, Down From The Mountain.

Kenny Baker

A sometime coal miner from east Kentucky, Baker was described by Bill Monroe as "the best fiddler in bluegrass". He was in the band, on and off, between 1957 and 1969, a longer tenure than any other player. He recorded classic fiddle tunes such as 'Jerusalem Ridge', 'Devil's Dream', and 'Salt Creek'. He was the son of an old-time fiddler, but grew up listening to Bob Wills, Stéphane Grappelli, and Glenn Miller. He had a sweet, full tone with a strong jazz influence. In 1969 he released an album, *Portrait Of A Bluegrass Fiddler*, on County Records. It was one of the first fiddle-led bluegrass albums, and proved highly influential in demonstrating "how it should be done". Bill Monroe had always dreamed of doing an album of the fiddle tunes he had learned from his uncle Pen, but felt he had to wait until the right fiddler came along; that man was Kenny Baker, and the album *Bill Monroe's Uncle Pen* was released in 1972.

Richard Greene

The first of Monroe's 'city fiddlers', Greene started out with a full classical training, moved into old-time, and then, on seeing Scotty Stoneman in LA, was turned on to bluegrass. He joined Monroe in 1966 at a time when his career was once more in the ascendant. In 1967, Greene moved on to form a pioneering bluegrass-country-rock band, Seatrain, in which he played electric violin. He played on some of the early 'newgrass' albums with David 'Dawg' Grisman, formed the Greene String Quartet and has done a mountain of session work. One of his most extravagant projects has been a concerto for violin and orchestra called *What If Mozart Had Played With Bill Monroe?* I'm not sure how you follow that.

Byron Berline

Brought up in the Texas contest fiddling tradition, Berline was a prodigy, entering his first contest at the age of five, and winning from the age of 10. He was greatly influenced by Benny Thomasson, pioneer and master of the contest style. He was turned on to bluegrass at university in Oklahoma, joining a local band called The Cleveland County Ramblers. In 1963 The Dillards played at his college, and he got to jamming with them afterwards. The band did not have a fiddler, and were knocked out by his playing; he was invited to LA the following year to record an album with them. The result was a groundbreaking fusion of his Texas fiddling with their bluegrass backing.

Around the same time, he both won Weiser (the nation's top fiddle contest) and appeared at the Newport Folk Festival. In 1967 he joined The Blue Grass Boys, bringing with him his full armoury of intricate double-stops, triplets, third-position fingering, jazzy phrasing, faultless tone and intonation. He was with the band only a short time, but was able to record two classics; 'Sally Goodin' and 'Gold Rush'. He was called up to the army, and on his return found his place filled by Kenny Baker. Undaunted, he set off to LA to become a session man, quickly landing a job with The Rolling Stones (he appeared on the classic 'Country Honk'). By 1971 he was playing with country-rock outfit The Flying Burrito Brothers; the band were loud and heavy, playing to huge audiences, but introduced a bluegrass segment to the middle of the gig, featuring Byron Berline playing 'Orange Blossom Special'.

The classic bluegrass line-up

Several fiddlers had already come and gone before Monroe put together the classic line-up that for many came to define bluegrass. In mid 1942, Monroe announced on his show that his latest fiddler, Howdy Forrester, was leaving to join the Navy. Hearing this, the young Florida fiddler Chubby Wise jumped on a train and was at the Opry the following Saturday, asking for an audition. Despite Wise's strong western swing influence, Monroe liked what he heard, and hired him on a trial basis. He brought a new smoothness and richness of tone to the band, used plenty of vibrato and was able to take hot, jazzy, improvised fiddle breaks. He was altogether a more modern-sounding player than many of his predecessors.

Around 1944, Monroe was joined by guitarist and singer Lester Flatt, from Sparta, Tennessee. He was a smooth, fluid guitarist and also a very fine singer with a voice that blended well with Monroe's. Flatt is credited with many lead vocals, to which Monroe would add a high tenor harmony. Also in 1944, Howard Watts (stage name Cedric Rainwater) joined as bass player; he added a four-beats-to-the-bar walking bass line to many of the medium and slower numbers.

In 1942, a fifth musician had been added to the band for the first time. Banjo player David Akeman, known as Stringbean, played clawhammer or frailing style as well as doing comedy, and added an extra 'down home' mountain touch to the band sound. When he left, in 1945, he was replaced by another banjo player, 21-year-old Earl Scruggs from North Carolina. Scruggs had perfected a North Carolina style of three-finger picking, which allowed him to combine a high-speed rolling rhythm with melody, producing one melody note out of every three. He could take breaks just like a fiddle player, and the Opry audience was astounded; Scruggs was an overnight sensation.

Here, finally, was the complete bluegrass sound. It drew on all the nostalgic elements of rural Appalachia: the hoedown fiddle and banjo; the gospel songs with rich harmonies and the 'high lonesome sound'; the country and string band sound from the guitar and mandolin; the strong modal and bluesy element to many of the songs. It featured soloists who could take breaks like a jazz or western swing band, and all this was underpinned by a driving bass rhythm. This was indeed a sound both ancient and very modern, and further commercial success was a foregone conclusion. Recordings of 'Mule Skinner Blues' and Monroe's composition 'Kentucky Waltz' were best sellers, and the band toured ever further afield, always to packed houses.

Sadly for Monroe, even this level of success was not enough to keep the band together. Within a short space of time, first Chubby Wise, then Flatt and Scruggs quit the band. Monroe bitterly resented their perceived lack of loyalty, and did his best to keep them out of the Opry. However, it was also the start of something more significant: the development of the musical style as an entity above and beyond the individual Monroe band. It was not yet being referred to as bluegrass, but it was already having a strong influence on other country musicians. The Stanley Brothers in particular began copying Monroe's sound. It was many years before Monroe could become reconciled to the fact that in copying his sound they were not so much stealing his ideas as honouring them. Through the 50s Monroe's own career, whilst never actually failing, was in decline. Rock'n'roll was on an unstoppable rise and popular taste, even in the rural south, was moving away from anything with hillbilly connotations.

The bluegrass revival

The end of the decade, however, saw the start of the 'folk revival' among students and the intelligentsia in New York and the northern cities. The revivalist movement had its roots in the left-leaning protest songs and union songs of the 1930s, centred around the singer Woody

Guthrie. Key figures on the intellectual side were the folksong collectors John Lomax and his son Alan, who both worked for the Archive of American Folk Song at the Library of Congress. Another father and son team was Charles Seeger, a Washington ethnomusicologist, and his son Pete, a revivalist banjo player and folksinger.

It's difficult to believe today, but to curious, music-loving urbanites like the Lomaxes and the Seegers, old-time music and bluegrass seemed exotic, distant, and semi-legendary. Mike Seeger, half-brother of Pete, was also learning banjo. In 1952 he was among the first to be exposed to bluegrass when he saw Flatt & Scruggs playing at a 'Country Music Park' (a type of open-air event that was becoming common and would be the prototype for the bluegrass festival). He described it as "Incredible! It was like a religious experience." Folk song collectors were already becoming familiar with the old-time fiddle and banjo playing of the Appalachians, but bluegrass, if they were aware of it at all, was seen as something modern and commercial. It took some time before they realised that this was a not only a direct descendant of traditional old-time, gospel, and blues music, but one which was no fossil, but was alive and kicking. Before long Mike Seeger had brought Scruggs-style picking to New York, where it was greedily devoured by an eager pack of 'citybillies' (a term coined by Charles Seeger).

By 1966, Bill Monroe, who had been slow to take part in the 'opening up' of bluegrass, had a band made up largely of energetic young northerners, including the singer Peter Rowan and the classically trained fiddler Richard Greene.

With this influx of new blood, the remainder of the 60s and 70s saw many changes in bluegrass. The seemingly unbreakable walls between country and rock, bluegrass and jazz, acoustic and electric, were crumbling. The Byrds, The Nitty Gritty Dirt Band, and The Flying Burrito Brothers were taking country-rock to large audiences, combining acoustic and electric instruments. Developments in pickup and amplification technology meant that it was now possible for fiddle, mandolin, or banjo players to stand in front of a drum-kit in front of thousands of baying fans, shake out the nits from their shoulder-length hair, and rock out with the best of them. Grateful Dead rock god Jerry Garcia went the other way; he could do a fine turn on the bluegrass banjo, and teamed up with mandolinist David Grisman, ex-Monroe singer/guitarist Peter Rowan, bassist John Kahn, and fiddler Vassar Clements to form Old And In The Way. This was hippy bluegrass at its best. Although short-lived, the band did a number of live recordings at West Coast gigs in the mid 70s. To my ears Vassar's fiddling in this band was as good as it gets, period.

It was in the late 70s when someone played me a copy of *Old And In The Way*, the band's album. I had been making my stumbling way as a jazz and rock fiddle player, and was only vaguely aware of the existence of bluegrass. From the very first notes I heard of Vassar Clements on this album, it was like Moses had come down from the mountain, bearing tablets of stone. Never mind the ten commandments, what I saw carved in stone was THOU SHALT LEARN THESE LICKS! Along with practically every other fiddle player who heard the album, I was in thrall to Vassar from then on, slavishly copying his every phrase. His style, unlike that of many of this predecessors in bluegrass, was not rooted in old-time fiddle music but in jazz; his playing soared and swooped like a bird of prey, aggressive, startling, effortless. He brought a unique blues element to what he played; not just playing flattened thirds, but flattened fifths and sevenths too, turning the chords inside out with consummate ease. Yet he was no musical intellectual; he did not read a note of music, and understood no theory. All of his bizarre chromatic twists and turns, his outlandish notes from Beyond The Chord were all instinctive, coming straight from the heart rather than from a calculating mind. He could shift position anywhere on the neck of the fiddle without batting an eyelid – indeed, when he played his eyes were closed, his calm square face like a granite-hewn socialist-realist statue – yet he was entirely self taught. This was The Man!

Vassar Clements

Vassar was born in 1928 in Kinards, South Carolina, but lived most of his life in Kissimmee, Florida. At the age of seven he was teaching himself guitar and fiddle. When Blue Grass Boy and family friend Chubby Wise called round at the house one day, he invited the young Vassar to jam with him, and a new world opened up: "I had been listening to those people (The Blue Grass Boys) for years on our old battery-powered radio, and I idolised them. Let me tell you, that was quite an experience for a young man."

Five years later he was invited to audition for Bill Monroe. Despite the fact that he had been mostly listening to jazz – Tommy Dorsey, Joe Venuti, and Stéphane Grappelli – Vassar had learned Chubby Wise's parts note for note, and landed the job, at the age of just 14. His early work in bluegrass was very much in the standard mould, but as his playing and confidence developed he began to push the boundaries and developed a unique and highly distinctive style. He was with Monroe on and off until 1956, when he went to work with Jim and Jesse McReynolds. The next decade or so was a grim time, when drink got the better of him, and he found himself surviving on blue-collar jobs. By 1967 he was back on form and moved to Nashville where he started getting session work. His big break came in 1972 when he was invited by The Nitty Gritty Dirt Band to play on their legendary album *Will The Circle Be Unbroken*. This was a symbolic moment in musical history, a joining of the circle between the new generation of commercial/country/rock/hippie musicians, and the 'old guard' of revered/legendary/bluegrass/uncommercial players such as Earl Scruggs, Doc Watson, Mother Maybelle Carter, and so on. The album was an instant classic, and Vassar got more than his share of the limelight, with demon versions of his trademark composition 'Lonesome Fiddle Blues' and the failsafe crowd-pleaser 'Orange Blossom Special'.

From this point on all doors were open, and work poured in, with sessions for The Grateful Dead, Paul McCartney, Linda Ronstadt, B.B. King, The Monkees, The Allman Brothers – more than 1,000 albums in all. Then came Old And In The Way. Playing a mixture of traditional bluegrass, rock covers ('Wild Horses'), and thinly disguised anthems to drug culture ('Panama Red'), this was the perfect band for a student audience. The live album released in 1975, *Old And In The Way*, was the best selling bluegrass album for decades, and secured immortality for Vassar. From here on he could do no wrong, and to his growing mountain of album credits he added a long string of solo albums, focusing on his own brand of 'hillbilly jazz'.

For many years he played a distinctive, ornate, and slightly mysterious instrument given to him by his longtime friend John Hartford. In place of the scroll is a carved, bearded head, and on the back is a beautiful painting of Sappho holding a lute. Around the side are letters that no one has been able to translate. The fiddle may once have belonged to a Russian prince, and may be the work of Gaspar Duiffoprugcar from the 16th century. If you take a look at the Vassar Clements official website you'll see the carved head of his fiddle; since his death in 2005, tears have dripped slowly from the eyes.

Bluegrass fiddle today
Since the 70s, there has emerged a new breed of highly talented genre-bending musicians who had grown up listening to bluegrass alongside jazz and rock. David Grisman pioneered his 'Dawg' music, and

ORANGE BLOSSOM SPECIAL

At a fiddle contest in Athens, Alabama in 1972, there was consternation backstage when a notice appeared over the fire alarm: "In case of Orange Blossom Special, break glass!" This is a tune so hot that it's become the stuff of myth and legend.

As a bluegrass fiddle player, the tune 'Lonesome Fiddle Blues' might be your right hook, 'Old Joe Clark' your trusty left jab; but when it comes to slaying your audience, 'Orange Blossom Special' is your knockout punch. The crowd goes wild, ding ding, match over.

There's nothing faster, flashier, and more action-packed, so every hour you spend honing those licks and sharpening that shuffle is time well spent, not to mention money in the bank. You kick off with some train noises: sliding double-stops make that lonesome whistle blow, sideways chops with the bow get those shiny wheels turning, and a bit of left-hand pizzicato rings the warning bell. The band comes chugging in behind you. You'd better hope they don't start too fast, because it's only going to get faster. You shoot off a string of repeating licks over the endless E chord, cue the band with a descending scale and bang, you're into the double shuffle, the syncopated 'hokum bowing' pattern that's so incandescent it's outlawed from every fiddle contest in the nation. The crowd are already going crazy; the guitarist, who normally speeds up on every number, is already begging you to slow down. Instead you shovel on more coal and it's back to the E chord mayhem. By now your fingers are a blur, you're crazed with power, quoting recklessly from the theme from *Dragnet*,

'Sweet Georgia Brown', the theme from *The Simpsons*, anything that comes into your head. You go skidding into the descending lick and it's the home straight.

Warp speed, sweat dripping, bow hairs flying and you pull into the station with a crashing climax and a squeal of brakes. The crowd acknowledge your divinity, the rest of the band bask briefly in your reflected glory. Five minutes later the adrenaline has stopped pumping, you're alone at the bar and it's all forgotten. "Welcome", as Stacy Phillips puts it in his book *Hot Licks For Bluegrass Fiddle*, "to the manic-depressive world of bluegrass fiddling."

This explosive piece of weaponry has been in circulation since 1938, when it was written by Florida fiddler Ervin T. Rouse. He named it at the time of the inauguration of the new Orange Blossom Special, a gleaming diesel-electric icon of progress, a confidant future, and the New Deal; a high-speed, fully air conditioned train that would run the thousand-plus miles from New York to Miami in the 'Orange Blossom State' of Florida. What better subject, then, for a train song?

The Special marked a turning point in the economic and social history of the South-East, but never mind locomotive history, the tune made bluegrass history. Ervin T. Rouse was a 'trick fiddler' who did a hillbilly vaudeville routine with his brother Gordon. "He could play the damn fiddle better between his legs and behind his back than most fiddlers could under their chin," according to fellow musician Gene Christian. His song had a double-shuffle instrumental break, a hot property that was soon taken up by every fiddler who heard it and a

guitarist Tony Rice his 'Spacegrass'; both were labels attached to a new style of music that had bluegrass instrumentation and many elements of bluegrass style, but was largely instrumental, and incorporated many jazz chords and extravagant extended solos. Bill Keith had revolutionised banjo playing in the 60s with his new 'melodic style' of playing, but Béla Fleck took it to a whole new level again. The dobro was taken to new heights by Jerry Douglas, and even the double-bass had its superman in the form of Edgar Meyer. On labels such as perfect showcase for a flashy fiddler like Rouse.

They say, "Where there's a hit, there's a writ" and this was no exception. Chubby Wise, Bill Monroe's fiddler in the golden years from 1946 to 1948, claimed throughout his life that he had a hand in writing it, and told a story that directly contradicted that of Rouse. According to Wise, he and Rouse, who were old friends, had met up at a gig in Jacksonville, Florida, and afterwards gone out on the town. They staggered into the station, where the train was being exhibited, and, having duly marvelled at it, Rouse said to his friend, "Chubby, let's write a fiddle tune and call it the Orange Blossom Special." Returning to Wise's home at three in the morning, "We got our fiddles out and wrote that melody in about 45 minutes, while my wife was cookin' breakfast." Rouse, excited by what they'd come up with, proposed that they immediately copyright it. Chubby, however, who had to get to work (as a cab driver), said "Ervin, I haven't got time to fool with a fiddle tune. … If you can do anything with it, buddy, it's all yours." "That was my first mistake," he later admitted. "About a $100,000 mistake!" Certainly the royalty cheques must have been eye-popping; the song has been covered by everyone from Bill Monroe to Charlie Daniels, Box Car Willie, Flatt & Scruggs, Alison Krauss, and The Nitty Gritty Dirt Band; one of the most famous versions was by Johnny Cash in 1965, with the great man playing the instrumental break on harmonica.

The story told by Ervin T. Rouse, much less often heard, is somewhat different. He had already written a tune called 'South Florida Blues', including the fiddle melody later incorporated into the Special. After viewing the train in Miami (not Jacksonville), Ervin's manager said to him "You know, that's going to to be another famous train like the Old '97; that is, if somebody does something about it." That very afternoon Ervin and his brother Gordon wrote some words for their old tune, which was copyrighted in its new name three days before the train began its exhibition tour.

This tale of two tales is told in glorious detail by Randy Noles in his book *Orange Blossom Boys: The Untold Story Of Ervin T. Rouse, Chubby Wise, And The World's Most Famous Fiddle Tune*. He concludes that, although neither of the two antagonists was a particularly reliable witness, most of the truth lay with Rouse. The latter's career went into decline, as did the man himself, troubled by alcohol and schizophrenia, and, despite the healthy flow of royalty cheques towards the end of his life, his story was seldom told or believed. Chubby Wise, on the other hand, stuck to his tale and capitalised on it through his long and relatively successful career. Certainly he was a great populariser of the tune. It became a centrepiece of the repertoire of Bill Monroe, Flatt & Scruggs, and just about every other bluegrass band and fiddler ever since. More often than not the words are left out: there's more than enough excitement in the instrumental section.

Since 1990 the train no longer runs, at least in any identifiable way, but as Rouse's manager predicted, thanks to the tune, the stainless steel marvel of 1939 is now surely immortal.

Rounder, Flying Fish, and Sugar Hill, these musicians collaborated in every possible combination to create an astounding array of bluegrass-infused textures and colours. Latin rhythms, jazz chords, and adventurous solos were all part of the mix. And into this melting pot went a new breed of fiddler. Richard Greene was among the first to bring a full classical training to the table. Vassar Clements created a whole new language of startling blues- and jazz-influenced licks that no one since has been able to avoid plundering. Mark O'Connor grew out of the Texas-swing contest fiddling style and, to the despair of hard-working fiddlers everywhere, has effortlessly mastered every fiddle style under the sun.

We can't close a chapter on bluegrass without mention of Alison Krauss. Despite women still being a bit of a rarity in the bluegrass world, this singer and fiddler from Champaign, Illinois, has dominated the commercial end of bluegrass for over a decade; every album of hers since 1995 has gone gold or platinum, and she stopped counting her Grammy awards at 20. With her band, Union Station, she has won virtually every country music award available, and she has collaborated with many artists outside of bluegrass and country, including Led Zeppelin singer Robert Plant.

Half a century after Bill Monroe assembled his childhood dreamscape of old-time fiddle tunes, gospel, and blues, bluegrass has moved from being one man's personal style, to a specialised but widespread genre of music, and finally to a whole post-modern spectrum of sounds and combinations. Is it bluegrass? Maybe not, but does it matter?

PLAYING BLUEGRASS FIDDLE

The first thing you need to know about playing in a bluegrass band is your place in the scheme of things. We all agree with Bill Monroe that the fiddle player is the Mr Big of the outfit, but don't forget that you're part of a well-oiled machine. Most bluegrass numbers are songs rather than instrumentals,

Alison Krauss

and apart possibly from an intro, an outro, and a very brief solo, your job is as backup. If you're looking for ten-minute solos, you might be lucky in the 'Spacegrass' or 'Dawg' division, but otherwise get yourself over to Jazz fiddle, Fusion Dept.

If you haven't already had a good look at the chapters on old-time and blues, do so now – they're both very relevant as the roots of bluegrass. We looked at the Nashville shuffle, Georgia bow, and open-string drones, all of which you're going to need, along with the major and minor blues scales.

OK, let's kick off with a kickoff. Although it didn't appear in much of Monroe's early work, this opening lick has become a staple of bluegrass fiddling, both for starting a number, and for launching into a solo.

EXAMPLE 8.1

CD 2 TRACK 1i

A few things to notice; it's a percussive little phrase, best played at the heel of the bow. Part of its function is to set the tempo, so don't get over-excited by your bluegrass debut and speed it up. A kick-off will usually have double stops or drones of one sort or another to set the old-timey feel right from the start.

Here's the same thing in the key of A. Notice the drone is now above instead of below the ascending scale:

EXAMPLE 8.2

CD 2 TRACK 1ii

There are endless minor variations. Here the scale is chromatic, the rhythm simpler, and no drone:

EXAMPLE 8.3

CD 2 TRACK 1iii

Notice the double-stop. This is an interval of a fourth played below the key note of G. This is a strident harmony which has bluegrass stamped all over it.

Here are a few choice phrases demonstrating this harmony in some other keys.

EXAMPLE 8.4

CD 2 TRACK 2i

EXAMPLE 8.5

CD 2 TRACK 2ii

EXAMPLE 8.6

CD 2 TRACK 2iii

EXAMPLE 8.7

CD 2 TRACK 2iv

Notice that for the last two examples it's easier to go into third position to get the double-stop. Using your third and fourth finger together for a double-stop is hard work!

We're going to come back to double-stops but first, one of the keys to successful bluegrass playing: blues scales.

EXAMPLE 8.8

CD 2 TRACK 3i

You can make good phrases with the pentatonic scale:

EXAMPLE 8.9

CD 2 TRACK 3ii

But much better if you add the flattened third, giving the major blues scale:

Here are a couple more bluesy riffs using the flattened third:

EXAMPLE 8.10

CD 2 TRACK 3iii

EXAMPLE 8.11

CD 2 TRACK 3iv

Note that when you're playing both the major and flattened third, you can either play them as separate notes, or slide one into the other. Eventually, it will become almost automatic to slide up to any major third:

EXAMPLE 8.12

CD 2 TRACK 4

Now let's try the flattened seventh:

EXAMPLE 8.13

CD 2 TRACK 5

The flattened seventh (in this case the G natural) is a powerful note, giving a modal sound. You can lean on it hard:

EXAMPLE 8.14

CD 2 TRACK 5ii

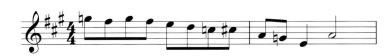

EXAMPLE 8.15

CD 2 TRACK 5iii

I could give you a scale to practise that includes both the major and flattened thirds and sevenths:

EXAMPLE 8.16

CD 2 TRACK 6i

But in fact this isn't particularly useful. Don't practise this scale! It demonstrates the available notes but doesn't give you access to useful phrases.

This scale, however, is dynamite. In my humble opinion it is the most important thing you will learn in this chapter:

EXAMPLE 8.17

CD 2 TRACK 6ii

This gives you the notes in an order that is useful; any set of adjacent notes from this scale will give you a usable lick.

Practise it with open string drones:

EXAMPLE 8.18

CD 2 TRACK 7i

Try taking it an octave down:

EXAMPLE 8.19

CD 2 TRACK 7ii

Now, using this same fingering, let's shift the pattern up to second position, key of F:

EXAMPLE 8.20

CD 2 TRACK 7iii

We're not using any open strings, but we can still play drones. This is a lot easier than it looks:

EXAMPLE 8.21

CD 2 TRACK 7iv

One of the great things about this scale is that it allows you to play drones even in the difficult keys. If you've ever tried playing a solo in any of the flat keys whilst staying in first position you'll know it can be hard. Getting that down-home country feel is just not possible without drones. Taking this 'closed' pattern and shifting out of first position solves the problem.

It also deals easily with the problem of the key of B, much beloved of the high and lonesome Mr Monroe:

EXAMPLE 8.22

CD 2 TRACK 7v

At this point you should realise that it's a whole lot easier to memorise the finger pattern than it is to read the dots. Practise that scale until it's second nature, and then practise it some more. Once you've mastered it, assuming you're also able to play accurately out of first position (and if you can't, this should give you good reason to learn), then you can play bluegrass in any key on God's green earth, to the amazement of all around you.

Now what happens if you put in the third blue note, a flattened fifth?

EXAMPLE 8.23

CD 2 TRACK 8i

This scale now has a flattened third, no major third, a flattened fifth and a perfect fifth, a flattened seventh and no major seventh. This is an A minor blues scale, but in a bluegrass context it can fit over an A major chord. It creates a lot of tension and excitement when you use this scale; it's one of the key elements of Vassar Clements' style. Because of the tension it creates, it's best to use it as a piquant sauce rather than the meat and potatoes; by moving subtly in an out of the minor scale, you'll have the audience following you like a bull with a ring on its nose.

EXAMPLE 8.24

CD 2 TRACK 8ii

Time to look at a real song. There's one piece of good news about bluegrass; you're not going to be kept up all night worrying about the chord sequence. This song, 'Roll In My Sweet Baby's Arms', has just three chords; the root (I), the fourth or subdominant (IV), and the fifth or dominant (V). This particular chord sequence is one you'll find in many other bluegrass standards: 'Kate Kline', 'Little Joe', 'My Dear Old Southern Home', 'New River Train', 'I'm Going', 'My Saviour's Train', 'The Saints Go Marchin' In', 'Will You Be Loving Another Man?', 'I'm Going Back To Old Kentucky', and 'It's Mighty Dark To Travel', to name but a few.

EXAMPLE 8.25

CD 2 TRACK 9

Here's the basic song:

Roll In My Sweet Baby's Arms

It's a 16-bar sequence, but be alert at the end of each section; the band will often add anything from half a bar to maybe two bars before starting the next verse. This curious practice stems from way bands used to play around a single microphone (and still sometimes do). Whoever is taking the lead steps up to the microphone, whilst the others step back. It's a beautifully co-ordinated ballet, though if you get it wrong you're liable to get decked by a banjo head in your chin. It also takes some extra time, hence the added beats or bars.

EXAMPLE 8.26

CD 2 TRACK 10

If you're playing the tune, you'll want to spice it up with some double stops, drones and shuffles:

It's then into a vocal or someone else's solo. Behind this you might play 'chops' – percussive two-note chords on the second and fourth beats of the bar. These are played very short and close to the heel of the bow. Your choice of notes will probably come from the root, third, and fifth of the chord. Here's where being familiar with the sequence starts to be important. (If you're a jazz player who's just come to this chapter after breezing through 'Giant Steps', I suggest you go and take a nap.)

OK, I got restless in bars four and eight.

An alternative strategy for backup is to play long notes, defining the chords with double-stops:

EXAMPLE 8.27

CD 2 TRACK 11

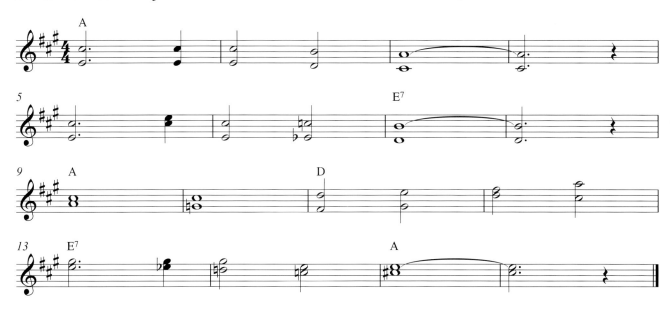

You can be as straightforward or adventurous as you like. In the first four bars I've slightly mimicked the melody. Bar six flags up the chord change, putting in a chromatic movement down to the two notes chosen for the E7 chord. Similarly in bar ten, a G-natural leads you down to the F-sharp note we're using for the D chord, and bars 13 and

EXAMPLE 8.28

CD 2 TRACK 12

14 lead you back down from E7 to A. Putting movement like this into your double-stop chord playing shows that you know where you are and you know where you're going.

EXAMPLE 8.29

CD 2 TRACK 13

The solo starts with a kick-off, and leads into a bit of the melody, before four bars of flattened third/flattened seventh runs. Bars eight and nine are a kind of yodel with a cutting rhythm. Bars ten and 11 go into a full minor blues run. Bars 13 and 14 both use double-stops which slide down a semitone and then back up. The last three bars bring us safely back home with a two-octave run down. This is a typical solo in that it is constructed mostly of licks – short phrases that can be learned and used as pre-formed building blocks. You can learn these licks from listening to other players, from books (Stacy Phillips's book, *Hot Licks For Bluegrass Fiddle*, is a goldmine), or even make up your own. The art, which takes some time to acquire, is to be able to transpose a lick automatically to any key, and to tailor its length and exact shape to fit the space required.

Finally, having given such a star billing to 'Orange Blossom Special', we've got to consider at least part of it. For reasons of National Security we can't bring you the whole tune, but here's a handy lonesome whistle:

EXAMPLE 8.30

CD 2 TRACK 14

And the indispensable double shuffle:

EXAMPLE 8.31

CD 2 TRACK 15i

This is a two bar pattern. Because the bow is rocking onto the upper string once in every three notes, the emphasis keeps changing, hence the sense of excitement. Once you've mastered the rhythm, you can be more adventurous with the upper string:

EXAMPLE 8.32

CD 2 TRACK 15ii

Or add double-stops:

EXAMPLE 8.33

CD 2 TRACK 15iii

With patience you'll be able to transpose this to other keys, and use it as a lick in your solos.

western swing fiddle

THE FIDDLE HANDBOOK

western swing fiddle

Of all the musical styles discussed in this book, surely none is more preposterous than western swing. The idea of combining old-time Texas fiddle music with a jazz horn section is plain crazy; when it was first described to me many years ago I though it was surely a joke. And as for the idea of a bandleader who rides on horseback up to the stage through an audience of thousands of dancers, wearing full cowboy regalia with gold and silver trim worth a considerable fortune … well, what can I say? He takes to the stage with his 20-piece band, picks up his Guadagnini violin, and when the music starts, proceeds to talk through half of the solos, warbling in an unearthly falsetto such comments as "Fiddle it up boy, fiddle it up!", "Aaaah haa!" and "Shoot low sheriff, he's riding a Shetland!" The bandleader could only be Bob Wills, and this could only be western swing. Even among musicians today this music is little known, let alone among the general public, yet there was a time and a place where this bizarre combination of musical styles grew completely naturally and became hugely popular. What's more, any fiddle player who comes into contact with western swing will have no choice but to acknowledge that there is no style in existence in which musicianship and pure fun are more equal partners.

It all began in Texas in the early years of the 20th century. Of all the states, this was the one with the most colourful history, the richest ethnic mix, and the strongest sense of individuality. Here were Mexicans with their mariachi trumpets and fiddles; black field workers with their country blues; Cajun fiddlers and accordionists; Germans, Poles, and Czechs with their polkas and waltzes; not to mention the Anglo-Americans with their old-time fiddle music.

The majority of the population were poor, hard-working rural folk, scraping a living on cattle ranches and cotton farms. There was a great deal of music around, but most of it was amateur or semi-professional. People loved to dance; German settlers had established a series of dance societies with large, purpose-built halls, later referred to simply as 'German clubs'. In west Texas, dances were held in the barns of large ranches, sometimes associated with rodeos. With the repeal of the prohibition law in 1933, honky-tonks sprang up across the state, often on county boundaries, since each individual county could choose whether to accept the return of alcohol. People would therefore drive from a dry county over the line to a wet one. Along with the much-needed beverage there would be a jukebox or, on a Saturday night, a local band playing. This, then, was the cradle of western swing.

Bob Wills

Bob Wills was born in 1905 in Limestone County, Texas, into a family of fiddlers; his father (John Wills) and both grandfathers played, and

Bob Wills

young Jim Rob, as he was known, was soon playing mandolin in the family band, travelling around the county to play at ranch dances. In 1913 the family moved the 500 miles to the town of Turkey in west Texas. They travelled by wagon, picking cotton and playing for dances along the route to pay their way. They played a repertoire of typical frontier fiddle music: 'Sally Goodin', 'Billy In The Lowground', 'Eighth Of January', and so on. At their new rented farm they lived the real western cowboy lifestyle, riding everything from bulls to wild mules, roping steers and attending rodeos. Jim Rob soon began playing fiddle (known in the 19th century as "the royal instrument of the frontier"), and quickly picked up a few tunes. One night he had been sent ahead to a dance with the instruments and his father, the bandleader and fiddler, failed to show. The 10-year old Jim Rob had no choice but to take the fiddle himself and play the same six tunes till two in the morning.

Texas had a long-established tradition of fiddle contests, and soon father and son were both competing; they usually both made the finals. Top of the tree and their chief rival at that time was Eck Robertson. One night at a big contest in Munday, west Texas, John and Eck were up against one another for a mouth-watering cash prize, worth two month's wages. Robertson led off with a barnstorming version of 'Beaumont Rag'. John Wills followed him with 'Gone Indian', and halfway through broke into a piercing and seemingly endless holler, harmonizing with the tune, driving the crowd into a frenzy, and winning him the contest. Afterwards, when the defeated Robertson was asked "Eck, did John out-fiddle you?", he replied "Hell, no! He didn't out-fiddle me. That damned old man Wills out-hollered me!"

The 'folk holler' frequently used by his father and other frontier fiddlers was to become a Bob Wills trademark. In addition to this, the young Wills spent a great deal of time listening to the black musicians who frequented the cotton farms, and as well as the bluesy fiddle style, he particularly liked the witty, free-and-easy banter they would use throughout a song. This again was something he made great use of later on.

At around the age of 17, tired of the daily grind on the farm, Bob Wills left home and spent several years sampling the delights of drinking, gambling, and brawling, before marrying in 1926 and making an attempt to settle down. He trained as a barber (a popular fall-back career for musicians at that time), and spent some time hairdressing in New Mexico, where he formed a band, mostly with Mexican musicians. It was here that he wrote 'The Spanish Two Step', which he would later rewrite as 'San Antonio Rose'. By 1929 he was back with his family playing regular Saturday night dances. One night he decided to organise and promote his own dance, and netted $190, more than he'd ever made in his life. This more than anything persuaded him to make a serious go at being a full-time musician. He had two attempts at playing with a minstrel show, playing fiddle and doing blackface comedy; with one of these, Doc's Medicine Show, he did a successful audition for a large Fort Worth radio station called WBAP. It was whilst doing this show that he met guitarist Herman Arnspiger, with whom he began working closely. With their combination of humour, showmanship, and lively dance tunes they soon gained widespread popularity, using radio performances to promote their dance shows, at which they were billed as the Bob Wills Fiddle Band. In 1930 they were joined by the singer Milton Brown and his brother, guitarist Durwood Brown, and soon after by New Orleans-style banjo player Frank Barnes.

They were by now playing for a more urban and sophisticated audience, and it was a natural progression for them to expand their repertoire from the old-time country fiddle music they had grown up with to include the swinging jazz that was increasingly dominating the airwaves. Fiddle music was popular for dances in Texas, but Dixieland was seen as music for the whole nation. By the end of 1930 the band had sponsorship for their WBAP show from the Aladdin Lamp Company, appearing as the Aladdin Laddies. With the five-piece line-up it was now possible to incorporate jazz solos from the guitar and banjo. Wills would never have the technique to play hot jazz solos on the fiddle, but this was clearly something he had in his sights for the future. The band also incorporated a lot of blues numbers (at the time referred to as 'race music'), including such well known numbers as 'St. Louis Blues', 'Basin Street Blues' and 'Jelly Roll Blues'.

Whilst this wide range of dance music was very popular with the fans, it gave a bit of a headache to promoters and record companies who had to describe the style; it was referred to variously as 'old-time music', 'hot string band', and 'novelty hot dance'. The term 'western swing' still lay some time in the future, but Wills had already established the idea of taking a core repertoire of 'western' music, and a core band of 'western' string instruments, and applying to them the jazz formula of swing rhythm and hot, improvised solos. It gave audiences a unique combination of the reassurance and comfort of 'traditional' American music, with the cosmopolitan pizzazz of modern jazz; and indeed the same thing was happening in other musical genres such as Cajun and klezmer. For the jazz musicians hired by Wills, particularly when he began expanding his band further, it also gave them a unique freedom. Having no formal training, and not being a jazz player himself, Wills was happy to allow his soloists to play whatever they wanted. There was a huge amount of fun involved in a Bob Wills performance, with schoolboy pranks happening both on and off-stage. And the music was always happy; in the words of Wills's younger brother Billy Jack, "Bob could play 'A Letter Edged In Black' and it would sound happy."

Light Crust Doughboys and Musical Brownies

In 1931 the Aladdin Laddies were taken on for a radio show by KFJZ, with sponsorship from the Burrus Mill And Elevator Company. The product they were advertising was Light Crust Flour, and during one show, Wills referred to the band flippantly as The Light Crust Doughboys, a name which stuck. The sales manager of the flour company was Wilbert 'Pappy' O'Daniel , a larger than life character who was to become something of a star in his own name, as songwriter, state governor, and senator. There is even a character called Pappy O'Daniel in *O Brother Where Art Thou?* At first O'Daniel was outraged when he heard the band, and cancelled their sponsorship. Wills appealed to him in person and eventually talked him round. O'Daniel was soon to become their greatest fan, appearing on their show himself, doing announcements and even writing songs for them. He began to think of the Light Crust Doughboys as his own personal band, and an outlet for his boundless ego and ambition. He raised their pay to $25 a week, and built them a studio in which they could rehearse eight hours a day.

However, like a jealous lover, he began to resent their dance work, which was independent of the radio show and his sponsorship, and insisted that they give it up. This created a crisis for the band. Bob Wills valued the security given by sponsorship from the mill, but the singer Milton Brown, who had become a crucial part of the band's sound, quit in protest. He took with him his brother Durwood (the guitarist), and they formed a rival band, Milton Brown & His Musical Brownies. Brown also hired Jesse Ashlock, a young swing fiddler who had been something of a Wills protégé, along with the banjo player Ocie Stockard and pianist Fred Calhoun.

There had always been some rivalry between Brown and Wills and, whilst they remained friends, the rivalry increased once they were in separate bands. Brown proved to be an able and innovative bandleader, and was responsible for introducing several of the features which were to become key to western swing. As well as being the first to use piano with a string band, he also added harmonised twin fiddles, bringing in the classically trained Cecil Brower to play with Jesse Ashlock. Perhaps most adventurous of all, in 1934 he brought in Bob Dunn on electrified steel guitar. This rather bizarre horizontal guitar, evolved from the lap guitar, had previously been used as a novelty instrument, mainly to play Hawaiian music. Brown saw the potential of using the steel guitar to imitate the riffs of a horn section, to harmonise with other melody instruments, and to take punchy and startling solos. With all these innovations, plus the freedom to play freely around the country, The Musical Brownies soon overtook The Light Crust Doughboys in popularity. Many see them as the first true western swing band, and had it not been for Milton Brown's untimely death in a car accident in 1936, it is arguable that it would be he, and not Bob Wills, who would today be seen as the icon of western swing.

Meanwhile, back at the Burrus Flour Mill, all was not well between Bob Wills and Pappy O'Daniel. After the loss of Brown, Bob Wills auditioned 67 singers before choosing Tommy Duncan. The broadcasts for O'Daniel continued, and the band, unbeknown to O'Daniel, continued playing dances outside Fort Worth, but Wills deeply resented the loss of income because he could not perform live in his local area. He was also drinking heavily, and after missing several broadcasts was fired (again) by O'Daniel. Duncan, along with guitarist/bass player Kermit Whalin, left with Wills, whilst Wills's original guitarist Herman Arnspiger and banjo player Sleepy Johnson stayed on as the Light Crust Doughboys, a band which, amazingly, is still operating today. If Bob Wills thought he was finally free of the heavy hand of O'Daniel he was sadly disappointed. Billing themselves as "Bob Wills & The Playboys, formerly The Light Crust Doughboys", the band were handed a $10,000 lawsuit by O'Daniel for misuse of his company name. O'Daniel lost both the suit and two appeals, but was still not satisfied, and with heavy-handed tactics persuaded several radio stations that it wasn't in their best interest to hire what was now

Bob Wills & His Texas Playboys. The band moved to Oklahoma City, and then to Tulsa, where in 1934 they began broadcasting on KVOO, eventually agreeing a very lucrative deal whereby, instead of working for a sponsor, they paid for the show themselves, but also marketed directly their own Play Boy flour. To their normal round of recordings and dances was now added a circuit of bakers' conventions and flour promotions.

'San Antonio Rose'

With freedom and financial security, Bob Wills was finally able to expand and develop the band. Perhaps inspired by Milton Brown, he hired Leon McAuliffe on pedal steel and Alton Stricklin on jazz piano, and he also lured back fiddler Jesse Ashlock. He then went an important step further than Brown, adding drums and a horn section. For dyed-in the wool country traditionalists this was a step too far. When some years later he arrived for the first time at the Grand Ole Opry, he was told, in no uncertain terms, "there will be no drums nor horns", at which Bob turned and said to the boys, "Pack up, we're going home." Fortunately the Opry was finally persuaded. So too was Art Satherley, a producer for Brunswick Records, who, in 1935, was shocked by the appearance of horns at what he thought was going to be a string band session, not to mention Wills's unnerving habit of talking over the music. The drums and horns were a groundbreaking concept at the time, but the logic behind it was simple. The big name acts across America in the mid 30s were the likes of Louis Armstrong, Bix Beiderbecke, and Fats Waller. They were smooth, modern, had big bands and horn sections. Bob Wills, with his down-home Texas background, had something of a chip on his shoulder, but felt that he could be as good as they were. By 1936 he had proved it by outselling all of them. In the years leading up to World War II the band continued to grow in every sense. They played to houses of over 1,000 every night. They had a vast repertoire, said to be over 3,000 numbers, ranging from fiddle breakdowns to blues, jazz, and pop. They could field up to 20 musicians, and Wills paid better than any of the other bandleaders. They also had a major hit in the form of 'San Antonio Rose'. This was a re-write of an early Wills instrumental composition, 'The Spanish Two-Step'. It was recorded again as 'San Antonio Rose' in 1938 and then with lyrics, in 1940, as 'New San Antonio Rose'. This became a gold record, and was the song which, in Bob Wills's own words, took him "from hamburgers to steaks". A year later Wills got onions and relish on his steak when Bing Crosby recorded the song, selling 1,500,000 copies.

Wills had achieved his chief goal of proving himself the equal of any other bandleader, but for the public, his unique selling point, which he was himself sometimes reluctant to acknowledge, remained his cowboy background. In 1941 he appeared with some of his band in the first of a long series of Western movies; mostly 'eight day wonders' (shot in Hollywood in no more than eight days filming), with titles like *The Last Horseman*, *Saddles And Sagebrush*, and *A Tornado In The Saddle*. He and the band relocated to California and revelled in the glitzy Hollywood version of the western lifestyle. The whole band bought horses, and Wills himself went in for some conspicuous consumption, buying himself a $4,300 cowboy outfit, a $3,500 saddle, and even a pair of $250 gold and silver spurs. He could clearly afford it; his earnings for 1945 were $340,000. He was always paid cash for his dances (by now attracting up to 4,000 paying customers per night), and would carry the money around in suitcases.

1944 was the year when Bob Wills fielded his largest band – 22 musicians and two singers – but in the post-war years good musicians were much harder to find and public demand for the big band sound started to diminish. He began to concentrate more on the string-band side of his operation. There had been numerous occasions when he had arrived at a gig with his big band and not even taken out his fiddle, only to be told, "If we had wanted Tommy Dorsey we would have hired him. But we hired Bob Wills. So get your fiddle, Bob!"

Despite a general decline in both swing and western music, in the face of rock'n'roll, and a decline in attendance at dances, due to the growth of cinema and television, Bob Wills remained popular and was still touring successfully up until 1969. Ill health and a series of heart attacks finally caught up with him, and he died in 1975. The plaque on his grave bears a line from his most famous song: "Deep within my heart lies a melody."

West Coast western swing

You would be forgiven for thinking that western swing as a genre was basically a one-man show, but in fact there were many other similar bands, not only imitating but also innovating. Although Bob Wills spent some years in California, his was basically a Texas band, but there was a whole separate offshoot of western swing thriving on the West Coast. Chief among the bandleaders in California was the colourful and controversial character Spade Cooley. Born in 1910, Donell Clyde Cooley was a quarter Cherokee, and went to an Indian school, where he received some classical musical training and acquired the nickname "Spade" due to his adept poker playing.

His first band, formed in 1942, mirrored the line up of Milton Brown's Musical Brownies; led by himself on fiddle, he also had vocals

Spade Cooley

(from Tex Williams), bass, guitar, steel, and piano. In 1943 he signed a recording contract with Columbia, and had a hit with the song 'Shame, Shame On You', which topped the country charts for two months. He added to his band, bringing in Andrew 'Cactus' Soldi and Rex Call on fiddles, a horn section, and, most unusually, accordion and harp. The sight of a harpist wearing a cowboy hat has to be one of the seven musical wonders of the world. The sound he created with this band was distinctly different from that of the Texas Playboys. He created complex, tight arrangements that were much smoother and more sophisticated than the Bob Wills sound. With his training he had a better understanding of musical theory, and could handle his horn section more competently. He had a disciplined and businesslike managerial style, but on stage had a relaxed and amiable persona. Whilst he never achieved fame in the East, he had a very successful and long running Saturday night TV show in California. It was for him that promoter Forman Phillips invented the term western swing in 1942, subsequently billing him as 'The King Of Western Swing'. His good looks got him a job as stand in for film cowboy star Roy Rogers, and he also appeared in films in his own right.

A wonderful nine-minute Warner Brothers movie short, currently to be found on YouTube, is as good an introduction as you will ever get to the humorous, wacky, cowboy-kitsch aspects of western swing. The text of the opening scene is also the height of irony. Narrated over scenes of bar room brawls, frontier shootouts, and lynchings, we hear:

"Back in the past and thrill-packed days of a roaring West, the old frontier, loud with life and sudden death. Overrun with warring redskins and ravaging whites, where it was the fate of many a brave man to feel the sting of hot lead or to swing at the end of a rope. Ah, but how times have changed! Today, the sons of the old West are still killers, but of another variety. They are killing them with hot music, and swinging them with swaying strains of rock solid rhythm."

Funny, yes, corny, undoubtedly. But ironic? It is when you discover that in April 1961 Spade Cooley beat his wife Ella Mae to death with his bare hands, suspecting her of having an affair with Roy Rogers. He served eight years of his sentence; on temporary release in 1969 he told a friend, optimistically, "Today is the first day of the rest of my life." He died of a heart attack that night.

Another successful West Coast bandleader was the singer Tex Williams. He had been with Spade Cooley's band until 1943, when he was offered a recording contract of his own by Capitol Records. Cooley was furious, and fired him. Aware that the same fate awaited any musician who displeased Cooley in any way, 11 of the 13 members of the band left along with him, setting up Tex Williams & The Western

Caravan, featuring the triple fiddles of Cactus Soldi, Gibby Gibson and Rex Call. Typical of the West Coast branch of western swing, they made a smooth, polished sound, less folksy than that of the Texas Playboys and similar groups.

The band had a big hit in 1946 with a recording of the Merle Travis song 'Smoke, Smoke, Smoke That Cigarette', which sold over a million copies, and put the band in the same league as Bob Wills and Spade Cooley. They continued until 1957, when, in the face of the popularity of rock'n'roll, the whole genre of western swing went into terminal decline.

From the mid 50s to the mid 70s there was little interest in western swing, and certainly the size of bands seen in the 30s and 40s was a commercial impossibility. People would no longer turn out in their thousands to pack the large dancehalls, and nostalgia for the old frontier spirit was brushed aside by the modern media of film and television. Nevertheless, western swing continued to make its mark within the realm of commercial country music, now largely centred in Nashville. Artists such as Willie Nelson, Waylon Jennings, George Strait, Charlie Daniels, and Merle Haggard have all included either some of the feel or some of the material of western swing within their repertoire, while studio session musicians like fiddler Johnny Gimble could always be called on to add some sparkle and shine to what were often otherwise bland country numbers.

Johnny Gimble

Cowboys on acid

As with virtually all the musical styles that were shelved during the rock'n'roll boom, the mid 70s saw a revival of interest in western swing. Whereas previously the musicians had been mostly from a rural, south-western background, the new breed of western swingers were mostly northern college kids to whom a cowboy hat was a cool piece of kit, and a haircut more of a theory than a reality. Commander Cody & The Lost Planet Airmen were a country-rock band formed in 1967, the Summer of Love. Their description of their early years ("We jammed, hung out, got high, and generally lived the life") suggests an approach not entirely in keeping with the cotton-pickin', ranch dancin', and rodeo ridin' on which Bob Wills was raised. Nevertheless they soon began including western swing along with honky-tonk and boogie into their set, aided by the dynamite fiddling of Andy Stein. At their first introduction to the 'real world' of country & western music, at a 1973 convention in Nashville, they recall that they were booed off stage with suggestions such as "Get a haircut!" and "Find a rock concert!"

Coming at it from a similar angle, and with a more direct take on western swing are Asleep At The Wheel. Formed in 1970 by singer Ray Benson, they have worked solidly ever since, chalking up nine Grammies over the years, along with the accolade (and I'm sure this would flatter them no end) of being the band in all the world that I would most like to play with. Dream on … They have used numerous fiddle players, but Jason Roberts has been their most regular fiddler and is still with the band. Among their most spectacular achievements has been the 1999 album *Ride With Bob*, a tribute to Bob Wills with a stellar cast of guest singers and musicians, including Willie Nelson, Merle Haggard, Lyle Lovett, Shawn Colvin, Dwight Yoakam, and The Dixie Chicks, not to mention Johnny Gimble on fiddle. Besides demonstrating the affection for Bob Wills within the country music establishment, the album also shows to great effect what old-fashioned western swing sounds like with modern production values and faultless accuracy of musicianship, which was not always a feature of the original sound. This is a band that swings like crazy.

A Who's Who of western swing fiddle players
Bob Wills

Bob Wills himself was as an old-fashioned 'breakdown' fiddler. When there was an old-time fiddle tune it would usually be led by Bob Wills on the fiddle. He played with little swing and did no jazz improvising, though he had a slightly bluesy edge to his playing. Despite the title given to him by Merle Haggard, "The best damn fiddle player in the world", on his 1970 tribute album, Wills was never even the best fiddle player in his band (unless he was the only one!) but his fiddling was nevertheless always very popular.

Jesse Ashlock

Jesse Ashlock was the first and longest-standing of Wills's fiddle players, and the first to do 'take off' solos. He had a considerable armoury of techniques, including the double shuffle, triplets, parallel fifths and lots of syncopation. He would sometimes go into third position, but not always with perfect intonation. Ashlock said of his playing, "I try to do the same thing on fiddle that jazzmen do on a trumpet." He initially learned fiddle as a teenager, sitting in behind Bob Wills. His idol, apart from Wills himself, was Joe Venuti. He was hired by Milton Brown in 1932 when he left to form The Musical Brownies, but joined The Texas Playboys after Brown's death.

Cecil Brower

Cecil Brower was a classically trained violinist. He never played country fiddle, but fully mastered the jazz idiom. He joined the Musical Brownies in 1933, forming the first harmonizing twin fiddle partnership in western swing, with either Jesse Ashlock or Cliff Bruner.

Joe Holley

Joe Holley was a hot and often frenetic jazz fiddler, much influenced by jazz player Stuff Smith, who did his first recordings with the Texas Playboys in 1942. Being left-handed, he always added an elegant symmetry to band photos when sharing a mike with Wills. He was one of the musicians who left the band with Tommy Duncan in 1948.

Louis Tierney

Louis Tierney was a great swing jazz player, smoother and more accurate than Jesse Ashlock; he was with the Texas Playboys from 1940 to 1947.

Cliff Bruner

Cliff Bruner was one of the few notable Texas swing fiddle players who did not play with Bob Wills. His first musical employment was with medicine shows. He joined Milton Brown in 1934, recording 48 sides with him. Following Brown's death he formed his own band, The Texas Wanderers, playing twin fiddles with J. R. Chatwell, (described by Johnny Gimble as a "gutbucket violinist"). He also worked with Texas Governor Pappy O'Daniel's band, The Hillbilly Boys, and Louisiana Governor Jimmie Davis.

Johnny Gimble

Johnny Gimble is considered by many to be the finest and most influential western swing fiddler of modern times. Born in 1926 in east Texas, he learned mostly by listening to the radio, for example to the Light Crust Doughboys' show. He was particularly influenced by Cliff Bruner's version of 'Draggin' The Bow'. He joined Jimmie Davis's campaign band in Louisiana, and during the war found himself in Vienna, Austria, where he developed an abiding love for the waltz. From 1949 he played for Bob Wills for two years. Then, in the early 50s, he began doing studio session work, mostly for Columbia producer Don Law; he also did regular TV work, hosting his own show in Dallas for three years. Though a western swing player at heart, most of his work was in commercial country music; in Nashville in the 60s and 70s he was the first-call player, recording with, among others, Willie Nelson, Merle Haggard, Charlie Pride, Dolly Parton, Loretta Lynn, Tammy Wynette, Chet Atkins, and George Strait. His playing is distinctive in its extreme smoothness and accuracy. He specialises in

PLAYING WITH BOB WILLS

As a fiddle player in the Texas Playboys, there were three jobs to cover:

1. Playing breakdowns – solo fiddle melodies. This job was usually taken by Bob Wills himself.

2. Playing twin fiddles or up to four-part arrangements with other fiddlers. These would be written, or at least organised arrangements.

3 Playing jazz solos.

The jazz solos were the most important and demanding part of the job. Some of the solos would be played behind a sung verse or chorus, in which case they would be partially 'off-mic'. Others would be breaks where the fiddle solo was the main focus. The order of soloing within a piece was never pre-planned, so that every soloist had to watch Wills like a hawk; he would turn round at a second's notice and point his bow at any member of the band. If you missed the signal, your job was on the line. Unlike in modern jazz, there was no such thing as an extended solo; one verse or chorus was all you got, and it had to be good. Every solo was expected to be fresh, new, and exciting. A story is told that a steel player, new to the band, missed his first solo cue because he was fiddling with his faulty amp. Wills warned him afterwards that he always had to be ready, and able to produce something "new and spectacular" at every solo. At the next show, as bad luck would have it, his amp failed again at the crucial moment. In desperation or frustration he kicked his instrument off the bandstand, demanding, "There, was that spectacular enough for you, Mr Wills?"

complex double-stop patterns, as exemplified in his compositions such as 'Gardenia Waltz' and 'Fiddlin' Around', both of which have become challenging contest standards. From the 70s onwards he has emerged from the anonymity of session work and is recognised as a performer and artist in his own right, picking up numerous awards and Grammy nominations.

PLAYING WESTERN SWING FIDDLE

At its most basic level, western swing involves playing standard 'old time' fiddle tunes, but with a degree of swing and syncopation. All the quavers are made into long-short pairs, and some notes are tied over the barline. Bob Wills recorded this tune, 'Liberty', in 1942. He used twin fiddles in harmony, but here we just add a few open string drones for that down-home feel.

EXAMPLE 9.1

CD 2 TRACK 16

Liberty

These techniques can be applied to any old-time tune.

Along with breakdown and blues numbers, rags are common in western swing. Over the page is a version of 'Beaumont Rag', based in part on the Bob Wills's 1938 recording.

On his fiddle break, Jesse Ashlock introduced the double shuffle into the B part on bars 17-24 (check back to the bluegrass chapter if you missed out on this); this shuffle has subsequently become standard in most versions of the tune.

EXAMPLE 9.2

CD 2 TRACK 17

Beaumont Rag

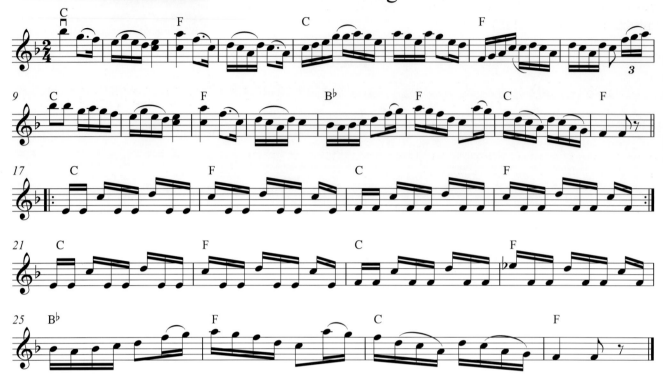

He also played this phrase when he got to bar 25:

EXAMPLE 9.3

CD 2 TRACK 18

The curious pattern in the second bar of this lick is part of an F diminished chord. Johnny Gimble says that hearing this lick was his first introduction to the diminished chord; it subsequently became part of his standard repertoire of licks.

The 'hot solo' – the jazzy break – is where the fiddler gets to strut his stuff. Here's a typical Joe Holley lick, where he adds triplets to the flow of his swing, along with a blue note:

EXAMPLE 9.4

CD 2 TRACK 19

A popular motif in western swing harmony is the sixth harmony, possibly an echo of the lonesome railroad whistle. Jesse Ashlock plays this phrase on 'Bob Wills Boogie':

EXAMPLE 9.5

CD 2 TRACK 20

Notice that we play the third (A) and sixth (D), rather than the root and sixth. This makes a much more effective harmony.

Here's another sixth harmony, this time in the key of A:

EXAMPLE 9.6

CD 2 TRACK 21

One of the characteristic features of singing in the Western style is the yodel, popularised by singer Jimmie Rogers, and this has been copied by the fiddler as a must-have lick. Here's a couple of examples:

EXAMPLE 9.7

CD 2 TRACK 22i

EXAMPLE 9.8

CD 2 TRACK 22ii

Bob Wills's insistence that his musicians play solos which were always short, snappy, and startling, led fiddlers to seek the 'outside' notes, those which don't lie within the chord being played. The effect is modern and exciting. In a break on 'Sugar Moon', in 1946, Joe Holley came up with this lick, putting a flattened ninth note onto a C chord:

EXAMPLE 9.9

CD 2 TRACK 23

In the early years of western swing, the soloing was mostly indistinguishable from jazz style being played by Joe Venuti, Stuff

Smith, and Stéphane Grappelli; most of the players in bands like The Texas Playboys had learned to play swing, but had no real experience in old-time 'frontier' fiddle music. When Johnny Gimble joined the band he was able to tie the two strands of fiddle music together, not only playing in a convincing old-time style, complete with drones and double-stops, but also pushing forward the boundaries of jazz fiddling with exciting 'outside' notes and chord substitutions.

The basis of the more modern style of western swing fiddling is the sliding double-stop. From your old-time playing you will know that every chord has a number of alternative first position double-stops. For C, for example, these are two alternatives.

EXAMPLE 9.10

Any of these simple shapes can be hammed up by preceding it with the same shape, but a half step down:

EXAMPLE 9.11

CD 2 TRACK 24i

The first two are very easy, but you'll notice that to do the third one you need to start in third position.

You can also take any of your first position patterns and slide up into third position, like so:

EXAMPLE 9.12

CD 2 TRACK 24ii

Put these two ideas together you have a hot western swing lick:

EXAMPLE 9.13

CD 2 TRACK 25i

The same fingering (first and third finger) is used all the way through the lick. Here it is again based on the second C pattern:

EXAMPLE 9.14

CD 2 TRACK 25ii

These simple parallel sliding licks are easy to construct once you get the hang of it. Johnny Gimble took the whole thing a step forward, creating suspended or 'hanging' harmonies, where one finger of the double-stop does what you expect it to do, whilst the other creates a temporary dissonance, a tension which is eventually released as the fingers change again. The effect is both startling and beautiful.

Gimble has written many tunes that demonstrate his advanced use of double-stop harmony; here are a few typical phrases you would find in a tune such as 'Gardenia Waltz':

EXAMPLE 9.15

CD 2 TRACK 26

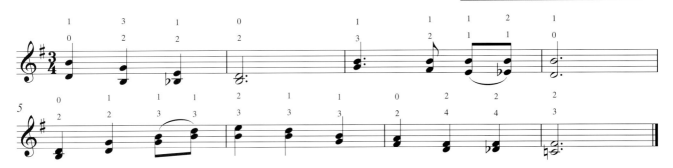

And here's Gimble's trademark killer lick, based on the augmented arpeggio. In the key of C, he would use it on the dominant (V) chord, ie, the G7. He would turn the G7 into a G+ (G augmented) by adding a sharpened fifth:

EXAMPLE 9.16

CD 2 TRACK 27

Master this lick, fit it casually into one of your solos, and you will be a god among fiddle players.

country fiddle

THE FIDDLE HANDBOOK

country fiddle

t's all a matter of definitions. In one sense country fiddle playing doesn't really exist at all; most if not all country fiddle players are actually bluegrass, old-time, Cajun, or western swing players who have sold, or at least temporarily rented, their souls to the devil, or perhaps Mammon. For some people country fiddle is an all-encompassing grab-bag which includes all the American styles; but the most widely accepted definition, and the one I'm going to use, is that country music is the commercial version of music that has grown out of the various genres already mentioned.

We're going to look at the birth of country music back in the 1920s, and see how the various commercial elements – radio, records, music publishing, and live performing – affected the music and the lives of the key performers. We'll trace the two main roots of country music: Appalachian or hillbilly, and western or cowboy music. And we'll look at the role of the Grand Ole Opry and the eventual dominance of Nashville and its studio system, where certain fiddlers became part of a factory production line of country hits. We'll see how traditional music evolved into western swing and bluegrass, and how honky tonk developed in the 40s. We'll note how the rise of rockabilly and rock'n'roll was countered by the growth of ever smoother and blander 'countrypolitan' music in the 50s and 60s, both trends which almost sounded the death knell for country fiddle. Finally we'll look at how the fiddle has survived and indeed thrived in the massive commercial expansion of country in the last few decades, when artists like Garth Brooks have managed to outsell even the biggest pop stars.

The birth of country music

Country music began on June 29 1922 when Texas fiddle champion Eck Robertson, along with his friend Henry Gilliland, also a fiddler, marched into the New York offices of the Victor Talking Machine Company and demanded an audition. The recording industry was in its infancy, and old-time music had never been recorded commercially, but the reception Robertson and Gilliland regularly received at fiddle contests persuaded them that stardom was just around the corner. They were not exactly welcomed with open arms.

Eck Robertson's recollections of the incident are quoted in Blanton Owen's sleeve-notes for *Eck Robertson: Famous Cowboy Fiddler*, a 1991 compilation of his recordings: "You couldn't fool that man [who] was running the shop in the Victor office … But then he come at me, he just come into the room in a hurry with a long piece of paper with names on it. He done that on purpose, you see, thought he'd get rid of me just like he had all the rest of them. He said 'Young man, get your fiddle out and start off on a tune.' Said, 'I can tell that quick whether I can use you or not.' Well, I said back to him, just as honest as I could, 'Mister, I come a long ways to get an audition with you. Maybe I better wait and come back another time. You seem like you're in an awful hurry.' 'No,' he said, 'Just start off a tune …' Well, I didn't get to play half of 'Sallie Gooden'; he just threw up his hands and stopped me. Said, 'By Ned, that's fine!' And just smiled, you know. Said, 'Come back in the morning at nine o'clock and we'll make a test record.'"

Whether Victor realised or not, Eck Robertson was the Real Deal, seen today as a pioneer of the modern Texas contest style of fiddling. He recorded 12 sides over the next two days, including such classics as 'Done Gone', 'Ragtime Annie', and 'Arkansas Traveler'. His 'Sallie Gooden' is said to be the earliest recording showing use of the 'Texas long bow', the smooth, fluid, slurring action which in Texas style was largely to replace the older, push-pull, sawing action of most old-time fiddling. Victor, unfortunately, had little idea about how to market these recordings, and it was a year before the first tracks were released, to a lukewarm reception.

Rival company Okeh, on the other hand, had their eye on the ball, and had realised that, just as poor blacks represented a strong market for 'race' records, so the white farmers of the southern states, particularly in the Appalachians, would lap up old-time music if it was offered to them. Talent scout Ralph Peer had been dispatched down south to seek out suitable performers of all kinds: black, white, secular, and gospel. In 1923 he struck gold when he came across Fiddlin' John Carson. Carson was not only a fine fiddler (though by no means as influential as Robertson), he was also a singer, albeit with a distinctly rough and creaky voice, a showman, and a natural entertainer. His first two sides, sung to the accompaniment of his own fiddle, were 'The Little Old Log Cabin In The Lane' and 'The Old Hen Cackled And The Rooster's Gonna Crow'. To everyone's surprise, the first 500 copies were sold out within days, and continued to leave the shelves as fast as they could be pressed. Carson became the first country music star, and proved that this was a major market which the record companies would have to take seriously.

Almost without exception, the bosses of the record companies, radio stations, and even talent scouts like Ralph Peer despised the music coming out of the Appalachians. It was raw, unschooled, and filled with crude double-entendres. They would have much preferred to deal with light classical, popular song, parlour music, or gospel choirs that had a degree of sophistication or respectability about them. Instead they were landed with backwoods yokels like Carson, who insisted that he had to be well oiled with moonshine and have a mouthful of chewing tobacco in order to perform. There was certainly little gentility in one of his later recordings, 'It's A Shame To Whip Your Wife On Sunday'.

One of the first problems to be dealt with was what to call this music. The term most widely used within the industry was 'hillbilly', which came with some powerfully negative connotations, as shown by this definition from *Variety* magazine in 1926:

"The 'hillbilly' is a North Carolina or Tennessee and adjacent mountaineer type of illiterate white. ... Theirs is a community all to themselves ... illiterate and ignorant, with the intelligence of morons." Clearly as a marketing term this would leave something to be desired. What was needed was some term that showed respect towards the sense of history, continuity, and old-fashioned values that this music appeared to represent. Among the terms tried out were 'old time', 'old fashioned', 'old familiar', and 'hill country'. The latter, though never widely used, may be significant in providing a missing link with the term 'country', which was eventually to become universal.

Soon Victor and Okeh representatives were making regular trips to the South, setting up temporary studios in empty shops or warehouses in regional centres like Atlanta, Georgia. Either through advertising or word of mouth, word would get round to local performers, who then turned up to audition and hopefully make a record, for which they would be paid between $10 and $25. At first the whole process was very hit-and-miss; the artists made little money out of even a successful record, and the record companies had little control over the material being recorded or the subsequent careers of the musicians. One aspect of the business that was problematic was publishing. In New York there was already a successful and well developed system; professional writers in Tin Pan Alley wrote new songs which could then be matched to suitable artists, earning good money for the publishers. With hillbilly music things were not quite so straightforward. Providing a song was 'traditional', it could be published by the first company to get its hands on it. The musicians themselves had no control over the process, as the publishers' society ASCAP was barred to performers who could not read music. This led to a frenzied 'strip-mining' of material, so that within a short time all the best-known songs had already been taken. What was then needed was people who could write new songs that still sounded authentic.

Polk Brockman was the Okeh representative in Atlanta, and it was he who had recorded Fiddlin' John Carson. He happened upon a blind newsboy called Andrew Jenkins, who, in the centuries-old tradition of the broadside ballads, was able to compose and perform songs about events in the news. In 1925, Brockman commissioned Jenkins to write a song called 'The Death Of Floyd Collins', about a man trapped in a Kentucky cave. The story filled the newspapers, all rescue attempts failed, Collins tragically died, and the song was dynamite. Brockman at first presented the song to John Carson, but the concept of quickly learning and convincingly performing new material was not second nature to the old-timer. He then offered it to Vernon Dalhart, an experienced, classically trained, operatic tenor who had no qualms about attempting a fake hillbilly accent. Dalhart had a huge hit with the song, becoming a major country star with a career largely based around sentimental disaster songs; others included the first million-seller in country music, 'The Wreck Of The Old '97', and a song which was still being played in my childhood, 'The Runaway Train'. Dalhart's success with this song provided two valuable lessons. Firstly, it showed the value of songwriting and publishing, even within hillbilly music, which by definition was supposed to be as old as the hills; and secondly it showed that, whilst authenticity was the cornerstone of old-time music, it was a cornerstone that could easily be fabricated or manufactured.

Gid Tanner & The Skillet Lickers were one of the first examples of a group of competent musicians put together specifically to make records, and one which furthermore played up the hillbilly image for all it was worth. Gideon Tanner, a fiddling chicken farmer from north Georgia, was in 1924 one of the first artists to record for Columbia after Fiddlin' John Carson's success. Tanner first recorded with singer/guitarist George Riley Puckett, then two years later was asked by Columbia to expand the group. They were joined by banjo player Fate Norris, and Clayton McMichen, 'The North Georgia Wildcat', an 18-times national fiddle champion, equally at home in jazz and hillbilly music. They recorded prolifically, churning out a series of hits, mixing fiddle tunes, songs, and comedy skits; their performance gave the impression of being rough and rowdy, but the fiddle parts were actually very carefully arranged. They were full of fun. 'Ya Gotta Quit Kickin' My Dog Around', for example, is punctuated with the howls of a maligned canine, while 'A Day At The County Fair' has some fine hog-calling and award-winning hogs. The band was joined in 1928 by fiddler Lowe Stokes. Aside from his fiddling, Stokes was something of a walking disaster area; on one occasion he was stabbed, almost in the heart, and on two separate occasions he was shot in the right hand, which was eventually replaced with a hook specially designed to hold his bow.

Radio barn dances

Radio played a vital role in the dissemination and evolution of country music. The first station of any size in the South was WSB (the call letters stood for "Welcome South, Brother") in Atlanta, which began broadcasting on March 16 1922. Fiddlin' John Carson was playing on the station within weeks, even though he had not yet had his first recording session. Country music on radio consisted almost entirely of live performances. Musicians were paid nothing more than expenses, but it was a vital medium for boosting their public profile and advertising their live performances. Hillbilly music was immediately popular with audiences, as measured by the response from listeners writing in. And for the programme schedulers, country fiddlers and singers were invaluable because they could play for as long or short a time as was required, unlike classical musicians who were tied to a fixed, prepared repertoire.

WSB soon had two major competitors: WLS ("World's Largest Store" – the original owners were Sears, Roebuck), which opened in Chicago in 1924, and WSM ("We Shield Millions" – the owner being an insurance company), which opened in Nashville in 1925. While WSB scattered its hillbilly music through the schedules, WLS made the shrewd decision to make Saturday night its country night, so that fans of this type of music would know when to tune in to hear what they wanted. The station's owners were aghast at the "disgraceful low-brow music" being aired, and would have pulled the show had it not been for the overwhelmingly positive response from rural farmers and homesick migrants from the south. The programme grew, and when it achieved national syndication, became known as the National Barn Dance. George Hay, a WLS presenter, was lured down to Nashville to launch a similar show for WSM. He booked Uncle Jimmy Thompson, a veteran fiddler already in his 77th year, who initially played the two-hour Saturday night slot on his own, churning out a seemingly inexhaustible string of breakdowns and hornpipes. With his white beard, his repertoire learned during the Civil War and his bluff, hard-drinking persona, he fitted the bill perfectly, and Hay could hardly get him to stop at the end of the show. However, although his show was popular, it was clear that solo fiddle was not as entertaining as someone like Fiddlin' John Carson, who could also sing. It was clear that to maintain an audience they were going to need variety, and soon Thompson was sharing the bill with singers, string bands, and other instrumentalists. The show, as at WLS, was referred to as a barn dance, but whereas Thompson had played what was authentic barn dance music, the show had soon become more of a country vaudeville performance. Hay established a regular cast of singers and musicians, and, like actors in a play, made sure that everyone had a name, a personality, and a part to play in the show beyond just producing music. Everyone dressed the part; they might turn up at the station dressed in their best Sunday suits, but on the show, even before it was performed before a live studio audience, it was smocks, dungarees, and straw hats all round. Hay named himself 'The Solemn Old Judge', presiding over an informal, hayseed knockabout show which eventually became known as the Grand Ole Opry.

Among the biggest stars of the Opry, almost from the beginning, was singer and fiddler Roy Acuff. He had joined the Opry in 1938; prior to his arrival most of the acts had been fiddle bands with occasional or incidental vocals. Acuff was the first to act as a lead singer with a backing band, and the crowds loved it. As Acuff himself modestly asserted, "I was the first one that came there with what they call a voice." He was always concerned with the image and entertainment value of his band. When he had established himself as a frontman and singer, rather than a fiddler, he hired former Blue Grass Boy Tommy Magness, the first fiddler to record 'Orange Blossom Special'. Acuff used his own instrument largely as a prop; one of his tricks was to balance his fiddle bow on his nose. By 1940 he had become the Opry's biggest attraction, often dubbed 'The King Of Country Music'. Legend has it (and who's going to disprove it?) that during World War II, Japanese troops used to go into action with the battle cry "To hell with Roosevelt, to hell with Babe Ruth, to hell with Roy Acuff!"

Roy Acuff

Jimmie Rodgers

Jimmie Rodgers, in his short career, earned the justifiable title of 'The Father of Country Music'. He was the archetypal country star, and perhaps the first to have a distinctive and iconic image that had nothing to do with the hillbilly. He was born in Mississippi, and in his formative years listened to a great deal of blues music. He wanted to become a singer from an early age, but for several years, at his father's insistence, worked on the railroads as a brakeman. He soon took to rambling, picking up casual work, and touring with minstrel shows. He had been singing with a group, the Tenneva Ramblers, when in 1927 they heard about auditions being held by Ralph Peer for Victor Records. The night before the audition they had a row, and Rodgers ended up auditioning on his own, accompanying himself on guitar. Many things would have made him stand out for Peer: his songwriting ability, his good looks and winning smile, his trademark yodel, and the simple sincerity of his singing. His first recordings were not a success, but his follow-up song, 'T For Texas' (released as 'Blue Yodel') went on to sell a million copies, making 'The Singing Brakeman', as he became known, into a household name. He built his freewheeling, romantic image around his hobo/railroad background, usually pictured wearing either a railroad worker's cap or a cowboy hat, and the material of his songs took in the lives of those on the wild side of American life: gamblers, drinkers, cowboys, and lost souls. He died young, of tuberculosis, in 1933, but not before he had written and recorded a string of hits. Whilst many of his songs were recorded just with guitar, he sometimes used fiddle, mostly Clayton McMichen (of Skillet Lickers fame); the song 'Peach Pickin' Time In Georgia' features McMichen playing an intro that mirrors the Rodgers yodel and places it firmly in the Essential Licks checklist of every country fiddler.

Singing cowboys

If Jimmie Rodgers was among the first country stars to move away from the hillbilly image, he was at the start of a profound trend. Soon America was in thrall to a new character: the Singing Cowboy. Whilst the Appalachian hillbilly and western cowboy are figures based in reality, they both have an equally strong mythology. From the beginning of the Depression, in the early 30s, the reality of the hillbilly, stuck on an isolated farm and facing foreclosure by the bank as commodity prices tumbled or forced into the cities to look for work, was a bleak one. The image of the cowboy, by contrast, had never looked more appealing and romantic; the solitary rider, untroubled by the complexity and hardship of the modern world, striving heroically against sun, wind, and the bad guy to do the right thing in his own way. It was an image ripe for exploitation, both by singers and Hollywood film-makers. Whilst the musical material inherited from actual cowboys was minute in contrast to that of the sons of the soil in the Appalachians, the clothes and accessories of the

Jimmie Rodgers

cowboy – the Stetson or ten-gallon hat, the boots, the spurs, the guns, not to mention the horse – practically wrote the songs themselves.

The first of the great singing cowboys, and certainly the only one who could ride a horse, sing, yodel, and play fiddle at the same time, was Ken Maynard. Born in Texas in 1895, he spent his early career as a trick rider with a series of touring wild west shows. A passable singer and an able musician, he played fiddle, guitar, banjo, and harmonica. With his rugged good looks he was the ideal candidate when Hollywood needed its first singing cowboy for what was to be a seemingly endless string of Saturday matinee westerns. His first was the 1929 film *In Old Arizona*, and he made many more throughout the 30s, including *The Fiddling Buckaroo*. He made only a handful of records, songs such as 'Home On The Range' and 'The Cowboy's Lament', and in 1934 he shot himself in the foot (not literally), when he invited Gene Autry to sing in his film *In Old Santa Fe*.

Unlike Maynard, Autry was an excellent singer, more of a Bing Crosby crooner than an honest-to-God rattlesnake-biting, tobacco-chewing horse-wrangler. He also wore a white hat, which guaranteed he would come out on top in any shootout. Autry already had a singing career before he got into films, having signed a record deal with Columbia in 1929, and had worked on the National Barn Dance show for four years. At first he sang a broad range of material, but when his future as the singing cowboy became clear, songs about moonshine and hogs were out; saddles, goldmines, and tumbleweed were in. To bolster his image as the Good Guy of western movies, Autry wrote a ten-commandment Cowboy Code, opening with "1. The Cowboy must never shoot first, hit a smaller man, or take unfair advantage." I think you get the picture. Possibly Columbia Pictures was not aware of the code. In 1938 Autry asked for a raise, having already made a fortune for Columbia; the company immediately began searching for a replacement, which they found in the shape of Roy Rogers and his faithful mount, Trigger.

Unlike Maynard or Autry (who was raised on a cattle ranch), Rogers had no genuine cowboy pedigree, having been born in Cincinnati, Ohio, and worked in a shoe factory. Nevertheless, with his boyish good looks he soon came to define the cowboy image for generations to come, eventually moving to television, and launching an armada of cowboy-related merchandise. (This was Woody from *Toy Story*, in flesh and blood.) He was, also, however, an excellent and experienced singer, working first with The Rocky Mountaineers, and then with the highly influential Sons Of The Pioneers. This was a group specialising in the romance of the old west: songs of tumbleweeds, campfires, bandits, and buckaroos, carefully arranged with the creamiest of harmonies. They also boasted a top dog of a fiddle player in Hugh Farr. Farr was a hugely talented musician, singled out as a fiddler from the outset. His parents performed as a duo, but had five daughters. At Hugh's birth, when he realised he now had a son, his father exclaimed "Well I'll be darned, there's my fiddler!"

By the age of nine, Hugh Farr had mastered the fiddle and learned the entire family repertoire of old-time material. Not content with this, he would sneak out of bed at night to listen to the radio, singling out jazzy groups like the Kansas City Night Hawks, and had soon picked up a first-class swing style. When Roy Rogers began to develop his film career, he left The Sons Of The Pioneers, though they would often accompany him on screen. They say old cowboys never die. Rogers made it to the age of 86. The Sons of The Pioneers are, remarkably, still performing. And at the Roy Rogers Museum, in Branson, Missouri, crowds still flock to see Trigger, stuffed.

Honky-tonk music

The dreamy nostalgia of western music wasn't going to last forever, and the 40s ushered in a more raw, down to earth style of country music: honky-tonk. The term had already been around since the early 1900s, referring to a style of piano playing, and it later became the common term for the new breed of roadhouses, bars, and juke joints that sprang up after the repeal of prohibition in 1933. They were rough and rowdy establishments, often on the outskirts of town, frequented by hard-bitten blue-collar workers determined to escape from the trials of life. Because honky-tonks were always so noisy, the proprietors and indeed customers wanted music that would cut through the hubbub. The immediate answer to this was provided by Ernest Tubb when, for his 1941 recording 'Walking The Floor Over You', he brought in Fay 'Smitty' Smith on electric guitar. It was still a novelty in country music but one which gave a new, harder edge to the sound. The song was a huge seller, and as well as setting him up for a long run of hits, it also won him a place on the Grand Old Opry, placing the new honky-tonk sound firmly at the heart of country music. Honky-tonk did not entirely overthrow the old order. The cowboy hats remained; it was still music largely from Texas, though now more urban than rural; and the fiddle still had a vital role, alongside the steel guitar, in anchoring the sound in country rather than mainstream music. Whilst Tubb didn't use fiddle until 1944, he used Johnny Sapp for three years until he moved to Nashville for the Opry; from then until the late 50s his fiddle work went almost entirely to the session men Tommy Jackson and Dale Potter. As we'll discover, these two would have country music recording sewn up between them for a decade or more.

Hank Williams

The biggest star of honky-tonk, and arguably of the whole of country music, was Hank Williams. He was born in 1923 in rural Alabama. He learned fiddle and guitar as a child, and, with a head full of cowboy films, named his first band The Drifting Cowboys. He was writing songs almost as soon as he began singing, and in 1946 he met Fred Rose, of the hugely influential Nashville publishing company Acuff & Rose. Rose was impressed by Williams's material and was able to get him signed, first to a minor New York record label, and then to the much larger MGM. Hank Williams was not an innovator, but he was an incredibly powerful and emotive performer, mesmerising audiences with the intensity and sincerity of his singing. He had a long string of hits, mostly his own compositions, with songs such as 'Hey Good Lookin'', 'Your Cheating Heart', 'Honky Tonk Blues', 'Cold, Cold Heart' and 'You Win Again'. Classics every one. He sang mostly bitter songs about heartache, remorse, personal doubt, and marital strife, themes which would be at the core of country music for decades to come. There was fiddle on most of Hank Williams' recordings. For the first few years he used Nashville sidemen Dale Potter and Tommy Jackson, and occasionally ex-Blue Grass Boy Chubby Wise. In 1949 he decided to establish a permanent backing band, and auditioned Jerry Rivers. Still proud of his own fiddle playing, Hank Williams opened the audition by taking Rivers's fiddle and playing a spirited version of 'Sally Goodin', before challenging him to "beat that!" Jerry was able to do so, and won a grudging compliment: "Well, anyone that can play 'Sally Goodin' better'n me is a darn good fiddle player. You're hired!" Rivers played on all the subsequent hits, using, at the encouragement of producer Fred Rose, a double-stop style which Williams referred to as "garden seed" fiddle. Hank Williams died a premature death from a mixture of heart problems, drink, and drugs in 1953; his current release was 'I'll Never Get Out Of This World Alive', which went on to be a Number One hit.

Another honky-tonk pioneer was Ray Price, who incorporated the walking bass and rock-steady drum patterns of western swing to create the 'honky-tonk shuffle' or 'Ray Price beat'. His first big hit was 'Crazy Arms', in 1956, featuring a powerful fiddle intro from Tommy Jackson. Hank Snow had one of the longest careers as a honky-tonk singer,

Hank Williams

lasting from the 30s to the 80s; Chubby Wise, who had been with Bill Monroe during the classic years of early bluegrass, toured extensively with Snow.

For most of its history, country music was mostly a male preserve, but in 1952 Kitty Wells put an end to that when she released 'It Wasn't God Who Made Honky Tonk Angels', a song that told the broken-hearts tale from the woman's point of view. It was a huge hit, and opened the way for subsequent female country artists. The song featured bluegrass fiddler Paul Warren, playing a classic country solo; restrained and smooth, artfully elaborating on the melody of the chorus with grace notes and double stops.

Honky-tonk was a style that to some extent brought together two sometimes disparate roots: country (the hillbilly music of the Appalachians, championed in the early Opry), and western (the cowboy music of Texas, western swing, and the Hollywood westerns). Fiddle and pedal steel supplied the distinctive element that differentiated it from the pop music of the day, but the electric guitar and eventually drums gave it a hard, modern sound. Add to that a singer with a southern twang and a Stetson, and you have a winning formula that still forms the basis of country music today. However, the mid 50s brought a challenge that was to shake country music to its core. To understand country music's response to that, we first need to see what had been happening back in Nashville.

The rise of Nashville

Since the early 30s, the Grand Old Opry in Nashville had been expanding and consolidating, acquiring big name sponsorship, gaining national syndication, and attracting the biggest country stars. In the early 40s it acquired a new home, the 2,300-seater Ryman Auditorium, where shows were held before a live audience. Members of the cast at the Opry had to perform regularly, if not weekly, so that Nashville was the natural base for many of country's top musicians. Performers were not well paid for appearing on the show, but it gave them huge prestige, publicity, and a way of promoting their careers. Opry artists The Vagabonds, a slick harmony singing group, had formed a company to sell first their own song books on the show and later those of other artists. Though their company did not survive the Depression, it inspired Roy Acuff, along with WSM pianist and aspiring songwriter Fred Rose, to form their own publishing company, Acuff-Rose, which would eventually become a cornerstone of the country music establishment.

Along with publishing there was a need for recording studios, either for recording demos of newly published songs, or for putting out finished product. The first of these in Nashville was Castle Recording Studio, opened in 1946. By 1954 it was getting so much work it needed new premises, and moved to 16th Avenue South, which was soon to become Nashville's music row as all the major record companies established studios and offices there. Managers, promoters, booking agents, and publicists all followed suit, and within a decade Nashville had become the undisputed heart of the country music business. Soon there wasn't a waiter, taxi driver, or delivery boy in Nashville who wasn't also an aspiring singer, musician, or songwriter.

Artists making records in Nashville tended to use the best musicians from the Opry cast as their backing band. This became the Nashville studio 'A team', a select group of pickers who could be guaranteed to learn a song and lay down a backing track in less time than it took to walk across the road and eat burger and fries. The first fiddler to reach this level was Tommy Jackson. He started exceptionally young; he was touring with Kitty Wells at the age of 12 and appearing at the Opry when he was 17, as part of Red Foley's band, The Cumberland Valley Boys. He was responsible for the fiddle parts on many of Hank Williams's classic tracks, including 'Lovesick Blues' and 'I Saw The Light'. His double-stop technique became known as 'walking fiddle', and he set the standard and style for country fiddle for decades to come. As fiddler Johnny Gimble put it, "When I moved to Nashville, Tommy Jackson's style was what sold on records. You sort of adhered to that." Jackson played on many of Hank Williams' early hits, as well as with Ray Price, George Jones, and a host of others. He also recorded under his own name; in 1953 he signed to Dot Records, and produced a long-running series of solo fiddle albums of standard breakdown tunes, directed at the resurgence in square dancing that was happening at the time. For many young fiddle players throughout the 50s and 60s it was his versions of these tunes that got them started. Dale Potter was another fiddler much in demand in Nashville; when twin fiddles were called for, Jackson would take the melody, but Potter, who had the better grasp of harmony, would find the higher or lower line. A great example of Dale Potter's playing is the solo on Hank Williams's 'Mind Your Own Business', a daring solo with lots of chromatic notes. His own composition, 'Fiddle Patch', is an exuberant improvisation on a blues sequence, packed with double-stop fireworks and an eye-watering chromatic run.

The whole recording process was managed, shaped, and controlled by a producer, who would book the studio, engineer, the backing musicians, and, if need be, an arranger. With the experience of an endless string of artists bringing in their songs to record, the whole process became extremely efficient, but arguably also stale and predictable. There was an element of the factory production line about it; and if Nashville was a machine, the spanner in the works arrived in 1954 in the shape of Elvis Presley.

Rockabilly versus the Nashville sound

If honky-tonk had been a kick in the pants for country music, then rockabilly was a dose of electric shock therapy. It was a rabid mixture of hillbilly, blues, and rhythm & blues, powered by electric guitar and slapped bass. It was high-energy music for a younger generation, delivered with a yelp, a sneer, and a raised finger to everything that had gone before. Rockabilly had close links with country; one of Elvis Presley's first recordings was Bill Monroe's *Blue Moon Of Kentucky*, played first as a waltz, then with a rocking 2/4 beat. Elvis was invited to appear at the Grand Ole Opry in October 1954; he was politely received by the audience, but afterwards one of the organisers, disapproving perhaps of the vulgarity of the performance, suggested that he return to Memphis and stick to truck driving. He vowed never to return. Rockabilly's country roots soon disappeared, merging into rock'n'roll with the use of drums, piano, and sax. What was definitely out were the fiddle and the pedal steel guitar, which to teenage fans represented everything old-fashioned and corny about country music.

With a huge slice of the audience decamping to rock'n'roll, Nashville faced a crisis. Rather than ignoring the problem and hoping it would go away (as indeed many people believed it would), Nashville producers started to change the direction of their own product, going for a smoother, more sophisticated and adult sound. With this change they hoped to open up to the mass market, taking it out of the relatively confined niche it had built for itself. The one man more than any other responsible for steering this change was producer, session guitarist, and one-time fiddler Chet Atkins. He had started out as a fiddle player for Archie Campbell and Bill Carlisle, eventually becoming known more as a slick, versatile guitarist and eventually a recording artist in his own right. In 1950 he settled in Nashville, first doing session work and then, by 1955, taking charge of RCA's new studio. Along with other producers like Owen Bradley and Don Law, Atkins created what became known as 'Countrypolitan' music, or simply 'The Nashville Sound'. Lush backing vocals, smooth harmonies, and 'legit' string sections were the order of the day. The chief casualty, along with the pedal steel, was the fiddle. Bluegrass guitarist Lester Flatt summed it up when describing the scene in the mid 50s; "Back then you couldn't *give* a fiddle away. No one liked a fiddle." The instrument had been rejected as old-fashioned by both younger and older audiences. Artists like Jim Reeves, Ernest Tubb, and

Patsy Cline, who started out as honky-tonkers, and had used fiddle extensively in the past, used it less and less. In 1953 (ironically the year of Hank Williams's death) the Nashville business elite decided to drop the 'western' from country & western, and it officially became plain old 'country music'.

New Country

One of the laws of physics states that every action has an equal and opposite reaction, and musical taste follows pretty much the same principle. It may take a decade or two, but everything always comes back into fashion eventually. By the mid 70s, rock'n'roll had split into dozens of sub-genres, one of which was country-rock. What simpler way to give a rock band a 'back to the country' feel than to add a fiddle? Two decades of rock was enough to leave large chunks of the population hankering after something simpler, rootsier, and more wholesome. Step forward bluegrass, old-time, Cajun, and western swing, which may have been hiding in the backwoods, but had never actually gone away. And within country music itself there was a reaction to the blandness and uniformity of the Nashville sound, as well as the stranglehold on the business by the major companies based there.

Established singers like Willie Nelson and Waylon Jennings had grown tired of having their careers directed and their records overproduced by suits in Nashville, and decided to take control for themselves. They used their own touring bands to record, instead of using session musicians, and they dubbed themselves the outlaws of country. Austin, Texas, became an alternative centre for musicians with a gritty, more progressive and less conservative outlook. Willie Nelson settled there and became a figurehead of the movement. Early on in his career, Nelson had met western swing fiddler Johnny Gimble, who at the time was working with Bob Wills. The two hit it off, with Gimble turning Nelson on to swing music such as that of Django Reinhardt. They began working together in Texas, both live and in the studio; Gimble features particularly strongly on the audacious 1980 *Somewhere Over The Rainbow* album of Hollywood soundtrack songs, while one of his own, most famous compositions, 'Fiddlin' Around', appeared on Nelson's 1980 *Honeysuckle Rose* album. Gimble had already spent ten years (from 1968 to 1978) as the first-call session fiddler in Nashville, working for a host of stars including Charlie Pride, Chet Atkins, Dolly Parton, Conway Twitty, Loretta Lynn, George Strait, Tammy Wynette, and Merle Haggard. The latter was one of the pioneers of the Bakersfield Sound, a California-based outpost of country with a hard, rock'n'roll sensibility.

Though by no means in Johnny Gimble's league as a fiddle player,

Charlie Daniels, leader of his own southern rock/country crossover band, left an indelible mark in 1979 with 'The Devil Went Down To Georgia'. Decades later, it is still one of the most insistent (and annoying) requests for any country fiddle player.

In 1986 there was a resurgence of traditional honky-tonk-based country music, with a string of debut albums for what would soon become the new country establishment: Steve Earle, Randy Travis, Dwight Yoakam, and Lyle Lovett. In 1988, Steve Earle's next album, *Copperhead Row*, included a track with Mark O'Connor, who in his turn had taken over as the top session fiddler in Nashville. On the 1999 album, *The Mountain*, Earle collaborated with The Del McCoury Band, adding a traditional bluegrass sound with Jason Carter on fiddle. Dwight Yoakam also features fiddle on many of his albums; Brantley Kearns was on the debut album, *Guitars And Cadillacs*, while more recently he has used Don Reed.

The country music sensation of the 90s was, like it or not, Garth Brooks. He was dismissed as a 'Hat Act', and widely sneered at by purists, who hated to see their music turned into a cross between TV evangelism and stadium rock; but no one can argue with sales of more than 80 million albums. He topped the mainstream charts, outselling the biggest pop stars, and did it moreover with a standard honky-tonk line-up including pedal steel and the fiddle of Jimmy Mattingly. Mattingly was a former US Grand Master fiddle champion, and had already worked with Dolly Parton from 1989-93; he toured and recorded with Brooks from 1996. Following Brooks's retirement in 2001, he has been working with award-winning bluegrass band The Grascals.

PLAYING COUNTRY FIDDLE

If you want to start playing country fiddle from scratch, don't start here! As we said at the outset, country fiddle is based on old-time, bluegrass, Cajun, western swing and a touch of blues. Get to grips with some or all of these styles (or at least go through the relevant chapters in this book, so you can pretend!), and then you'll already be most of the way towards being a country fiddler.

Most country fiddling involves being a backing musician for a singer. As such, your job is:
- Playing some intros or outros.
- Playing behind the singing, either shuffles or melodic lines between the vocal phrases.
- Taking short solos.

Here's a typical honky-tonk style chord sequence:

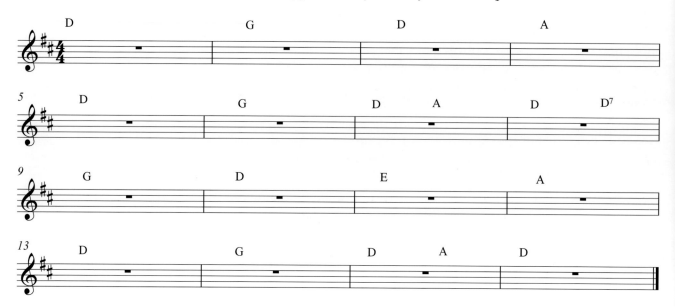

EXAMPLE 10.1

CD 2 TRACK 28

Typically with country music, the chords are very simple and predictable, so you should find them easy to follow.

The first thing you need is a selection of double stops to use for each chord. Here are a few possibilities:

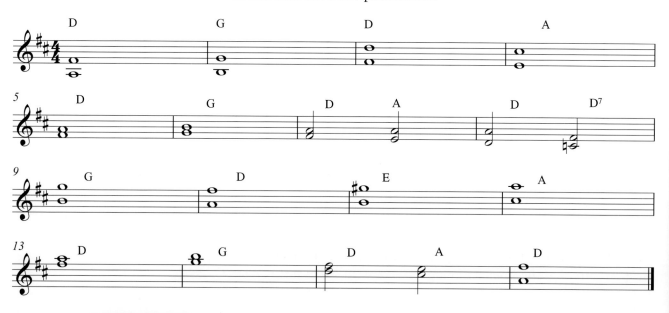

EXAMPLE 10.2

CD 2 TRACK 29

As you can see, there's no need to stick to one shape or pattern for each chord; I managed to find nine different inversions of the D chord, using only the root, third and fifth. In choosing which double stops to

236   THE FIDDLE HANDBOOK

use, try to find some logic as you move from one to the next; in terms of hand movement, less is more. The change from bar one to bar two, for example, is neat and economical, whilst the move to bar three is unwieldy. The four patterns through bars seven and eight show a good sense of musical direction as the lower note moves down the scale. An exercise like the above is useful for trying out possibilities but it's not exactly musical. We need to narrow down the range of double stops we're going to use, and also add some rhythm.

The Nashville shuffle is a repetitive bowing pattern widely used in playing traditional old-time, Cajun, and bluegrass tunes. It was in use long before the rise of Nashville country, but acquired its name, probably some time in the 60s, when fiddlers doing session work started using it in a generic way as a backing for songs. You can hear a good example on Ray Price's 1956 recording of 'Falling, Falling, Falling'.

Here it is applied to our chord sequence.

EXAMPLE 10.3

CD 2 TRACK 30

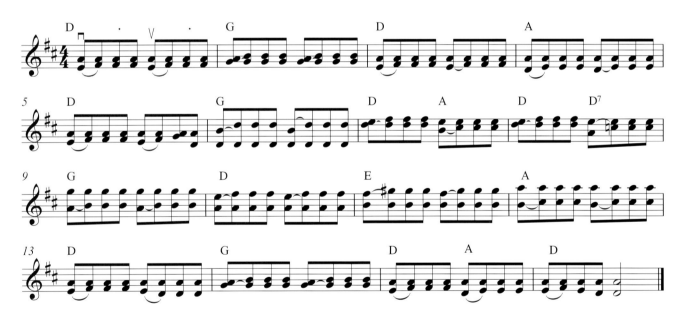

There are a few things to notice about this example. Firstly, to match the backing, we've applied a swing to the shuffle. Again the choice of double-stops has some logic to it, in that we try to avoid big jumps from chord to chord, choosing finger patterns that lie close to one another. Notice that whilst most of the fingerings use only root, third, or fifth notes, in bar eight on the D7 chord we've emphasised the C-natural, the seventh note of the chord. This is important as it is acting as a signpost that the bridge or middle section of the tune is coming up. In bar 11, on the E chord, it's important to get the G-sharp note, emphasising the third note of the E chord; it's the only time this appears in the sequence so make the most of it. You'll see that some of the double-stop patterns, such as in bars two and seven, start with a discord. Played on its own this would sound wrong, but in the context of the pattern it's fine.

A more interesting and sophisticated approach is the 'walking fiddle' style of Tommy Jackson. He left the rhythm up to the guitar and bass, but played either two or four shapes or patterns for every bar, depending on the tempo. This could be messy and over-complicated, but by having direction to the movement you can instead make it purposeful and straightforward. For example, if you're moving from a D chord to a G chord, and back to a D, you could effectively play an ascending and descending scale:

EXAMPLE 10.4

CD 2 TRACK 31

In the example above we've used a C-natural in the first bar. The C-sharp would sound too schmaltzy, whilst the C-natural effectively creates a temporary D7 chord, sign-posting the G chord to follow.

EXAMPLE 10.5

CD 2 TRACK 32

This use of double stops looks tricky, but once you've mastered the 'scale in sixths', there's nothing to it; you simply use the upper note as your melody, and let the lower note follow:

This scale (and of course like any other scale you need to try it lots of different keys) is immeasurably useful in many styles of fiddle playing. Here's the walking fiddle applied to the whole sequence. You can hear good examples of this style on Hank Williams's 'I Can't Help It' or 'Crazy Heart'.

When played as a whole this again is not very musical, because now the rhythm has become monotonous. In practice you need something more melodic, using the walking fiddle to link phrases:

EXAMPLE 10.6

CD 2 TRACK 33

EXAMPLE 10.7

CD 2 TRACK 34

How much movement, rhythm and melodic interest you put in depends partly on what else is going on. If you're playing this behind a verse or chorus, it's fine to keep it bland, maybe playing a bit in the gaps between vocal phrases. If this is your fiddle break, you can liven it up a bit.

Much of what we now regard as country fiddle evolved in the 50s and 60s in conjunction with the steel guitar; on Hank Williams recordings for example, they almost always feature together. As a result the fiddle will often mimic the steel's way of playing. One neat way to achieve this is by sliding up to one note of a double stop:

EXAMPLE 10.8

CD 2 TRACK 35

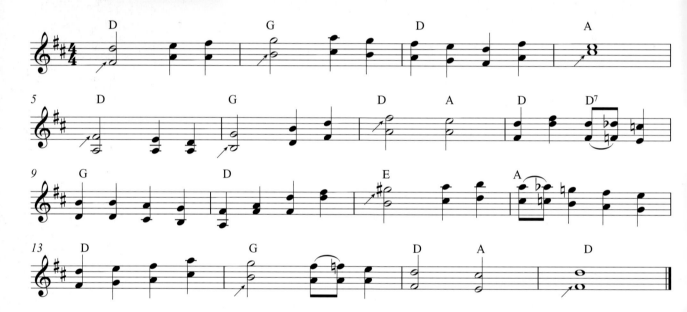

In addition to the upward slides on the double stops, in bars 8, 12, and 14 we've also done a smooth downward slide. Finally, the pedal-steel effect has been enhanced by a rich, creamy vibrato.

blues fiddle

blues fiddle

When it comes to choices for a musical career, blues fiddle ranks right up there in the popularity stakes with bluegrass trombone, Cajun harpsichord, baroque harmonica, and ambient trance bagpipes. It wasn't always so. At the turn of the last century, when the blues was in its formative years, fiddle was among the primary instruments used by the rural black musicians who were performing in this style. By 1930 more than 50 different black blues fiddle players had their work on wax. Even as the guitar was rising in prominence, many of the star players, such as Lonnie Johnson and Big Bill Broonzy, played both guitar and fiddle.

In many ways fiddle is the ideal blues instrument; closest to the human voice, capable of great passion, and able to deal easily with the uncertain and sinuous areas 'between the notes', all of which are crucial to the blues. Yet by the end of the Depression years, in the mid 30s, the blues fiddle was virtually a thing of the past, leaving no trace except some dusty old recordings. Why then, in a contemporary book on fiddle playing, include a chapter on the blues? Where are the blues fiddle tune books, the blues fiddle contests, blues fiddle festivals? Pretty thin on the ground, to put it mildly. However, although in itself very much a minority genre, blues remains a core element of rock, country, western swing, bluegrass and jazz, and without it you will never really get to grips with any of these styles.

What is the blues?

You can answer this question in at least three different ways.

First of all, it's a song structure, normally 12 bars in length, and with just three basic chords; the root (I), subdominant (IV) and dominant (V). The chords are arranged like so:

```
I  /  /  /   I  /  /  /   I  /  /  /   I  /  /  /
IV /  /  /   IV /  /  /   I  /  /  /   I  /  /  /
V  /  /  /   IV /  /  /   I  /  /  /   I  /  /  /
```

We'll come back to this sequence in more detail later. If a song is called

'Something Blues', there's a good chance that it will be a blues in the structural sense, but that's by no means guaranteed; at the time when blues became popular, writers and publishers would happily jump on the bandwagon, adding the word blues to a title, regardless of the song's content. In the jazz field, musicians have found blues a good vehicle for improvisation, but often many substitute chords are used, so that a 'jazz blues' might be a lot more complex harmonically.

Secondly, blues is a scale, or to be more precise, a set of scales, based on the idea of flattened, flexible or 'blue' notes. It is not uncommon in folk music around the world, whether Celtic, American, Scandinavian, Asian, or African, to have notes that do not appear on the standardised 12-note scale as presented on the piano keyboard. As a general rule, such notes have not fared well in recent years; as soon as they are confronted with a fixed-pitch instrument such as the accordion or piano, they see the writing on the wall and take early retirement. Not so with the blues. The tension created by bending notes to create a flattened third, fifth, and seventh (the three blue notes) remains absolutely central to the blues. The simplest and most common explanation for the origin of blue notes is the attempt by black slaves brought to America from Africa, to reconcile their traditional minor pentatonic singing scales with the major western harmony they were confronted with in the colonies. Unfortunately, as we'll see, there are several different interpretations of what the blues scale actually is.

Finally, the blues can be regarded not as a musical structure or scale but as a feeling; the yearning and longing of the downcast and oppressed. The lives of bluesmen were never easy and their songs were rarely trivial or cheerful; the blues was a way of expressing and dealing with the hardships of life.

The roots of the blues

There were plenty of hardships for the black slaves in colonial America. Slavery had been expanding since the mid 17th century on the tobacco plantations of Maryland and Virginia, and soon spread throughout the southern states. A highly profitable 'triangular trade' developed. Ships laden with goods sailed from England to West Africa, where the goods were exchanged for slaves. They then sailed the 'middle passage' to the Caribbean and America, exchanging the slaves for money or more goods, before returning to England.

The banjo, based on a group of plucked stringed instruments found in west Africa, quickly became popular on the plantations as an accompaniment for the singing of semi-improvised songs that the whites found comical. It was clear that the slaves had a good deal of natural musical ability, and that black musicians could entertain not only their fellows, but their masters as well. The owners soon introduced them to European instruments, most notably the violin, which gained rapid popularity among the slaves. Some would have taught themselves to play the fiddle, but many were also given formal musical training by their masters, or learned in a church or choir.

One slave-holder wrote, "I have a good fiddler, and keep him well supplied with catgut, and I make it his duty to play for the negroes every Saturday night until 12 o'clock."

By the 18th century, black musicians were playing jigs, reels, and fandangos, as well as religious and classical music. In the 1880s, southern writer George Washington Cable was able to state that "the banjo is not the favourite musical instrument of the negroes of the southern states of America. Uncle Remus [the black character created by Joel Chandler Harris] says truly that it is the fiddle."

By the beginning of the 20th century blues was beginning to coalesce as a style, with roots in spirituals, humorous secular songs, field hollers, work songs, ragtime, and jug band music. The guitar was the primary blues instrument but the fiddle was also very common. W.C. Handy, the first artist to have major commercial success with the blues, commented how in the old times "country gals and their mirthful suitors got as much enjoyment out of a fiddle at a breakdown or square dance as jitterbugs or rug-cutters get nowadays from a swing band".

Early blues recordings

The record industry was quick to jump on the blues bandwagon, signing up many artists for what it called its 'race' labels. Among the performers to record were many fiddle players. Lonnie Johnson was one of the most influential and prolific, cutting more than 20 sides for the Okeh label, starting in 1925. He had already been a professional musician for a decade; having started with his family band, he had played string band music and jazz as well as blues. He performed on both guitar and fiddle, working with a popular band, the Mississippi Sheiks. Winning a blues contest in St Louis gave him his big break, the prize being the contract with Okeh. From here on he concentrated on the blues, working both as a bandleader and session man. He was best known as a pioneering virtuoso guitarist, but his violin playing, as heard for example on 'Memphis Stomp', is powerful and expressive .

Another notable blues guitarist/fiddler was Big Bill Broonzy. He was born on a Missouri plantation in 1898, and was one of many players who started off with crude, home-made instruments. As he explained to the song collector Alan Lomax, "Every night I would bring some cornstalks together, and I'd go out in back of the barn and rub them cornstalks together and make music and the children would dance.

That was my 'cornstalk fiddle'. I rubbed it hard when I wanted a loud tone and I rubbed it easy when I wanted to play soft." From this he moved up to a cigar-box fiddle, and finally a mail-order violin from Sears, Roebuck. To start with he mostly played music for white audiences – old-time breakdowns and waltzes – but when he moved to Chicago in 1920 there was already a big demand for blues; he took up the guitar and began a long and successful career as a blues singer. Although his dirty, muscular fiddling was heard on some of his early recordings, Broonzy played little violin from then on. The blues historian Paul Oliver records having had the rare privilege of hearing Broonzy pick up a fiddle someone had left backstage at a concert in London: "During the next few moments that violin played notes it will never play again. … With his powerful fingers twisting, sliding and releasing strings, Big Bill played pure alley fiddle, grinning broadly as the strangely remote sounds filled the room."

Another notable blues fiddler was Eddie Anthony, also known as 'Macon Ed'. Like Broonzy and Lonnie Johnson, he had a broad musical background, including rags and country stomps as well as blues. A remarkable recording of his is the 'Moanin' And Groanin' Blues', where he scrapes and whines on the fiddle along with a sung chorus of, as the title suggests, wordless growls and groans from the singer, Joshua 'Peg Leg' Howell. Another example of music so intense and bizarre it seems to have come from another planet.

Blues fiddle of the period around 1900 to 1930 can be described as being earthy, energetic, and rhythmic. The use of flattened and bending notes, and loose and flexible phrasing, closely mimics the singing style. It was rarely slick and polished, but often exciting and impassioned. By the early 30s more than 50 different black blues fiddlers had been recorded, but the blues was changing. The hardships of life in the south led many blacks to move north in the 20s and 30s, to cities like Chicago, where there was more chance of factory work and the repression and prejudice were at least less institutionalised. Blues was big in Chicago, but the new style developing there in the nightclubs was loud and heavy, dominated by the newly developed electric guitar, often with piano, harmonica, and drums. The fiddle, which had not yet been successfully amplified, had no place in this new sound; as we have already seen, people like Big Bill Broonzy abandoned the instrument in favour of the guitar. Many black fiddlers in the cities found work in small theatre orchestras, but the advent of recorded music on film, with the release of Al Jolson's *The Jazz Singer*, put paid to these jobs almost overnight. From being one of the key instruments among black musicians in general, and blues players in particular, the fiddle went into rapid decline and virtually disappeared in these fields. For genres such as western swing, country, and old-time music the fiddle, for all the competition from new sounds, remained a potent symbol of 'the good old days'. For the blacks there were no good old days, and the idea of misty-eyed nostalgia for the early days on the plantations was laughable.

Despite all this, the violin remains a natural instrument for the blues, and it wasn't much more than a decade after the Depression years and the boom in Chicago blues that amplification of the violin became possible. Three great black artists carried the torch for blues violin through most of the rest of the century: Papa John Creach, Don 'Sugarcane' Harris, and Clarence 'Gatemouth' Brown.

Three great blues fiddlers

Papa John Creach was born John Henry Creach in Beaver Falls, Pennsylvania, in 1917. He began playing violin in Chicago bars in 1935, and then moved to LA in 1945, making his living playing cabaret spots, on ocean liners, and making occasional film appearances; he described his profession modestly as "sawing wood".

In 1967 he met rock drummer Joey Covington, who was struck not only by Creach's playing but also by his great gentlemanly charm. The friendship led to Papa John recording and gigging with the band Jefferson Airplane, which later became Jefferson Starship, and the spinoff group Hot Tuna, a much more rootsy blues combo.

These collaborations lasted from 1970 to 1974, and left him with a ready audience for his own blues albums, including *I'm The Fiddle Man*, *The Cat And The Fiddle*, and perhaps his best work, *Papa Blues*, released in 1992.

He played with a warm, breathy tone; restrained and controlled, but with a rough edge. He often used an aggressive tremolo and had a wide, insistent vibrato. In his solos a lick would be played repeatedly, punctuated with frequent trills and wild upward swoops.

Don 'Sugarcane' Harris, from Pasadena, California, was born in 1938. By his teens he was playing rhythm & blues guitar and violin with Dewey Terry, under the name Don & Dewey. In the 60s they separated, and Harris began to concentrate on electric blues violin. He made many appearances as a sideman, with artists such as John Mayall

Papa John Creach

& The Bluesbreakers, Johnny Otis, John Lee Hooker, and Little Richard. He is probably best remembered, though, for his work with Frank Zappa in the 1970s, notably the grinding, take-no-prisoners, rocking blues 'Weasels Ripped My Flesh'. Here he makes the most of his raw, shredding sound, frequent 'harmonica' trills, tremolo and double stops. His playing can be fast and fluent, but is most effective on slow numbers, where his distinctive thin tone and shaky vibrato come across as vulnerable and sensitive.

One of his lesser-known but most interesting recordings was the *New Violin Summit* recorded in Germany in 1971, alongside jazz violinists Jean-Luc Ponty (veteran of the original *Violin Summit*), Michal Urbaniak from Poland, and the Austrian Gypsy jazz fiddler Nipso Brantner.

Clarence 'Gatemouth' Brown was born in Louisiana, but raised in Texas, and the musical influences of those two states are clear in his music; along with the blues he enjoys playing zydeco, Cajun, swing, country, and rhythm & blues. Although frequently pigeonholed as a bluesman, with T-Bone Walker as his biggest single influence, Gatemouth Brown referred to his music as "American music, Texas style". He was a highly versatile musician; alongside the fiddle, he also played a lot of electric guitar, sang, and played some mandolin and harmonica. He was a larger-than-life, gregarious character, and I had the good fortune to meet him in the 80s. Along with my group, I was giving a workshop on blues and western swing at a British festival. Halfway through, in strode Gatemouth; with a huge grin he grabbed a fiddle and proceeded to show the audience how music was *really* played in Texas.

He was a popular rhythm & blues artist in the period 1948-58, having hits with swinging numbers such as 'Okie Dokie Stomp' and 'Gate's Salty Blues'. His first big break had come in 1947 when T-Bone Walker was taken ill during a concert in Houston. Gatemouth stepped on to the stage, grabbed a guitar, and went on to steal the show with a number he composed on the spot; the promoter was so pleased he offered him a job right there.

After a dry patch in the 60s, his career took off again in the early

Clarence 'Gatemouth' Brown

70s when he was invited on the first of many tours of Europe, where his genial personality won him many friends. He continued to tour extensively up to his death in 2005, collecting a Grammy and a pile of other awards along the way. A fine example of his playing style can be heard on 'Song For Renee', from his 1983 album *One More Mile*, which was also a popular feature of his live set. He plays clean jazzy lines in unison with the wind section, then launches into a playful solo, full of rhythmic excitement. His scratchy, attacking tone is tempered by a very minimal vibrato, but he is not short on technique, as demonstrated by the dramatic solo fiddle cadenza which swoops fearlessly up into the higher positions.

PLAYING BLUES FIDDLE

EXAMPLE 11.1

CD 2 TRACK 36

The first thing to get your head round is the 12-bar blues sequence. You can do this by playing arpeggios for the chords:

The G chord is the I or root chord; the C is the IV or subdominant, and the D is the V or dominant. Using these relationships you can work out the 12-bar blues easily in any key.

Let's play the same thing again but with three changes. We'll have a two-bar phrase instead of a one-bar phrase, making it more of a scale than an arpeggio. We'll make it swing a bit by splitting up the first note of the phrase into a longer and shorter note, and we'll add a flattened seventh note (for the G chord this means an F-natural instead of F-sharp).

This is now more like what you would call a boogie.

It's approximately what a pianist's left hand might be doing when playing the blues. It's important to understand this 'bottom end' of the blues machine, but it's not what the violin would play in a blues band. In a song, the fiddle will be either following or replacing the vocal line. A typical line for the singer might be:

EXAMPLE 11.2

CD 2 TRACK 37

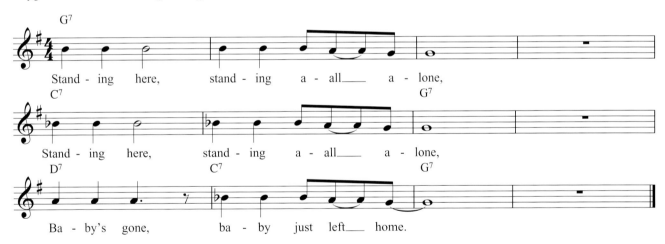

Stand - ing   here,   stand - ing   a - all___   a - lone,
Stand - ing   here,   stand - ing   a - all___   a - lone,
Ba - by's   gone,   ba - by   just   left___   home.

That's so sad it makes you weep. Notice how the first line comes twice, but the main melody note, the B-natural (which is the third note in the G chord), has to come down to B-flat in the second line. As a B-flat it is acting as the flattened seventh of the C chord. If the note had stayed as a B-natural in line two, it would have been the major seventh note in the chord – a most un-bluesy sound. This semitone movement, and the idea of keeping line two very similar to line one, is very typical of blues. The third line is the answering phrase which brings it all back home.

EXAMPLE 11.3

CD 2 TRACK 38

EXAMPLE 11.4

CD 2 TRACK 39

Now it's time to look at the scales used in blues. First of all check out the pentatonic scale; this is the foundation of much European and American folk music, and it is also found widely in Africa. Here's what the G major pentatonic scale sounds like played over a 12-bar blues:

You can improvise over the whole sequence using this scale, and being able to do so is the simplest and easiest introduction to improvisation in general. However, it's not very bluesy, and if you play with your hot combo like this all night, it'll be a case of the bland leading the bland.

EXAMPLE 11.5

CD 2 TRACK 40

However, as soon as you add a flattened third to your pentatonic scale, it gets a lot more interesting.

This is what I call the major blues scale; a major pentatonic scale plus a flattened third. It is invaluable for any kind of improvisation-country, bluegrass, jazz or blues. What's special about the flattened third is that it implies a minor chord:

EXAMPLE 11.6

CD 2 TRACK 41i

When both these notes occur in the same scale, over the same chord, it sets up a tension. The major chord is 'happy' sounding, whilst the minor chord is sad. It's one of the great mysteries of music how a single note can create a distinct emotional response, but there's no question that it does. By manipulating this note you have your finger on the G-spot of the blues; handle it with care! Being a fiddle player, you can easily bend between the two notes:

EXAMPLE 11.7

CD 2 TRACK 41ii

A guitarist can achieve the same effect by bending the strings or using a bottleneck; all the poor pianist can do is to hit the two adjacent notes simultaneously. The note he wants is actually in the crack between them.

Here's an example of a blues solo making use of this scale. It uses lots of blues licks – phrases that you can store up to use over and over again. In particular notice the 'harmonica lick' over the D7 chord. This is bread and butter for the bluesman.

EXAMPLE 11.8

CD 2 TRACK 42

The flattened third isn't the only blue note. We've already seen that the seventh can be flattened. In fact the chords we're using are all seventh chords, so they imply that the F should be natural rather than sharp.

Here's a couple of phrases using flattened sevenths:

EXAMPLE 11.9

CD 2 TRACK 43

The second of these has both a flattened third and a flattened seventh.

Now let's look at one more blue note, the flattened fifth. In the key of G, the fifth is D, so the flattened fifth is D-flat (or C-sharp):

EXAMPLE 11.10

CD 2 TRACK 44i

The second of these combines the flattened fifth, flattened seventh and, as part of the slide, the flattened third:

EXAMPLE 11.11

CD 2 TRACK 44ii

Now what happens if we make a scale that has these three blue notes, but does *not* have the major third at all?

EXAMPLE 11.12

CD 2 TRACK 45

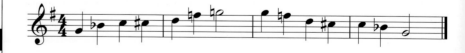

This is the G minor blues scale. It is not as flexible as the G major blues scale, because it won't work over jazz or country songs that have a major feel to them. However, in a proper blues, this is the real thing; dirty, low-down, up-to-your-neck-in-Mississippi-mud blues.

One frequent source of confusion with blues scales is that this minor blues scale is the first thing that many rock and blues guitarist learn when they start playing lead. In fact in many cases that's *all* they ever learn. If you're taught about blues scales by a guitarist they will tell you that this is the blues scale, full stop. However, if you try this G minor blues scale over a jazz tune like 'Dinah', or a country song like 'Hey Good Looking', you'll soon see that it doesn't work, whilst the G major blues scale does. When you've had plenty of experience playing blues, you'll find you don't have to give it a moment's thought, but meanwhile it's important to differentiate between the two.

If you have an enquiring mind, two final question may occur to you. What happens if the song actually is in a minor key; 'Black Magic Woman', for example? That's no problem. If the song is in G minor, the G minor blues scale will work just fine. You may also have been wondering about the fact that we've played a single scale throughout the three-chord 12-bar sequence. Couldn't you play three different scales instead of one? The answer is yes, you can; here's what it sounds like.

EXAMPLE 11.13

CD 2 TRACK 46

We've taken the blues scale for G, with its flattened third, fifth, and seventh, and transferred it first up to C and then D. This is a more sophisticated way of dealing with the chords. It's a technique you would definitely want to learn, particularly for playing in country and jazz. The extent to which you use it in blues is entirely up to your own taste. Don't forget, blues is music from the heart, not the brain. Don't get too clever!

EXAMPLE 11.14

CD 2 TRACK 47

THE FIDDLE HANDBOOK

rock fiddle

What is rock violin? ■

Fiddlers in bands ■

Effects for electric violin ■

Playing rock fiddle ■

rock fiddle

In 1976 I joined my first band, The Speedy Bears, destined by the gods to be the Masters of the Prog-Rock Universe. I was playing my pride and joy, a cherry Gibson SG Special, having abandoned the violin a year previously as being Insufficiently Cool. My talents on the guitar, in the mould of Led Zeppelin's Jimmy Page, were blindingly obvious, but sadly only to myself.

After a few months of rehearsal and a few gigs, belatedly inspired by Curved Air and The Mahavishnu Orchestra, I decided to include a few numbers on my violin, dusted off and amplified with a crude acoustic guitar pickup. The effect on the rest of the band and the fans (now approaching double figures) was immediate and dramatic, and taught me a valuable lesson. In the context of a rock band, a violin is like a talking frog or a tap-dancing nun; a freak of nature, but one that people would cross the street – and even pay money – to see. To musicians and punters raised on three chords and a blues scale, a violin was a Touch Of Class, and a classically trained musician who can play a G major scale in three octaves through a fuzz box is a wonder to behold.

Let's face it, to the uninitiated, one roller-skating polar bear looks very much like another, so it was no time before people were saying of the violinist in The Speedy Bears, "Have you *seen* that guy? He sounds *just like* the bloke that plays with Frank Zappa!"

But what of the success of my band? A quick glance at your almanac of rock history will show that 1976 was not an auspicious year to launch a progressive rock band; it was the year when wizards' capes and waist-length hair were traded in for Mohican haircuts and slashed leather trousers. Magic mushrooms were out and glue sniffing was in; 15-minute keyboard solos were out, The Sex Pistols were in. To cut a long story short, the gods did not smile on The Speedy Bears.

This was, however, by no means the final curtain for the violin in rock music. Whilst there is no such thing as 'rock violin' as a style, in one way or another the instrument has found its way into rock and pop records from the 60s right up to the present day. It would be unfair to refer to tracks hauled out from the dusty corners of my record collection, so most of what is mentioned below is currently available on YouTube for your listening pleasure.

As we've already seen, playing violin in a rock band is a gratifying experience; you never quite escape from the idea that you're doing something slightly naughty, and you hope your old teacher doesn't find out. So how do you go about making sense of your new role?

What is rock violin?

First of all, let's decide what isn't rock violin. There are lots of songs packed with violins, but in the 'string section' sense; that is to say, the producer has hired a string arranger to write some parts, and then got in some session players to play them on the record. Prominent examples would be The Beatles' 'Eleanor Rigby' or The Verve's 'Bitter Sweet Symphony'. They will be 'straight' players, moonlighting from some chamber orchestra. This is definitely not what we're looking for in the concept of rock violin. I had a taste of this when I was hired for one of my most bizarre sessions – to play on an album entitled *Punk Hits For String Quartet*. Not my finest moment.

An improvising violinist will often be brought in to a recording session just to provide a flavour for a particular track. Petra Haden, for example, adds some tasteful but restrained playing to Green Day's 'Time Of Your Life'; she got more chance to let rip during live work with Foo Fighters. Sometimes a guest fiddle player will make the song, as was the case with London fiddler Bobby Valentino's contribution to The Bluebells' 'Young At Heart'. His opening country-style lick was a key hook to the song, and he also got a rollicking solo. The song was a double hit, first on release in 1984, and again in 1993, following its use on a Volkswagen TV advert. Where there's a hit there's a writ, and the Clark Gable lookalike took the band to court, claiming that his session fee in no way reflected his contribution to the song. He won.

Fiddlers in bands

Often the violinist will not be a session musician but a member of the band. Ideally the violinist will double on something else – singing, keyboards, or guitar, for example – or there'll be a fair bit of standing around to do. Slade's first Number One single, the stomping 'Coz I Luv You', saw bass player Jim Lea making

Sarah Neufeld and Owen Pallett with Arcade Fire

a rare appearance on violin. In a lot of situations the violin will find some way of locking into the rhythm and chord structure, with chops, arpeggios, long notes, and so on. Sean Mackin, fiddle player with contemporary American band Yellowcard, does a lot of this. Most of the time he's acting as singer and frontman, playing simple backing lines on his skeletal Fender electric violin. His lack of musical gymnastics is, however, more than compensated for by his ability to do backwards somersaults whilst playing; that's something I'm still working on.

There's a similar situation in Canada's art-rock band Arcade Fire; violinist Sarah Neufeld is mostly a singer, using her instrument for structural string lines that could otherwise be happily handled by a string quartet. She is sometimes joined on stage by Owen Pallett, and he's quite a different kettle of fish. With a whole string of bands in Montreal, and most recently with his own Final Fantasy, Owen has pioneered the very effective use of looping pedals. He will start a number off on his own, playing a couple of bars of percussive pizzicato, which is 'sampled' by his pedal and immediately played back. He will then superimpose several more lines of pizzicato, and then arco, until he has a full backing track which he can sing over. The effect is very full, as percussive and lush as you like; and when done live and with no safety net it is, as his fans would no doubt state, "totally cool".

Some violinists make effective use of their classical training and repertoire within a rock setting. In the early 70s Darryl Way of British rock band Curved Air had a showcase number called 'Vivaldi'. This consisted of a series of improvised classical motifs, a quick tour of his array of effects pedals, and a final section dragged kicking and screaming from *The Four Seasons*. Way's party-piece was to set his bow alight, and then hurl it across the stage into an archery target. This was not, presumably, a technique he acquired from his classical training.

Boyd Tinsley

Perhaps the most successful band deliberately to include classical elements was ELO (The Electric Light Orchestra). Formed in 1970 by Roy Wood, it was an attempt to build on the type of orchestral textures used in such Beatles songs as 'Strawberry Fields' and 'I Am The Walrus'. The band used not only violin but two cellos onstage (and a spaceship, which hovered over the stage but never quite landed). The band had numerous personnel changes, but violinist Mik Kaminski was with them in their 1973-9 heyday, and again in the 80s. Video footage shows him with his trademark blue electric violin, for example playing the lush Gypsy-style intro to 'It's A Livin' Thing'. He had a brief foray in 1977/8 with a solo project, Violinski, best remembered for their hit single, the jolly if lightweight jig-cum-boogie, 'Clog Dance'.

The sawing rhythms of country fiddling can often work in a rock context; Boyd Tinsley of the Dave Matthews Band uses lots of old-timey double-stops on his Zeta electric violin, for example on 'Tripping Billies' and 'Ants Marching'. Violin can also be used to add a flavour of romance and nostalgia, as for example in violinist Billy Currie's contribution to Ultravox's biggest hit, 'Vienna'.

What a rock violinist really wants is a good old-fashioned, let-your-hair-down, improvised 'guitar hero but with a violin' solo, where at last he's in the driving seat. They don't come much better than the solo on The Who's 'Baba O'Riley'. Guest violinist Dave Arbus was given free rein at the end of the song to 'blow' over an F chord for about 40 seconds; that's a long time on a pop single. Arbus was also in East Of Eden, who had a UK hit with the extraordinarily adventurous 'Jig A Jig' (1971), a jazz/folk/rock extravaganza based on a set of Irish reels, 'Jenny's Chickens', 'Drowsy Maggie', and 'The Ash Plant'.

Eddie Jobson, who replaced Darryl Way in Curved Air, got a similar opportunity during his tenure with Roxy Music. On the live version of 'Out Of The Blue' he belts out a soaring solo, demonstrating the useful fact that

Eddie Jobson

a healthy dose of echo and reverb will cover a multitude of sins in the intonation department. This must have been an off-night, because Jobson also worked successfully with Frank Zappa, Jethro Tull, and the all-star cast of UK.

The best way to guarantee you get a good featured solo is to form your own band, as did David LaFlamme from Connecticut. He already had a taste for the spotlight as classical soloist with the Utah Symphony Orchestra, but was soon working with the likes of Janis Joplin, Jerry Garcia, and an early version of Dan Hicks & His Hot Licks.

EFFECTS FOR THE ELECTRIFIED VIOLIN

One of the most seductive things about rock violin is the possibility of using effects pedals. Though most of these are designed with the guitar in mind, almost all will work well with the fiddle.

I've summarised some of the more common examples below. Without hearing them, you can't get much of an idea of the effect. There's no better way than to go to a music shop and try them out. I'd recommend you go down first thing in the morning. That way you'll avoid the wannabe rock guitarists showing off their 'Smoke On The Water' and 'Stairway To Heaven'. I've never known a guitarist who could get up before 11am.

You'll probably find there are lots of effects that you like. Boss, in particular, does a very comprehensive range of pedals. However, if you are thinking of buying several, add up the cost and compare it with a multi-effects unit. You'll quite likely find that for the cost of three or four pedals, you can get a single unit that will do the job, not just of these but of a dozen other pedals as well.

Chorus, phasing, and flanging

These effects fatten up the sound, giving an effect of several violins playing in unison.

Chorus adds a copy of the original sound, slightly delayed and pitch-shifted (ie, out of tune; it's very much like working with a viola player). Phasing does a similar thing but alters the tone rather than pitch of the copied signal. Flanging is a more sophisticated combination of the two effects. With all three of these the depth and intensity can be altered.

Wah

This is an effect well known from the electric guitar. As the name suggests, it produces a voice-like 'wah' sound. This can be controlled by a foot pedal, in which case each wah can be phrased as you want it, or it can be automatic – an 'auto wah' triggered by the attack of the notes.

Delay

This adds an echo to your playing. You can use delay to simulate playing in different sizes of room, from bedsit to cathedral, to infinity and beyond. The options include: a short 'slapback' effect of a few milliseconds; a second or so, allowing you to harmonise a run; or more than ten seconds, allowing you to make a start on 'looping' – creating complete phrases which you can use as your own backing.

Loop pedals

As digital echo effects have become more and more sophisticated, it has become possible to 'sample' a whole section of playing, from seconds to minutes. This can then be immediately played back or 'looped' repeatedly, so that you can play over the top of it. Some systems allow multiple loops so that you can build up a complex multilayered sound.

Overdrive, distortion, and fuzz

These are all different ways to achieve or describe the dirty sound that guitarists first acquired by playing too loud through their valve amps. It's an aggressive, raucous effect that makes you believe that, despite all those violin lessons and allowing your mum to pay for your instrument, you're a true rebel at heart. The biggest problem with 'fuzz violin' is that it can be difficult to maintain any clarity or edge to your sound. What sounds great played solo may just disappear in a band context.

Pitch shifting

This is an effect that alters the pitch of what you're playing by a fixed interval. The simplest kind is an octaver, which will play everything one or two octaves down. More complex is the harmonizer, which will play both your original note, and a note in harmony with it. By setting it to the key in which you're playing, you can get it to play in thirds, for example; the interval will automatically change from minor to major third depending on what note of the scale you play.

In 1967 he formed It's A Beautiful Day, and had a hit with the melancholy single 'White Bird'. This opens with some pizzicato and features two extended violin solos – mostly in the Mixolydian mode – always a good bet to add a slightly dreamy and folky dimension to a solo.

Irish fiddler Steve Wickham made his name playing with The Waterboys in the 80s; he can be heard to good effect on one of the band's most successful singles, 'Fisherman's Blues'. He also got to play on one of U2's biggest hits, 'Sunday Bloody Sunday'; he had met guitarist The Edge at a bus stop and asked him on the off-chance whether they needed a violin player. Amazingly, they did. I've tried this technique myself, but so far with little success – we just don't have that quality of bus stop in my part of London.

A similar chance meeting led to American violinist Scarlet Rivera working with Bob Dylan on his 1975 album, *Desire*; he spotted her walking through Greenwich Village with a violin case on her back. They chatted, and he invited her round to his rehearsal studio, where they tried out several numbers. Her sweetly-toned playing, with equal measures of blues and Gypsy influence, features heavily on the whole album; she also went on to tour with his Rolling Thunder Revue.

Chicago-born violinist Jerry Goodman was one of several jazz/rock/fusion violinists around in the early 70s. He joined The Flock for their 1970 album, *Dinosaur Swamps*, playing fast, fluent, and adventurous solos on songs such as 'Clown'. He was poached from this band by John McLaughlin when he formed the first version of his all-star Mahavishnu Orchestra. His first choice had apparently been Jean-Luc Ponty, who was unable to get a working visa in time. Though short-lived, this band was a perfect showcase for Goodman. The ten-minute 'Dance for Maya', for example, opens with an extended bluesy pizzicato solo, going on to feature an extended violin solo using wah-wah. He remains on top form today, as shown by his work with The Dixie Dregs, for example on the track called 'Take It Off The Top'.

A strong contender for the best ever genuine rock violin solo has to

Steve Wickham and Mike Scott of The Waterboys

be from the Canadian Ben Mink on 'Losing It', a 1982 song by Rush. On this track, which kicks off at a brisk pace in 5/8 time, Mink is in from the start, playing mellow electric violin with heaps of delay, which gives a sparkle to simple rippling scales. Rhythmic chops and tremolo passages punctuate the singing, before he launches into the Big Solo. He doesn't break sweat over the 11/8 time signature, soaring and gliding effortlessly into the highest registers, maintaining perfect intonation throughout. In recent years Mink has worked with singer k.d. lang.

And what about the worst rock solo? Well, naturally, I couldn't possibly comment. But if you happen to check out 'Dust In The Wind' by Kansas, be sure to sit down and take a stiff drink first.

PLAYING ROCK FIDDLE

Show me a rock violinist who says he isn't really a frustrated lead guitarist, and I'll show you a liar. You can put in as many fancy Vivaldi licks as you like, and show off your finger-crunching expertise in ninth position, but when it comes down to it you just want to make a lot of noise and annoy the neighbours.

So, apart from spending your college fund on a scarlet sunburst electric violin and a roomful of effects pedals, how do you go about sounding like a guitarist?

Remember the harmonica lick we looked at in the blues section? That also makes a killer rock lick, especially if you put some harmonics on it. Get the trill going, and then start reducing the pressure on your bow. You should hear the notes starting to whistle and break up, just like a guitar on the edge of feedback. If you don't get the effect you want, try bringing the bow closer to the bridge. Start with a slide up and finish the phrase off by dragging the note down:

EXAMPLE 12.1

CD 2 TRACK 48

THE FIDDLE HANDBOOK

The minor blues scale is really useful for this kind of playing. This next phrase runs up and down the scale bending notes and slipping into and out of harmonics. It's completely out of tempo, so don't take too much notice of the length of the written notes. When you get into this type of playing you're in a world of your own. All time stands still as the audience gazes on in rapt amazement.

EXAMPLE 12.2

CD 2 TRACK 49

The minor blues scale is also useful in constructing crunchy power chord riffs. You'll also need lots of syncopation:

EXAMPLE 12.3

CD 2 TRACK 50i

You can fatten up this kind of riff by playing a parallel fifth harmony. This sounds impressive but is really easy:

EXAMPLE 12.4

CD 2 TRACK 50ii

You don't have to stick with the minor blues scale. The Mixolydian mode is useful for getting an 'over the hills and far away' folky vibe. It's the scale Dave Arbus used for his solo on Baba O'Riley. Here's the mode in D:

EXAMPLE 12.5

CD 2 TRACK 51i

If you know the scale well, you can do fast scalar runs which sound impressive but require minimum brain power:

EXAMPLE 12.6

CD 2 TRACK 51ii

Simplify the scale and you get something with an instant Indian flavour:

EXAMPLE 12.7

CD 2 TRACK 52i

EXAMPLE 12.8

CD 2 TRACK 52ii

Sadly, you're not going to be in the spotlight the whole time, so you'll need some rhythmic phrases to lock in with the rhythm section.

A pattern which works well over a straight 4/4 drum rhythm is a two-bar triplet pattern; it's a slowed down version of the double shuffle used in bluegrass. Sean Mackin of Yellowcard uses this kind of pattern on 'Ocean Avenue'.

EXAMPLE 12.9

CD 2 TRACK 53

Darryl Way used the same rhythm on the intro to Curved Air's 'Propositions'. Play it right down at the heel for maximum attack:

EXAMPLE 12.10

CD 2 TRACK 54

Here's a more classical sounding pattern. Again it will work well with a rock drum beat, and you can modify it to follow a chord sequence. Mackin uses this on the intro to 'Believe'.

EXAMPLE 12.11

CD 2 TRACK 55

Here's a handy riff with a bit of a country rock feel. The middle part is a bit of a finger-cruncher, but worth the effort.

EXAMPLE 12.12

CD 2 TRACK 56

jazz fiddle

Joe Venuti

Eddie South

Stuff Smith

Stéphane Grappelli

Svend Asmussen

Bebop and beyond

Jean-Luc Ponty

Jazz fusion

THE FIDDLE HANDBOOK

jazz fiddle

You would be forgiven for thinking that jazz violin is a one-man show, the one man being the late, great Stéphane Grappelli. There can't be a jazz fiddler alive today, amateur or professional, who doesn't get compared to him. If you've just come off the stage, having played some jazz violin, the chances are that some well-meaning but often woefully ignorant member of the public will come up and congratulate you on sounding "just like Stéphane Grappelli". If your band is called 'Swing 39' or 'The Hot Club Of Wherever', and you closed your set with 'Sweet Georgia Brown', you'll probably be quietly flattered. If, however, you're just unplugging your seven-string Perspex glow-in-the-dark electric violin, and your band is called Voyagers Into The Fourth Dimension, you'll probably accept the compliment through gritted teeth. The truth is that there have been, and still are, hundreds of highly skilled jazz violinists, covering virtually the full range of the jazz spectrum, from Dixieland through swing, Gypsy jazz, bebop, jazz rock, free jazz, and experimental jazz. Grappelli may be the best known, but his style represents only a narrow slice of the vast range of the musical colours, techniques, and approaches available to today's jazz violinist.

In the formative years of jazz, at the end of the 19th century and start of the 20th, the violin was in widespread use by black musicians in the South of the USA. Whether in blues, ragtime, jug-band, or early jazz, the violin was a natural instrument for improvisation, with its ability to bend and slide freely between notes and its closeness in expression to the human voice. The violin was as important as the clarinet and trumpet in vaudeville, ragtime, and dance bands, doing both section and front-line solo work. To name just one example, Armond J. Piron's Novelty Orchestra was a New Orleans band in the 20s, featuring saxophones, clarinet, trumpet, trombone, banjo, piano, and drums. It was a pretty standard line-up from today's perspective on New Orleans jazz, apart from the fact that Piron led the band himself on fiddle. However, in bands like this, particularly in larger line-ups, there was an obvious problem in that the violin could not compete in volume with the brass instruments. So in mainstream dance music the jazz violin gradually declined. It was in smaller groups and more specialised niches that the violin was to make an impact in jazz. If there is one man who deserves the title of the father of jazz violin it is Joe Venuti.

Joe Venuti

Joe Venuti (1903-1978) is widely regarded as the first great jazz violinist. Born to Italian parents who emigrated to the States (he claimed to have been born on the boat, though, as we'll see, all his stories are to be taken with a pinch of salt), he learned classical violin as a child. The fruits of that training can be clearly seen in his exciting melodic and rhythmic technique.

In 1913, at school in Philadelphia, he met guitarist Eddie Lang; they started playing together, at first playing polkas, inventing and trading variations, and quickly moving into jazz. It was a rewarding partnership. From 1926 to 1933 they made many recordings in a variety of small band line-ups, and became internationally famous, not least because the novelty of the guitar/violin combination.

Venuti's technique was ground-breaking; he had a sharp, bright tone, excellent intonation, and an ability to play in any key, anywhere on the violin. He developed what has become known as the 'violin capo' technique, using his first finger as the root and fifth of whatever key he was playing in. In A-flat, for example, he would start with his first finger on the low A-flat on the G-string and E-flat on the D-string, playing one octave up to the fourth finger on the D-string. If he wanted to move higher he would move to fourth position, replacing the top A-flat (fourth finger) with his first finger; this gave him a new octave on the D- and A-strings. Moving up again gave him yet another octave on the A- and E-strings. This made playing in any key easy, as well as allowing double-stops and rocking bow patterns anywhere up and down the neck.

Joe Venuti

He was probably the first violinist to popularise the 'double shuffle' (a 123, 123, 123, 123, 12, 12 pattern rocking across two or three strings, and extending across two or more bars), which was quickly adopted by western swing and, later, bluegrass fiddlers.

He made frequent use of clean, accurate harmonics; both true harmonics and the more difficult artificial harmonics (created by 'stopping' the string with the first finger, and lightly touching the same string with the fourth finger, a fourth interval higher). He used frequent choppy double-stops, and could do extended swinging pizzicato solos. His playing was always punchy, aggressive, inventive, and playful. Perhaps his most famous technique, rarely copied because it is at the same time very difficult and completely wacky, was to unfasten the hairs of his bow, then wrap them round the top of his fiddle, with the bow underneath. This enabled him to play all four strings simultaneously, allowing lush four-part harmonies.

His approach to playing was mirrored very much in his character; he was a notorious prankster, and there are countless stories (often spread, exaggerated, and quite possibly invented by himself) of madcap adventures and escapades. He is said to have pushed a piano out of a fifth-floor window in order to see what key it would play when it hit the sidewalk; to have nailed a pianist's shoes to the floor because he wouldn't stop tapping his feet; and to have given a fellow musician directions to a gig which involved a 200 mile journey, ending up round the block from where he started. Most famously, he is said to have called up 26 (or was it 46?) tuba players (or was it double-bass players?) to an imaginary gig in Hollywood (or was it Manhattan?), just for the fun of seeing the confusion as they all arrived at the same place at once.

Many of Venuti and Lang's compositions bear wacky titles, such as 'Black And Blue Bottom', 'Kickin' The Cat', 'Beatin' The Dog', 'Add A Little Wiggle', 'Have To Change Keys (To Play These Blues)', and 'Bull Frog Moan'. Among the backing instruments that appear on their recordings are bass saxophone, comb, hot fountain pen, kazoo, and a remarkable instrument called the goofus. A majority of the numbers they recorded and performed were self-penned, frequently integrating flashy 'set piece' fiddle tricks into the main melody. 'The Wild Dog' is a playful number with alternating sections, either slow, lazy, and carefree, or completely frantic, whilst 'Wild Cat' is a showcase for the breathtaking speed of which Venuti was capable, always performed with absolute neatness and precision of bowing. 'Raggin' The Scale', one of their best known tunes, has them apparently practising scales within the melody.

At the time of the Great Depression this brilliant, irreverent, light-hearted approach was just the kind of thing the American public wanted. Venuti and Lang achieved great success, fulfilling many recording sessions for a variety of labels, most frequently as Joe Venuti's Blue Four. In addition they worked with many important artists of the day, including Louis Armstrong, Benny Goodman, Paul Whiteman, the Dorsey Brothers, and Jack Teagarden.

This productive period was brought to a tragic close by the sudden death of Eddie Lang in 1933; he died in hospital during an operation for tonsillitis. Venuti then formed his own big band, but this did not prove a big success, whether because he missed Lang's steadying influence and more astute business sense, because of his increasing drinking problem, or simply because musical tastes were changing. His career went into a rapid decline, and after the war he folded his band and moved to the West Coast to concentrate on anonymous Hollywood studio work. The only notable feature of this largely bleak part of his career was his numerous appearances during the 50s on Bing Crosby's radio show, where he was able to show off his quick wit, outrageous stories, and gruff repartee to best advantage.

His fortunes changed once more in 1967; building on an electrifying appearance at the annual Dick Gibson Colorado Jazz Party, he resumed his recording career, working with artists such as Earl Hines, Bucky Pizzarelli, and, most notably, the swinging tenor saxophonist Zoot Sims. In 1969 he recorded a fine album (*Venupelli Blues*) with Stéphane Grappelli, who acknowledged that it was seeing Venuti perform in Paris in 1935 that was one of his major inspirations.

He continued working, appearing at major jazz festivals round the world, until his death from cancer in 1978.

Eddie South

Whilst Venuti is widely admired and named as an inspiration by many younger players, Eddie South, arguably an equally talented player, has received relatively little attention. Born in 1904, just a year after Venuti, he showed prodigious talent as a child and studied classical violin at Chicago Music College. Being black, he quickly found that no amount of talent or education would qualify him in the world of classical music, so he moved into jazz, working in Chicago with artists such as Erskine Tate, Charles Elgar, and Jimmy Wade's Syncopators. In 1927 he formed his own band, Eddie South & His Alabamians. His horizons were opened in 1928 by a visit to Europe; he studied at the Paris Conservatoire, further honing his technique, and in Budapest picked up a love for Gypsy music, as demonstrated by such numbers as 'Tzigani In Rhythm', 'Hejre Kati', and 'Zigeuner'.

A return visit to Paris in 1937 saw him collaborating with Stéphane Grappelli and Django Reinhardt. The Frenchmen were always delighted to meet visiting American jazz musicians. South would often sit in with the band (while Grappelli went off for a drink!), and there were also several exciting recording sessions. These included a fascinating South/Grappelli duet on the first movement of the Bach double violin concerto (I have no doubt that the composer would have heartily approved), and a three fiddle extravaganza on 'Sweet Georgia Brown', with Michael Warlop on the third violin.

Eddie South's jazz playing showed a rich, warm tone, superb technique and intonation, and great aptitude for improvisation. He used a wide and extravagant vibrato, perhaps as a result of his love of

Gypsy music, and to the modern ear his style perhaps suffers from being excessively flowery in its ornamentation and a little stiff in his phrasing. Although he earned himself the nickname 'The Black Angel Of The Violin', South never received the recognition or success that he deserved in America. He died in 1962 in Chicago.

Stuff Smith

Stuff Smith was undoubtedly one of the great swing violinists of the early 20th century. He was black, born Hezekiah Leroy Smith in Ohio in 1909; his nickname came from his habit of referring to other people whose names he couldn't remember as "Stuff".

His first notable work was with the Alphonso Trent Orchestra in the 20s, but it was not until 1936 that he got his major break; he formed a sextet with his lifelong friend, trumpeter Jonah Jones, and they took a residency at New York's Onyx club. There their driving rhythm, exciting performance, and good humour made them a hit with audiences and critics. Two of their most successful recordings of the time were the jive-talkin' 'I'se A-Muggin'' and 'You'se A Viper', while 'Desert Sands' was a favourite he recorded at least three times between 1943 and 1945.

Smith's comedy vocals were an important part of the formula, as was his eccentric habit of wearing a top hat on stage, with either a stuffed monkey or a parrot on his shoulder. However, this comic presentation belies the quality of his playing, which was virtuosic and technically adventurous.

Though not considered a bebop violinist, he definitely had leanings in that direction; trumpeter Dizzy Gillespie was a great admirer of Smith, and credited him with many of the harmonic innovations that pointed him towards bebop. Stuff Smith jammed with the likes of Charlie Parker, something which I'm sure would have daunted Venuti or Grappelli. Whilst Venuti explored the fiddle-orientated aspects of jazz (with his use of rocking bows, country shuffles, harmonics and open strings), and Eddie South came from a classical angle, Stuff Smith had a far more horn-like approach. He phrased as if he were a trumpeter or sax player. He also had a much more progressive and adventurous approach to harmony than his predecessors, exploring with glee the mysterious 'outside' notes that would become the meat and potatoes of bebop and post-bebop jazz. As Barry Ulanov put it in a review in 1944, "He plays so much – the craziest damn double-stops, the weirdest intervals!"

Stuff Smith is credited as being the pioneer of the electric violin. Although today we take amplification of the violin for granted, in the days of the swing bands it was a serious problem for a violinist to be

Stuff Smith

heard on a noisy bandstand. In the 20s, with the Alphonso Trent Orchestra, he used a Stroh fiddle, which incorporated a metal horn like that on an old-fashioned gramophone. He experimented unsuccessfully with a pickup and homemade amplifier "as big as a room", and then, whilst at the Onyx Club, he was presented with a purpose-built National Dobro Vio-Lectric, which he then endorsed and used extensively.

After two years in New York, he went to Hollywood to appear in the film *Swing Street*; this was the end of his Onyx Club run, but he continued to find work with a variety of line-ups, including recording sessions with Dizzy Gillespie, Oscar Peterson, Nat King Cole, Ella Fitzgerald, and even Sun Ra.

He moved to Europe in the 1960s and was still playing up to his death in Munich in 1967.

Stéphane Grappelli

It is rare with any jazz instrument that the field is so dominated by one musician as is the case with Stéphane Grappelli and the jazz violin. True, the field is not large; jazz violinists with an international reputation are numbered in the dozens rather than the hundreds. Nevertheless, through his style and technique, the longevity of his career, the vastness of his discography, not to mention his personal charm, Grappelli has earned a place among the giants of jazz.

Born in 1908 in Paris, he had a hard upbringing. His mother died when he was four, and his father was forced to put him in an orphanage when he was called up to fight in World War I. He was given his first violin at the age of 14, and his father taught him to read music and play scales; he soon started making money, busking around the courtyards of Paris. It was in one such courtyard, in 1929, that he first encountered the Gypsy guitarist Django Reinhardt, also busking, and they started arguing about who would get to play. Grappelli studied piano at the Paris Conservatoire from the age of 16 to 20, working in his spare time as an accompanist to silent films in the cinema. He later became a member of Gregor & His Gregorians, the leading French showband of the time, again playing piano. It was Gregor who heard Grappelli playing violin one night, and realised that here was not just a good pianist but an outstanding violinist. He persuaded him to play the violin full-time.

The most important turning point in Grappelli's career came in 1934, when he again encountered Django Reinhardt in the Croix du Sud nightclub in Montparnasse. In the words of Grappelli, "One day he was strumming his guitar, and I started to improvise with him." Both were already familiar with the work of the American duo, Joe Venuti and Eddie Lang, and they quickly realised that here was an opportunity for them to try and make the same kind of hot, swinging, string-band jazz music. With the addition of two rhythm guitars and a double-bass they created a band. Since their first engagement was organised by the Hot Club de France, they became known as the Quintette du Hot Club de France.

Django and Stéphane were an unlikely partnership. Reinhardt was an illiterate, tempestuous Gypsy, as likely as not to miss a recording session in order to go fishing, but nevertheless regarded as a true genius on his instrument; Grappelli was punctilious, urbane and sophisticated. The band was an immediate success, and was quickly recognised as the first of its kind; a string band, and one with a distinctively European rather than American voice. They played together until the outbreak of World War II, performing widely, recording extensively, and writing what were to become the standards of the Hot Club style: numbers such as 'Minor Swing', 'Djangology', 'Nuages', and 'Swing 39'.

At the outbreak of war they were performing in London; Reinhardt returned to Paris, but Grappelli stayed in England, where he began playing with the blind pianist George Shearing. Grappelli and Reinhardt were reunited in 1945, but by this time Reinhardt's musical direction was changing, with more use of electric guitar and more of a bebop sensibility. The Quintette was never really re-established, and Grappelli's career went into a slow decline. He lived in England for some years before moving back to Paris to take up a long-running residency at the Le Toit club in the Paris Hilton.

Two events were to bring Grappelli back to prominence. The first was an appearance in 1971 on BBC Television's *Parkinson* chat show with classical violin virtuoso Yehudi Menuhin; the idea was to put together two musical opposites to see how they would make out. In fact it was a huge success with the public, and led to a series of further appearances and six albums. The partnership is still talked about today. Among jazz musicians there is a tendency to sneer at Menuhin's less than perfect attempt to swing (all his solos were written out and played note-for note, whilst Grappelli, of course, was completely in his element and could relax). It has to be said that as a meeting of two styles, the territory was very much Grappelli's, and Menuhin was surely very brave in playing completely outside his own field – the number they played on the first occasion, 'Jealousy', was chosen

Stéphane Grappelli

because it was the only jazz tune that Menuhin had ever heard. The partnership gave a huge boost to Grappelli's flagging popularity, and introduced him to a huge middle-class public who may previously have had little interest in jazz, let alone jazz violin.

In 1973 Stephane Grappelli was invited by British guitarist Diz Disley to appear at the Cambridge Folk Festival, and he caused a sensation. The way was now clear for a return to performing at the highest level; he played constantly from then on, first with Disley, then with a variety of other line-ups, including many with guitarist Martin Taylor. He was still performing right up to his death in 1997.He left a prodigious body of recording; apart from those with the artists mentioned above, he recorded albums with guitarists Barney Kessel and Joe Pass, pianists Oscar Peterson, Earl Hines, and McCoy Tyner, and vibes player Gary Burton. He had a particular liking for working with other violinists, and recorded with Eddie South, Joe Venuti, Stuff Smith, Svend Asmussen, Jean-Luc Ponty, Mark O'Connor, Vassar Clements, and the Indian virtuoso L. Subramaniam.

Stéphane Grappelli's playing style can best be described as elegant, relaxed, and flowing. He produced a constant stream of perfectly executed melodic phrases, often at very high speed and with a minimum of effort. He rarely practised, apart from when he was rehearsing with a band, and said of his performances "you play better when you're not thinking of what you're doing". He had a very distinctive fast, tight vibrato, which he used deliberately but sparingly, and used very light finger pressure. He often used a mute, and particularly on ballads he employed a soft, intimate, whispering tone. His bow rarely left the string, and he was a master at producing great flurries of notes with only a tiny amount of bow movement, mostly near the tip. His improvisational style was very melodic, mostly using diatonic scales based around the tonal centre. He constantly used phrases from the major blues scale, with flattened thirds and fifths. He drew on a huge stockpile of riffs and melodic motifs, which become very recognisable when you've listened to enough of his recordings. There are certain 'trademark' techniques he used repeatedly, such as playing a series of third-position harmonics; playing runs in double-stopped fifths across two strings, and playing left-hand pizzicato across the open strings at the start or end of a phrase or section. He made frequent use of repeated triplets, and often played phrases that climbed dizzyingly to the very top of the neck, whilst always maintaining perfect intonation. His tone, apart from when he was deliberately playing very softly, was bright, warm, and clean. Although he would mostly swing, with great accuracy and precision, he also made very effective use of rubato, gliding lazily across the beats and the barlines. His on-stage persona was part of his charm; always elegantly dressed, he played with his eyes half closed with a look of pure bliss and serenity on his face – a feeling he readily transmitted to his audience. Undoubtedly a large factor in his enduring popularity is the nostalgic association between him and the lost, romantic dream of pre-war Paris.

Svend Asmussen

Another fine European jazz fiddler with a long and fruitful career is Svend Asmussen. He is an all-round musician, singing and playing the vibes as well as the violin. That he has never become internationally famous is mainly due to the fact that he chose to remain in his native Denmark, rather than relocate to America, or perhaps France or England, where he would have had more impact. Born in 1916, he was influenced at an early age by the records of Venuti, echoes of whose style can be heard in his early playing. Among other techniques, he mastered Venuti's trick of wrapping the loosened bow hairs around the fiddle so that he could play all four strings at once. His first jobs were on Scandinavian cruise ships, where he got the opportunity to work with such artists as Fats Waller and Josephine Baker. When Stuff Smith visited Denmark, Asmussen's eyes were opened to a whole new angle on jazz fiddle, and, like Smith, he began using his instrument more like a horn or a voice than a violin.

After World War II he achieved considerable fame in Denmark, becoming something of a vaudeville performer. He developed an act that would appeal to the general public as well as jazz aficionados; he played numerous instruments as part of his act, including the rare alto and tenor violins, and such oddities as the musical saw. He incorporated various calypso numbers, and had comedy skits as part of his act. Despite this 'family entertainment' side to his work, he remained a well respected jazz musician, and was much admired by Stéphane Grappelli. His playing was shown to good effect when he shared the stage with Grappelli, Stuff Smith, and Jean-Luc Ponty at the 1966 Jazz Violin Summit in Switzerland.

Bebop and beyond

Whilst the 30s had been the decade of swing, the 40s saw the birth of a new jazz form: bebop. This differed from swing in many ways; whereas swing was primarily dance music, musically accessible to the listener, and with usually steady tempos, bebop was fast, furious and uncompromising. Instead of being based around melody, with bebop the chords were all-important, with the soloist outlining each chord carefully, as well as deliberately stepping outside the chords to create

CONTEMPORARY GYPSY JAZZ

The music of Django Reinhardt and Stéphane Grappelli is usually referred to either as 'Hot Club' or 'Gypsy jazz'. The Gypsy element of the music – the minor keys, furious tempos, and chromatic runs – came from Reinhardt. Grappelli outlived his partner by many years, and gradually moved away from the style he had used in the 30s. Gypsy jazz, however, has grown and developed vigorously since Django's death, among Gypsies and non-Gypsies alike.

A visit to the Samois festival, held every June in the French town on the Seine where Django spent his final years, or any other Gypsy jazz festival, will quickly show you that the genre is dominated by guitarists, who gather in their hundreds to compare string gauges, plectrum designs, and chord substitutions. Yes, they're an exciting lot. As a fiddle player, you'll be a rare but highly valued species.

Among the best contemporary Gypsy jazz violinists is Romanian-born Florin Niculescu. He received a full classical training at the George Enescu music school in Bucharest, before moving to Paris in the early 90s where he began working with Boulou and Elios Ferré, two of the top Gypsy jazz guitarists, with Babik Reinhardt's New Quintette du Hot Club de France, and with Biréli Lagrène's Gypsy Project.

Dorado Schmitt is a French fiddler and guitarist, noted for his fine melodic compositions and mastery of the Gypsy bossa style; his tune 'Bossa Dorado' is now widely played. Also worth discovering are the blind Belgian violinist Tcha Limberger; the German Titi Winterstein; Watti Rosenberg from the famous musical Gypsy family from Holland; and, from Amsterdam, Tim Kliphuis, who is not a Gypsy but a talented and dedicated Grappelli stylist.

dissonance and tension. Further challenge for the listener came from the complexity of the chords, and the jumpy and fragmentary syncopated melodies. All together this was an entirely more challenging style of jazz. If you like your jazz violin smooth, elegant, and nostalgic, read no further; it's all downhill from here. Musicians such as Coleman Hawkins, Charlie Parker, and Dizzy Gillespie blazed the trail, while established swing musicians looked on with varying degrees of wonder, admiration, and disgust. Of the jazz violinists of the time, Stuff Smith was the one closest to bebop, though it was something he never fully embraced, referring to it as "the illegitimate child of swing".

One of the earliest true bebop violinists was the little-known Ginger Smock, a black woman and a protégé of Stuff Smith. In 1946, with an all-female group and sporting a solid-body Rickenbacker electric violin, she recorded a no-nonsense album of hard violin bop. Another interesting pioneer was Harry Lookofsky, a classical orchestral player. He produced two bebop albums, the 1954 *Miracle In Strings,* and the 1959 *Stringsville.* He was not an improviser, and all his solos were composed and played from music. Unable to find other string players who could swing, let alone play bebop, he multi-tracked string sections himself, treating violins like a horn section. Elek Bacsik was a Gypsy musician of Hungarian descent who studied violin at Budapest Conservatory, moving to Paris in 1959 and the US in 1966. Although he started out performing classical and Gypsy material, he soon developed an interest in bebop. He was also a guitarist, and did most of his work as a sideman, though he released some excellent bebop violin, including the album *Bird And Dizzy: A Musical Tribute.* Though fascinating to other jazz violinists, the efforts of such as Smock, Lookofsky, Bacsik and others largely go to prove that the musical world as a whole has little interest in bebop violin; if you're looking for fame and fortune in that direction, you will be sadly disappointed! Oh, and if you find bebop violin hard going, check out the work of Ornette Coleman, saxophonist, free-jazz pioneer and violin owner, for whom concepts such as rhythm, key, intonation, and tone are mere abstractions. Stuff Smith generously commented on Coleman's violin playing: "I think he should stick to his alto sax."

There were other experimenters in the field, but it wasn't until the arrival of Jean-Luc Ponty that bebop violin had its first star, and even he didn't spend long on bebop before moving on to more rewarding musical pastures.

Jean-Luc Ponty

Jean-Luc Ponty was born into a family of musicians in Avranches, France, in 1942. His father taught him violin from the age of five, and at the age of 13 he quit school in order to practise intensively. At 16 he entered the Paris Conservatoire, where he graduated two years later as the prize student. He was immediately hired by a symphony orchestra, with which he played for three years.

Whilst still in Paris with the orchestra, he started playing clarinet with a local college jazz band, soon switching over to violin. He began playing jazz purely for fun, but was quickly seduced by both the freedom and the intellectual challenge of improvisation. He knocked on Stephane Grappelli's door and introduced himself; Grappelli subsequently came to see him play, and was very encouraging. However, Ponty had no intention of following the footsteps of the older player; he avoided the sentimentality and nostalgia of 40s

Parisian swing, turning instead towards the more cool, modern, and challenging sounds of American bebop, particularly Miles Davis and John Coltrane. He was also particularly inspired by Stuff Smith's 1957 album, *Swinging On A String*.

He was among the first violinists to make the break successfully. In terms of playing technique it meant avoiding the linear, melodic sweetness that is so natural to the violin, seeking instead angularity and punchy, horn-like phrasing. He cut vibrato out of his playing almost completely, even on ballads, giving his playing a compellingly stark quality. His approach to chords was very modern, with many altered notes such as flattened and sharpened ninths, chords extended to 11ths and 13ths, and many chromatic passages. He made extensive use of octaves, often combined with aggressive, choppy rhythms, and would sometimes play unison notes on two strings, (fingering a note on one string with his first finger, and on the next string down with his fourth, requiring an added stretch). One ornament that became something of a trademark is the dragging or sliding down of a note at the end of a phrase.

Jean-Luc Ponty

His abandoned his classical career to pursue jazz full-time, though he was very grateful for his classical technique, which, though a hindrance at first, gave him superb control of bowing and intonation.

He released two landmark bebop albums, *Jazz Long Playing* in 1964 and *Sunday Walk* in 1967. He favoured a piano/bass/drums accompaniment rather than the guitar-led combos typical of Grappelli or Venuti; and the material consisted mostly of bebop standards, though he was already beginning to introduce his own compositions. An important milestone in his career was his appearance at the legendary Violin Summit in Basel, alongside Grappelli, Svend Asmussen, and Stuff Smith. Smith had this to say about Ponty: "Keep an eye on this youngster; he is a killer! He plays on violin like Coltrane does on sax!"

In 1969 he began working with Frank Zappa, appearing first on one track of the *Hot Rats* album; Zappa then wrote and produced a solo album for Ponty, entitled *King Kong*. When invited to tour live with Zappa's Mothers of Invention, Ponty left Paris and moved to LA. Other

JAZZ VIOLIN COLLABORATIONS

Perhaps because they have always been seen as an exotic novelty, there is an abiding fascination with putting two or more violinists together at once, to see what happens. Among the earliest such occasions was the pairing of Stéphane Grappelli and Eddie South on their 1937 recordings in Paris.

Duke Ellington had been using Ray Nance since 1940. He was a gifted trumpeter, violinist, and singer, perhaps best known for his famous trumpet solo on the first recording of 'Take The A Train', but also for his many fine jazz violin contributions to tracks such as 'Come Sunday' and 'Moon Mist'. In 1963 Ellington teamed Nance with Stéphane Grappelli on violin and Svend Asmussen on viola, creating a heady mix. Sadly it wasn't released until 1977, but is now available as *Duke Ellington's Jazz Violin Session*. I can't help thinking that Nance must have welcomed Grappelli to the Ellington fold through gritted teeth; despite being on home ground, he was left looking timid and ham-fisted by the suave Frenchman, while Asmussen stuck to the viola, playing low down and funky.

The most famous jazz fiddle grouping was the 1966 'Violin Summit' in Basel, Switzerland, which brought together the three veterans, Grappelli, Smith, and Asmussen, along with the young Jean-Luc Ponty. An electrifying live concert saw each of the violinists on top form: Grappelli as elegant as ever, Asmussen relaxed and witty, while Smith and Ponty battled it out to see who could produce the most explosive bebop solo. Sadly, the recording, *Violin Summit*, can now be most accurately filed as 'hard to get'. The concept, and indeed the title, of a jazz violin summit has proved a popular one. A 1999 release by Legacy, entitled *Jazz Violin Summit*, has Grappelli, Smith, and Ponty together, but is in fact a welding together of two widely separated recording sessions, rather than a single event.

More interesting is the *New Violin Summit* from 1971, presided over by Ponty, but also featuring Polish fusion player Michal Urbaniak, Gypsy Nipso Brantner, and blues legend Don 'Sugarcane' Harris.

collaborations at the same period included an appearance on an Elton John album, and, more significantly, a pairing with John McLaughlin's Mahavishnu Orchestra.

His playing by this time was taking a different direction. He was already beginning to find bebop old-fashioned and restrictive, and was moving into jazz-rock fusion. When he moved to the States he began using electric violins, which were ideal for playing with loud bands and provided more possibilities for manipulating the sound. He championed Barcus Berry violins, and was particularly taken with the

REGINA CARTER

One of the hottest new names in American jazz violin is Regina Carter. Born in Detroit, Michigan, she learned violin from an early age using the Suzuki method. This she found a useful foundation for her jazz playing, because it encourages the learner to play by ear and improvise rather than being stuck to the written music from the outset. She studied first at the New England Conservatory, and then at Oakland University. Playing in the big band there, she was put in the sax section and told to play the alto sax parts. This gave her valuable experience in various aspects of jazz that violinists often struggle with. She learned to play in the flat keys, to control her vibrato, and to phrase like a horn player. The result is a punchy, riff-laden, bluesy style with a rich tone and vibrato ranging from minimal to wide and wild.

After graduating from Oakland she began working with the all-female quartet Straight Ahead, before going solo, releasing records for Atlantic and Verve. The material in her solo albums, though definitely jazz, includes strong elements of soul, funk, latin, and blues. In 2001 she was given the opportunity to travel to Genoa in Italy to perform and record with the city's famous Guarneri violin, known as "The Cannon" due to its enormous tone. The violin was once owned by Paganini, and the resulting album is entitled *Paganini: After A Dream*.

Regina Carter

baritone version of the violin, which could play an octave lower and was good for playing unison melodies with sax or electric guitar. Ponty began to forge a unique sound using effects pedals, particularly chorus and phasing. Through the 70s he released a series of solo albums with psychedelic titles such as *Imaginary Voyage, Enigmatic Ocean,* and *Cosmic Messenger.* The material on these albums consisted of largely self-written, sprawling compositions based on minimalist, repeated melodic units. The extended solos were often modal in nature, the overall feel tense, dark, and introspective. Unlike such predecessors as Stuff Smith or Joe Venuti, Ponty has never been one to include much lightness or humour in his playing.

As technology developed, he continued to stay at the forefront, switching to the solid-bodied Zeta violin, which has an individual pickup for each string. When the Zeta finally became MIDI-capable, he was able to shape the sound in any way he wanted.

Since the 80s, Ponty has begun to change direction again, experimenting with West African rhythms (his *Tchokola* project), with Indian jazz fusion (working with L. Subramaniam), and finally making a return to acoustic music with Al Di Meola, Stanley Clarke, and Béla Fleck.

Jazz fusion

The direction chosen by Ponty, moving from bebop towards rock and fusion proved irresistible for others too. Bebop and the violin have always been unlikely bedfellows, the violin naturally gravitating towards melodic rather than chordal playing. And in the flow of popular culture, jazz in the 60s and 70s was gradually being pushed into a ghetto, whilst anything with psychedelic or rock connotations had a ready audience. Miles Davis led the way, creating music more open in form than bebop, with simpler chord sequences and extended solos often on a single mode. Whilst the acoustic violin would be lost among the pounding grooves, wailing guitars, and washes of keyboards, the electric violin was ideal, especially when combined with distortion, echoes, chorus, phasing, and any number of other mind-bending effects.

Among the violinists taking this road was Michal Urbaniak, yet another disciple of Stuff Smith. Born in Warsaw, Poland, he studied classical violin and jazz sax. He formed a fusion group with singer Urzula Dudziak, and moved to the US in 1973. He has incorporated some Polish folk rhythms into his compositions.

Didier Lockwood is a classically trained violinist who was transfixed by Jean-Luc Ponty's work with Frank Zappa. In the mid 70s he played with the prog rock band Magma, and went on to record a series of jazz-rock albums under his own name.

Zbigniew Seifert was another Pole, and one of the instrument's brightest hopes until his untimely death at the age of 32. Like Urbaniak, he initially played both violin and sax. He was deeply influenced by the playing of John Coltrane, and transferred the style and technique he learned from Coltrane to his violin. The result was a manner of phrasing and articulation quite unlike that achieved by most violinists. He worked first in Poland, then Germany, and finally the US, and recorded five albums under his own name between 1974 and 1978. Despite being one of the most advanced modern jazz violinists of his day, Seifert never achieved the success of someone like Ponty, and his recordings are now rarities.

PLAYING JAZZ FIDDLE

Before you start this, check back over the Blues Fiddle section; the pentatonic scale, blue notes, and major blues scale are essential foundations for jazz playing.

However, the first thing to get a handle on is how to make things swing. You'll find that whenever jazz melodies (often referred to as the 'head'), are written down, they appear without swing; in other words, the quavers (eighth-notes) are written as equal notes. Here's an example of a simple jazz head:

EXAMPLE 13.1

CD 2 TRACK 57

Before we do anything with it, just take a look at the form of the tune. It starts with an eight-bar sequence (the A section), which is repeated. Then comes a different eight-bar sequence (the B), followed by another A. This sequence, AABA, is typical of most jazz tunes, and it's something you need to be familiar with.

Play it through and you'll find it feels stiff and wooden. We need to make it swing.

Take the first bar, for example:

EXAMPLE 13.2

CD 2 TRACK 58i

EXAMPLE 13.3

CD 2 TRACK 58ii

It would actually be played more like this:

On each pair of quavers, the first note is lengthened and the second shortened. Another way of writing it would be:

EXAMPLE 13.4

CD 2 TRACK 58iii

Neither of these is strictly accurate, which is just as well, because it would make the written music very messy and hard to read. Instead the music is left 'straight' and it's up to you to put in the amount of swing that you think appropriate. The feel of it is something that comes with practice and a lot of listening.

There are some other fundamental things you need to do to make your playing sound like jazz.

Vibrato If you've had any classical training, you'll automatically find yourself putting an even vibrato on every note, without even thinking about it. You may have sweated blood to learn that vibrato, but from now on it's going to be more of a hindrance than a help. Use it deliberately, but only occasionally, to give shape to an individual note. A wide, crazy vibrato at the end of a punchy phrase can be very effective; this was something Joe Venuti used a lot. Grappelli had a smooth, fast vibrato, but always very controlled. Most modern players, such as Ponty or Urbaniak, use little or none.

Bowing Another bad habit you've probably got into is playing long, smooth, even bows. Whilst you will need to use long bows sometimes, for most of your playing you won't need more than four inches (10cm) of bow, and a lot of notes need only an inch (2.5cm).

Slides Whereas you will have learned to hit a note squarely and precisely, with jazz it's common to slide up to some notes, particularly longer notes or those at the start of a phrase. This will usually be a small and subtle slide, not an extravagant swoop.

Articulation You're aiming for very precise articulation of notes; you can aid this by giving each new bow a little 'dig' of pressure with the first finger of your bow hand.

With swing playing, the accent usually occurs on the beat (ie, with the first of a pair of eighths). For example bar 15 becomes:

EXAMPLE 13.5

CD 2 TRACK 59i

Remember to lengthen the first note of each pair.

The exception is where the second of each pair is tied with a longer note as at the end of bar eight. When this happens the accent will normally lie on the second note, even though the first of the pair is still longer.

EXAMPLE 13.6

CD 2 TRACK 59ii

Syncopation is an important part of swing playing; it involves placing the accent of a phrase off the beat instead of on the beat, creating surprise and a sense of urgency. This may be written into the melody; we've already seen a simple example in bar eight, where the last note of the phrase is brought forward or anticipated.

A more complex and interesting example is in bars 10 and 11:

EXAMPLE 13.7

CD 2 TRACK 60i

The same phrase could have been written without syncopation:

EXAMPLE 13.8

CD 2 TRACK 60ii

But then you lose all the interest. It's important with jazz fiddling to be able to create your own syncopations, both when playing the head, and in your solos.

Messing with the tune

We've already seen that what you play on the head isn't necessarily what's written. Make yourself at home in the tune; think of it as your own house, not a rented hotel room. Your aim is to find ways to personalise it, and make it comfortable for yourself.

We've looked at ways of adding swing to the eighth-notes. Supposing it's a very simple tune without many eighths, but you want to give it a strong swing feel. You can easily split the notes wherever you want.

Bar seven, for example, has four straight quarter-notes (crotchets):

EXAMPLE 13.9

CD 2 TRACK 61i

You could split them like this (remembering to swing the pairs of eighth notes):

EXAMPLE 13.10

CD 2 TRACK 61ii

Or for more interest you could make a triplet, leave two quarter-notes straight, and split the last one into a pair:

EXAMPLE 13.11

CD 2 TRACK 61iii

The aim of these changes is to add interest, swing and variety to the melody. Where a rhythmic phrase appears several times in the original melody, you should aim to give it a different treatment each time it reappears.

Here's an example of how you might play the whole head, with split notes, syncopation, and triplets.

So far we've changed the length, position, and number of notes in the melody, but not the pitch. Now we'll look at how we can add extra filling notes to a melody by using adjacent notes from the scale. Since we're in the key of G, we can fill a gap between two adjacent notes with whatever note from the scale comes in between.

EXAMPLE 13.12

CD 2 TRACK 62

So bar two could change from:

EXAMPLE 13.13

CD 2 TRACK 63i

to:

EXAMPLE 13.14

CD 2 TRACK 63ii

Obviously if you're going to add a note, you have to subtract from something else. In this case we've shortened the first of the two notes whose gap we decided to fill.

Similarly bar four could change from:

EXAMPLE 13.15

CD 2 TRACK 63iii

to:

EXAMPLE 13.16

CD 2 TRACK 63iv

Pretty radical stuff! We can be even bolder by using chromatic notes rather than notes from the major scale. So bar four could become:

EXAMPLE 13.17

CD 2 TRACK 63v

or:

EXAMPLE 13.18

CD 2 TRACK 63vi

Endless small variations like this can make every performance unique.

Improvisation

So far we've looked at small changes to a melody that give it a jazz feel. That, unfortunately, is the easy part. The real crux of jazz is improvisation, where you leave the melody behind completely and compose your own lines with nothing for guidance but the chords and rhythm. If you've never tried this before it can be very intimidating. What is also intimidating is the way that many jazz courses try to teach improvisation, insisting that every chord has its own scale or mode and that you have to change scale every time the chord changes. With the straightforward chord sequences that you find in most swing-era jazz tunes, there's a much easier approach that will serve you very well. Start off by playing the G major scale all the way through the chord sequence to the head we've been looking at. Here it is, played through the chords of the A section:

EXAMPLE 13.19

CD 2 TRACK 64

You can do this all the way through the sequence. First play the scale straight, then start playing around with it, adding swing and syncopation, making patterns from the scale. What you'll find is that all the notes from the scale will sound OK on any chord of the sequence. Even the odd chords like C-sharp diminished, A9, or D augmented seventh don't sound too bad. This discovery gives you a great deal more freedom than you thought you had. You've got to listen to the chords, but at this stage you don't have to know every chord inside out.

A more useful, interesting, and melodic scale to use is the pentatonic scale:

EXAMPLE 13.20

CD 2 TRACK 65i

As with the major scale, you can use this freely throughout the chord sequence. It will give more shape and logic to your phrases, and make it easier to create simple melodies. For a novice jazz fiddler this scale is invaluable. Spend as much time as you can learning it, eventually in every key.

More useful still is the major blues scale. For more on this scale check out the blues chapter, but here it is in G:

The flattened third (B-flat) is the blue note; when combined with the major third (B) it gives you the two options; a happy or a sad sound. This gives you control of a great deal of musical tension and expression.

Practise this scale not only in first position but in higher positions as well. Learn the fingerings in each position as follows:

Third position:

The top note (the D) available in third position is a fourth finger. Replace this with your first finger and you're in sixth position:

There are fewer notes easily available in this position.

Again replace the top note fourth finger with your first. You're now in ninth position. Don't look down; you're perfectly safe.

You might think this is a bit of an academic exercise and that you're never going to go that high. The point of these fingerings is that once your fingers have learned them, you can cover the full neck and play in any key with ease, no matter how many sharps or flats. Once you're out of first position you don't even need to know what notes you're playing. The American swing fiddler Paul Anastasio learned this technique from Joe Venuti and called it the 'violin capo' method. Just like a guitarist with a capo, or a keyboard player with a pitch-change switch, it makes your life a whole lot easier when it comes to dealing with nightmare keys like D-flat or F-sharp.

Chords

So far we've studiously ignored chords, even though they're of critical importance to jazz. I could write a whole book about chords; it would be a publishing phenomenon to rival *Harry Potter* or the Bible. However we'll have to settle here for a quick skim through the basics. A chord is a group of notes that harmonise with one another. In practice this usually means three or four notes. In a three-note chord they are the root (or tonic), third, and fifth. If the third is three semitones (half-steps) above the root, then it's a minor chord. If it's four semitones (half-steps), that makes it a major chord. Some chords also have a seventh. If the seventh is one semitone (half-step) below the octave of the tonic, it's called a major seventh chord. If it's two semitones (half-steps) below, it's called a seventh chord. Other notes can also be specified, such as flattened fifth, sharpened ninth and so on. To some extent you don't need to pay much attention to the finer points of these chords. If you play D instead of D6, don't expect everyone to turn around and look at you with raised eyebrows. However, a word of warning. The method of dealing with chords we've used so far is fraught with hazards. I discovered this the first time I tried to improvise on 'The Girl From Ipanema', using my tried and tested, but extremely naïve, method of playing it by ear with a single pentatonic scale. Let's just say I've hated the tune ever since.

Here's the root, third, and fifth of a G major chord. To hear it properly play it as an arpeggio:

EXAMPLE 13.25
CD 2 TRACK 69i

Here's a G7 chord:

EXAMPLE 13.26
CD 2 TRACK 69ii

And here's Am7 (A minor seventh):

EXAMPLE 13.27

CD 2 TRACK 69iii

So how do we incorporate this knowledge into playing over chords? All the notes in the Am7 chord, and indeed most of the chords in our 'head' are a part of the G major scale, which is why we were able to use this scale to play through the sequence.

However, whereas this sounds fine:

EXAMPLE 13.28

CD 2 TRACK 70

It doesn't sound nearly as good over Am7:

EXAMPLE 13.29

CD 2 TRACK 71

So what you really want is to play a phrase starting on A, not G:

EXAMPLE 13.30

CD 2 TRACK 72

This sounds much better. So if you're playing up and down with a single scale, use your ear to tell you which notes sound best to start and end your phrases. If you want to understand the chords fully, a good approach is to play through the whole sequence using arpeggios.

Here are bars five to eight treated as arpeggios:

EXAMPLE 13.31

CD 2 TRACK 73

THE FIDDLE HANDBOOK

It'll sound more musical if you go down as well as up, and also if you don't always start on the root:

EXAMPLE 13.32

CD 2 TRACK 74

It's useful to try this whenever you learn a new tune. It can also serve as the starting point for an actual solo, if and when you come across an unforgiving sequence such as 'The Girl From Ipanema'.

Playing outside

Jazz is like life. If you're learning from scratch, my advice is to start off making it as easy for yourself as possible, playing by ear and not paying too much attention to chords. Think of this as your carefree, tearaway youth where you avoid all responsibilities. The next stage is to find out all about chords, and learn to treat them with respect; that is to say get a haircut, get a job, get a mortgage. The third stage is when the kids have grown up, there's money in the bank, and we're bored with sticking to the straight and narrow. It's time to buy a Harley Davidson and take to the open road. Or, in jazz terms, it's time to start living dangerously, and deliberately play outside the chords.

This is an idea that developed gradually over decades through the history of jazz, starting with the idea of 'leading notes' or 'passing notes' that don't belong in the chord but lead to notes that do. Bebop was all about extending and altering individual chords, whilst fusion allowed the soloist to do pretty much what he felt like. This again is something that deserves a book to itself. Instead here's a single example. It uses a whole-tone scale where, instead of having a mixture of tones and semitones (whole steps and half-steps), all the intervals are whole tones. It means that on an ascending scale you will start off 'in' (ie, safely within the chord), but quickly end up 'out', and sounding pretty weird. The normal practice is to start a phrase in, move out, and then, to prove that you know what you're doing, end up safely back inside. This is Michal Urbaniak territory:

A final word of warning. When playing 'outside', context is everything. Jazz is a wide spectrum, and 'outsidedness' definitely belongs at the more modern end. If you're playing with The Purple Warriors Of Zebulon, with accompanying chords that are open and ambiguous, a bass player who has sworn never to play the same note twice in four bars, and a drummer who sounds like his kit is falling down stairs, your outside licks are going to sound just fine. If, however, you've landed a plum job with the New Dixieland Revival, with a rumpty-tum rhythm section and a beetle-browed banjo accompanist who has a deep suspicion of major seventh chords, you'd better start checking the 'fiddle player wanted' ads.
CONTEXT IS EVERYTHING!

EXAMPLE 13.33

CD 2 TRACK 75

on the CDs

CD1

TRACK

1. Ex 1.1: 'Julia Clifford's Polka'
2. Ex 1.2
3. Ex 1.3
4. Ex 1.4
5. Ex 1.5
6. Ex 1.6
7. Ex 1.7
8. Ex 1.8, 1.9
9. Ex 1.10
10. Ex 1.11
11. Ex 1.12
12. Ex 1.13
13. Ex 1.14
14. Ex 1.15
15. Ex 1.16
16. Ex 1.17
17. Ex 1.18
18. Ex 1.19
19. Ex 1.20
20. Ex 1.21
21. Ex 1.22: 'Paddy Fahey's Jig'
22. Ex 2.1
23. Ex 2.2
24. Ex 2.3
25. Ex 2.4
26. Ex 2.5
27. Ex 2.6
28. Ex 2.7: 'I Prefer The Kilt'
29. Ex 2.8
30. Ex 2.9
31. Ex 2.10, 2.11
32. Ex 2.12, 2.13
33. Ex 2.14, 2.15. 2.16

34. Ex 2.17: 'The Laird O' Drumblair'
35. Ex 2.18, 2.19
36. Ex 2.20
37. Ex 2.21
38. Ex 2.22: 'Earl Haig (The Laird O' Bemersyde)
39. Ex 2.23, 2.24
40. Ex 2.25
41. Ex 2.26: 'The Fairy Dance'
42. Ex 2.27: 'Da Ferry Reel'
43. Ex 3.1: 'Shepherd's Hey'
44. Ex 3.2: 'Sir Roger de Coverley'
45. Ex 3.3: 'Hod The Lass Till I Run At Her'
46. Ex 3.4: 'John Of The Green, The Cheshire Way'
47. Ex 3.5: 'The Savage Hornpipe'
48. Ex 3.6: 'The High Level Bridge'
49. Ex 4.1, 4.2
50. Ex 4.3
51. Ex 4.4
52. Ex 4.5: 'Tantz, Tantz, Yidelekh'
53. Ex 4.6
54. Ex 4.7, 4.8
55. Ex 4.9
56. Ex 4.10
57. Ex 4.11: 'Bessarabian Hora'
58. Ex 5.1: 'Korobushka'
59. Ex 5.2: 'Kolomyjka Lubka'
60. Ex 5.3
61. Ex 5.4: 'One Kitten, Two Kittens'
62. Ex 5.5

63. Ex 5.6
64. Ex 5.7
65. Ex 5.8
66. Ex 5.9: 'Ozwodna (Goralski Polka)'
67. Ex 5.10: 'Hora Femeilor'
68. Ex 5.11: 'Madro'
69. Ex 6.1, 6.2
70. Ex 6.3: 'Old Joe Clark'
71. Ex 6.4
72. Ex 6.5, 6.6
73. Ex 6.7, 6.8, 6.9
74. Ex 6.10, 6.11
75. Ex 6.12
76. Ex 6.13: 'Fisher's Hornpipe'
77. Ex 6.14, 6.15
78. Ex 6.16, 6.17
79. Ex 6.18, 6.19
80. Ex 6.20: 'Granny Will Your Dog Bite?'
81. Ex 6.21
82. Ex 6.22: 'Greenback Dollar'
83. Ex 7.1
84. Ex 7.2
85. Ex 7.3
86. Ex 7.4
87. Ex 7.5, 7.6
88. Ex 7.7, 7.8, 7.9, 7.10
89. Ex 7.11
90. Ex 7.12
91. Ex 7.13
92. Ex 7.14
93. Ex 7.15: 'Jolie Blonde'
94. Ex 7.16: 'Allons A Lafayette'

CD2

TRACK

1. Ex 8.1, 8.2, 8.3
2. Ex 8.4, 8.5, 8.6, 8.7
3. Ex 8.8, 8.9, 8.10, 8.11
4. Ex 8.12
5. Ex 8.13, 8.14, 8.15
6. Ex 8.16, 8.17
7. Ex 8.18, 8.19, 8.20, 8.21, 8.22
8. Ex 8.23, 8.24
9. Ex 8.25: 'Roll In My Sweet Baby's Arms'
10. Ex 8.26
11. Ex 8.27
12. Ex 8.28
13. Ex 8.29
14. Ex 8.30
15. Ex 8.31, 8.32, 8.33
16. Ex 9.1: 'Liberty'
17. Ex 9.2: 'Beaumont Rag'
18. Ex 9.3
19. Ex 9.4
20. Ex 9.5
21. Ex 9.6
22. Ex 9.7, 9.8
23. Ex 9.9
24. Ex 9.11, 9.12
25. Ex 9.13, 9.14
26. Ex 9.15
27. Ex 9.16
28. Ex 10.1
29. Ex 10.2
30. Ex 10.3
31. Ex 10.4
32. Ex 10.5
33. Ex 10.6
34. Ex 10.7
35. Ex 10.8
36. Ex 11.1
37. Ex 11.2
38. Ex 11.3
39. Ex 11.4
40. Ex 11.5
41. Ex 11.6, 11.7
42. Ex 11.8
43. Ex 11.9
44. Ex 11.10, 11.11
45. Ex 11.12
46. Ex 11.13
47. Ex 11.14
48. Ex 12.1
49. Ex 12.2
50. Ex 12.3, 12.4
51. Ex 12.5, 12.6
52. Ex 12.7, 12.8
53. Ex 12.9
54. Ex 12.10
55. Ex 12.11
56. Ex 12.12
57. Ex 13.1
58. Ex 13.2, 13.3, 13.4
59. Ex 13.5, 13.6
60. Ex 13.7, 13.8
61. Ex 13.9, 13.10, 13.11
62. Ex 13.12
63. Ex 13.13, 13.14, 13.15, 13.16, 13.17, 13.18
64. Ex 13.19
65. Ex 13.20, 13.21
66. Ex 13.22
67. Ex 13.23
68. Ex 13.24
69. Ex 13.25, 13.26, 13.27
70. Ex 13.28
71. Ex 13.29
72. Ex 13.30
73. Ex 13.31
74. Ex 13.32
75. Ex 13.33

bibliography

Irish

Peter Cooper *Mel Bay's Complete Irish Fiddle Player* (Mel Bay 1995)

Miles Krassen *O'Neill's Music Of Ireland: Over 1000 Fiddle Tunes* (Oak 1976)

Paul McNevin *A Complete Guide To Learning The Irish Fiddle* (Waltons 1998)

Gearóid Ó hAllmhuráin *A Pocket History Of Irish Traditional Music* (O'Brien 2003)

Captain Francis O'Neill *Irish Folk Music: A Fascinating Hobby* (Norwood Editions 1973)

June Skinner Sawyers *The Complete Guide To Celtic Music* (Aurum 2000)

Scottish

Tom Anderson *Ringing Strings* (The Shetland Times 1997)

Tom Anderson and Pam Swing *Haand Me Doon Da Fiddle* (University of Stirling 1979)

Pete Cooper 'James Scott Skinner (1843-1927). Reflections on the life and music of one of Scotland's greatest fiddle composers' in *Musical Traditions* online magazine, 2002 (www.mustrad.org.uk/articles/skinner.htm)

Liz Doherty 'Bringing it all back home? Issues surrounding Cape Breton fiddle in Scotland.' An article in *Play It Like It Is: Fiddle And Dance Studies From Around The North Atlantic*, ed. Ian Russell and Mary Ann Alburger (Elphinstone Institute 2006)

Burt Feintuch 'Music In The Margins: Fiddle Music In Cape Breton.' An article in *Play It Like It Is: Fiddle And Dance Studies From Around The North Atlantic*, ed. Ian Russell and Mary Ann Alburger (Elphinstone Institute 2006)

Alistair J. Hardie *The Caledonian Companion* (The Hardie Press 1992)

Stuart McHardy *MacPherson's Rant And Other Tales Of The Scottish Fiddle* (Birlinn 2004)

J. Murray Neil *The Scots Fiddle (Volume 1); Tunes, Tales And Traditions Of The North East and Central Highlands* (Neil Publishing 1999)

English

Chris Bartram *The Fiddle In Southern England* (Free download from Yorkshire Dales Workshops, www.ydw.org.uk)

Paul Burgess and Charles Mentieth *The Coleford Jig (Traditional Tunes From Gloucestershire)* (Self-published 2004)

Pete Cooper *English Fiddle Tunes: 99 Traditional Pieces For Violin* (Schott 2006)

Philip Heath-Coleman '"Here's One You'll Like": Stephen Baldwin, English Fiddler', *FiddleOn Magazine* 18 (Autumn/Winter 2005)

John Offord *John Of Green, The Cheshire Way: A Collection Of Hornpipes* (Green Man Music 1985)

Paul Roberts 'English Fiddle Styles 1650-1850: Reconstructing Pre-Victorian Technique' (www.village-music-project.org.uk/roberts.htm)

Klezmer

Ilana Cravitz *Klezmer Fiddle: A How-To Guide* (Oxford University Press 2008)

Stacy Phillips *Mel Bay's Klezmer Collection For C Instruments* (Mel Bay 1996)

Seth Rogovoy *The Essential Klezmer* (Algonquin Books 2000)

Henry Sapoznik *Klezmer! Jewish Music From Old World To Our World* (Schirmer 1999)

Henry Sapoznik *The Compleat Klezmer* (Tara Publications 1987)

Mark Slobin (ed.) *American Klezmer: Its Roots And Offshoots* (University of California Press 2002)

Eastern European

Balkan Dance Music Book (Eliznik 1997) From www.eliznik.org.uk

Donna A Buchanan 'Wedding Musicians, Political Transition, And National Consciousness In Bulgaria.' In *Retuning Culture: Musical Changes In Central And Eastern Europe*, ed. Mark Slobin (Duke University Press 1996)

Hudit Frigyesi 'The Aesthetic Of The Hungarian Revival Movement.' In *Retuning Culture: Musical Changes In Central And Eastern Europe*, ed. Mark Slobin (Duke University Press 1996)

Gundula Gruen *Gypsy Fiddle Collection* (Spartan Press 2007)

Janos Manga *Hungarian Folk Songs And Folk Instruments* (Corvina Press 1969)

Bruno Nettl *Folk And Traditional Music Of The Western Continents* (Prentice-Hall 1965)

Bálint Sárosi *Gypsy Music* (Corvina Press 1970)

Carol Silverman 'Music And Marginality; Roma (Gypsies) of Bulgaria And Macedonia.' In *Retuning Culture: Musical Changes In Central And Eastern Europe*, ed. Mark Slobin (Duke University Press 1996)

Philip Thornton *Where Did It All Begin?* (Balkan Plus)

Old-Time

Joyce H Cauthen *With Fiddle And Well-Rosined Bow – A History Of Old-Time Fiddling In Alabama* (University of Alabama 1989)

Craig Duncan *Mel Bay's Deluxe Fiddling Method* (Mel Bay 1981)

Bill Shull *Cross-Tuning Your Fiddle* (Mel Bay 1994)

Marion Thede *The Fiddle Book* (Oak 1967)

Cajun

Barry Jean Ancelet and Elemore Morgan *Cajun And Creole Music Makers* (University Press Of Mississippi 1999)

John Broven *South To Louisiana: The Music Of The Cajun Bayous* (Pelican 1992)

Craig Duncan *The Cajun Fiddle* (Mel Bay 1995)

Rick Foster *Louisiana Music* (Da Capo Press 2002)

Bluegrass

Randy Noles *Orange Blossom Boys: The Untold Story Of Ervine T. Rouse, Chubby Wise And The World's Most Famous Fiddle Tune* (Centrestream Publishing 2002)

Stacy Phillips *Hot Licks For Bluegrass Fiddle* (Oak Publications 1984)

Neil Rosenberg *Bluegrass: A History* (University of Illinois Press 2005)

Richard D Smith *Can't You Hear Me Callin': The Life Of Bill Monroe* (Little, Brown and Company 2000)

Western Swing

Jean A Boyd *The Jazz Of The Southwest; An Oral History Of Western Swing* (University Of Texas Press 1998)

Stacy Phillips *Western Swing Fiddle* (Oak Publications 1994)

Charles R Townsend *San Antonio Rose: The Life And Music Of Bob Wills* (University Of Illinois Press 1986)

Country

Stacy Phillips *Mel Bay's Complete Country Fiddler* (Mel Bay 1992)

Richard A. Peterson *Creating Country Music: Fabricating Authenticity* (University of Chicago Press 1997)

Kurt Wolff *Country Music: The Rough Guide* (Rough Guides 2000)

Blues

Craig Duncan *Blues Fiddling Classics* (Mel Bay 1994)

Julie Lyonn Lieberman *Blues Fiddle* (Oak, 1986)

Jazz

Matt Glaser and Stéphane Grappelli *Jazz Violin* (Oak 1981)

Raymond Horricks *Stéphane Grappelli* (Hippocrene 1983)

Martin Norgaard *Jazz Fiddle Wizard* (Mel Bay 2000)

Dave Reiner and Glenn Asch *Mel Bay's Deluxe Anthology Of Jazz Violin Styles* (Mel Bay 1982)

discography

Irish
Altan *The Best Of Altan* (Green Linnet)
Kevin Burke *If The Cap Fits* (Mulligan Records)
Liz Carroll and John Dole *In Play* (Compass Records)
Martin Hayes and Dennis Cahill *The Lonesome Touch* (Green Linnet)
Eileen Ivers *Wild Blue* (Green Linnet)
Tommy Peoples *High Part Of The Road* (Shanachie)
The Wheels Of The World, Vol. 1: Early Irish-American Music? (Yazoo)

Scottish
Scottish Tradition Volume 4: Shetland Fiddle Music (Greentrax)
Scottish Tradition Volume 9: The Fiddler And His Art (Greentrax)

English
Rig-A-Jig Jig: Dance Music Of The South Of England. Volume 9 of *The Voice Of The People* series (Topic)

Klezmer
Khevrisa *European Klezmer Music* (Smithsonian Folkways)
Itzhak Perlman *In The Fiddler's House* (EMI Angel)
Alicia Svigals *Fidl: Klezmer Violin* (Traditional Crossroads)

Eastern European
Taraf De Haidouks *Musique Des Tziganes De Roumanie* (Cramworld)
The Trebunia Family Band *Music Of The Tatra Mountains* (Nimbus)
Ukrainian Village Music: Historic Recordings 1928-1933 (Arhoolie)

Old-Time
American Fiddle Tunes (Library of Congress/Rounder)
Eck Robertson *Old-Time Texas Fiddler: Vintage Recordings 1922-1929* (County)
Traditional Fiddle Music Of Kentucky (Rounder)

Cajun
Harry Choates *Fiddle King Of Cajun Swing* (Arhoolie)
Michael Doucet *Learn To Play Cajun Fiddle* (Homespun Video DVD)
Dennis McGee *The Complete Early Recordings Of Dennis McGee* (Yazoo)

Bluegrass
Bill Monroe & His Blue Grass Boys *All The Classic Releases 1937-1949* (JSP Records)

Western Swing
Stompin' Singers And Western Swingers (Proper Box)
Bob Wills & His Texas Playboys *Take Me Back To Tulsa* (Proper Box)

Country
Johnny Gimble *The Texas Fiddle Collection* (CMH)
Ray Price *The Essential Ray Price 1951-62* (Columbia)
Eck Robertson *Old-Time Texas Fiddler: Vintage Recordings 1922-1929* (County)
Hank Williams *40 Greatest Hits* (Polydor)

Blues
Folks, He Sure Do Pull Some Bow! Vintage Fiddle Music 1927-1935: Blues, Jazz, Stomps, Shuffles & Rags (Old Hat)
Violin Sing The Blues For Me; African-American Fiddlers 1926-49 (Old Hat)

Rock

Final Fantasy *Has A Good Home* (Tomlab)

The Flock *Flock Rock: The Best Of The Flock* (Legacy/Columbia)

It's A Beautiful Day *It's A Beautiful Day* (San Francisco Sound)

Rush *Signals* (Island Def Jam)

Violinski *Clog Dance: The Very Best Of Violinski* (Castle Music)

Darryl Way *Saturation Point* (Esoteric Recordings)

Jazz

Duke Ellington's Jazz Violin Session (Wounded Bird Records)

Stéphane Grappelli and Joe Venuti *Venupelli Blues* (Charly)

I Like Be I Like Bop; Odds And Svends Of Early Bebop Violin And Contemporary Violin Curiosities (AB Fable)

Tim Kliphuis *The Grappelli Tribute* (Robinwood)

Eddie Lang and Joe Venuti *The New York Sessions 1926-35* (JSP)

Didier Lockwood *Tribute To Stéphane Grappelli* (Sony)

Jean-Luc Ponty *Electric Connection/King Kong* (Gott Discs)

Jean-Luc Ponty *Jazz Long Playing* (Universal)

Stuff Smith *Time And Again* (Proper)

Eddie South *The Dark Angel Of The Fiddle* (Soundies)

Michal Urbaniak *Fusion* (Columbia/Legacy)

Violin Summit (MPS)

appendix

Key signatures

Six flats (B♭, E♭, A♭, D♭, G♭, C♭) = G♭ major or E♭ minor

Five flats (B♭, E♭, A♭, D♭, G♭) = D♭ major or B♭ minor

Four flats (B♭, E♭, A♭, D♭) = A♭ major or F minor

Three flats (B♭, E♭, A♭) = E♭ major or C minor

Two flats (B♭, E♭) = B♭ major or G minor

One flat (B♭) = F major or D minor

No sharps or flats = C major or A minor

One sharp (F♯) = G major or E minor

Two sharps (F♯, C♯) = D major or B minor

Three sharps (F♯, C♯, G♯) = A major or F♯ minor

Four sharps (F♯, C♯, G♯, D♯) = E major or C♯ minor

Five sharps (F♯, C♯, G♯, D♯, A♯) = B major or G♯ minor

Six sharps (F♯, C♯, G♯, D♯, A♯, E♯) = F♯ major or D♯ minor

index

Words *in italics* indicate album titles unless otherwise stated. Words 'in quotes' indicate song titles. Page numbers in **bold** indicate illustrations.

acknowledgements

Author's thanks

I'd like to express my deep gratitude for the many people who've helped me with various aspects of this book, including Paul Butler, Pete Cooper, Dave Townsend, Rick Townend, Roger Wilson, Emma Reid, Bo Chomenko, Emese Hruska and Alicia Svigals.

Picture credits

Pages 8, 9, 10, 11, 13, 15, 16, 17, 18: Lebrecht Collection. Pages 34, 35, 41, 65, 66: Redferns/Getty Images. Page 89: EFDSS. Pages 92, 93, 94: Redferns/Getty Images. Page 107: Tina Chaden. Pages 109, 127, 134: Redferns/Getty Images. Page 135: Lebrecht Collection. Pages 152, 169, 171, 172, 180, 188, 192, 204, 209, 211, 226, 227, 230, 246, 247, 257, 258, 259, 261, 267, 270, 272, 277, 279: Redferns/Getty Images.

About the author

Chris Haigh began playing classical violin at seven, before discovering that fiddle was more fun. A prolific and versatile musician, he has gigged and recorded in an astonishing range of genres and styles, from western swing to African jive, and has played on more than 70 albums. He has written three albums of TV production music, tracks from which have been used in more than 300 films, shows, and commercials. He teaches playing and improvisation in schools, universities, and in workshops, and has written extensively about the instrument. Chris can be contacted through his website, www.fiddlingaround.co.uk.